Communities and the Environment

Communities and the Environment

Ethnicity, Gender, and the State in Community-Based Conservation

edited by

ARUN AGRAWAL

CLARK C. GIBSON

RUTGERS UNIVERSITY PRESS

New Brunswick, New Jersey, and London

Library of Congress Cataloging-in-Publication Data

Communities and the environment : ethnicity, gender, and the state in community-based conservation / edited by Arun Agrawal and Clark C. Gibson.
p. cm.
Includes bibliographical references and index.
ISBN 0-8135-2913-1 (cloth)—ISBN 0-8135-2914-X (pbk.)
1. Nature convervation—Citizen participation. 2. Conservation of natural resources—Citizen participation. I. Agrawal, Arun, 1962– II. Gibson, Clark C., 1961– III. Title.

QH75.C58 2001
333.7'2—dc21   00-045729

To
Fiona and Connor
Welcome to the world

Contents

Foreword by Elinor Ostrom   *ix*
Acknowledgments   *xiii*

Introduction   The Role of Community in Natural Resource
Conservation   *1*
ARUN AGRAWAL AND CLARK C. GIBSON

Chapter 1   Invoking Community: Indigenous People and Ancestral
Domain in Palawan, the Philippines   *32*
MELANIE HUGHES MCDERMOTT

Chapter 2   Gender Dimensions of Community Resource
Management: The Case of Water Users' Associations
in South Asia   *63*
RUTH MEINZEN-DICK AND MARGREET ZWARTEVEEN

Chapter 3   The Ethnopolitics of Irrigation Management in the
Ziz Oasis, Morocco   *89*
HSAIN ILAHIANE

Chapter 4   Reidentifying Ground Rules: Community Inheritance
Disputes among the Digo of Kenya   *111*
BETTINA NG'WENO

Chapter 5   Communities, States, and the Governance of Pacific
Northwest Salmon Fisheries   *138*
SARA SINGLETON

Chapter 6   Boundary Work: Community, Market, and
State Reconsidered   *157*
TANIA MURRAY LI

Conclusion   Community and the Commons: Romantic and
               Other Views   *180*
               BONNIE J. MCCAY

               About the Contributors   *193*
               Index   *197*

Foreword

ELINOR OSTROM

Many lessons are to be learned from the pages of this book. Let me heartily recommend that both academics and practitioners read it carefully. The study of conservation policy has been filled with too many wild chases after the chimera of the ideal way to achieve conservation. But there simply are no ideal conservation policies. Unquestionably, community-based conservation efforts have been highly successful in many places. The structure of each of these successful programs differs, however, and the reasons for success are quite diverse. Further, many community-based conservation efforts have failed.

Failure is almost guaranteed when policymakers think that they can design a rapid, foolproof blueprint for achieving the difficult goal of conservation. For those researchers who have tried to substantiate the *feasibility* of self-governing communities and their potential capability of sustainably using natural resources over long periods of time, seeing our own research used to support simplistic programs to hand over natural resources to local communities is of major concern. Even if legislation or policy boasts a "participatory" or "community" label, it is rare that individuals from the community have had any say at all in the policy. Further, many of these centrally imposed "community" programs are based on a naive view of community. It is unlikely that any policy based on such views has a chance to produce more than a few minor successes.

Thus, this is an important book for all to take seriously.

Arun Agrawal and Clark C. Gibson's introduction provides a good overview of the findings of each chapter. It is not the purpose of a foreword to repeat that introduction. Puzzles of lasting significance are identified in many chapters of this book. I would like to call attention to some of these crucial puzzles.

One puzzle of substantial import is how to achieve a transition from a colonial and authoritarian past to a democratic future involving more voices and organizations at all levels. The transition to democracy is a major puzzle of modern life. All modern democracies have themselves been through long periods of development in which democratic powers were wrested from centralized and authoritarian regimes. The last half of the twentieth century witnessed many efforts to speed up this process and to impose presumably democratic institutions from a national capital. Many of these efforts faltered, while some notable successes have been achieved.

Where multiple peoples have lived in a region for centuries with varying languages, institutions, and ways of life, trying to involve communities in the general governance of local territories as well as in the management of natural resources has proven to be particularly thorny. A major source of the problem has been that the processes of colonial rule and its aftermath of overly centralized regimes have taken away the legitimacy and formal powers of local communities. Although many groups have continued to sustain their local institutions, one does not re-create a functioning community by fiat. Melanie Hughes McDermott's case study of Palawan illustrates these puzzles extraordinarily well. When did the national government of the Philippines decide to establish Certificates of Ancestral Domain Claims (CADCs)? For many years, lowlanders had an escape valve from ever denser and growing population in the shape of migration to upland areas. During these years, the national government failed to stop massive deforestation resulting from this settlement process and from commercial logging. Then, after all of this, the Department of Environment and Natural Resources was instructed to develop a community-based forest management program at the same time that the formal code still declared all forest residents to be illegal squatters on public land. The legislation identifies indigenous communities themselves as having a particular right to resources and presumes that they are automatically capable of organizing to exercise these rights responsibly. The stylized conception of communities built into this legislation, as homogeneous societies that have lived in a bounded area and have shared customs and traditions for many centuries, is exactly the naive conception of community criticized by all of the authors of this book.

It is tragic indeed when naive, oversimplified conceptions are actually used in legislation. Instead of setting in place a process in which communities composed of people with heterogeneous interests, human skills, and knowledge could gain the experience of managing resources together, legislation requires the drafting of a management plan in a language that only external actors such as NGOs and state foresters can understand. While McDermott points out the conflict and contestation that resulted from this creation of community by fiat, she also points to contemporary processes that bring some encouragement to the reader. Through networks reaching outward to others in similar situations, the people of Kayasan on the island of Palawan are slowly developing new capabilities that may indeed make them better stewards of local forests than the national government was for many years. This will not be accomplished, however, because some extant homogeneous, unchanging community is now allowed to exert once again its long-standing capabilities to manage forest resources. If a new and better stewardship happens, it will occur as a result of struggles, contestation, and cooperation among a network of peoples. Basing their plans on inadequate conceptualization, policymakers have set in place new policies designed around imaginary beings and capabilities. After years of colonial and authoritarian rule, new self-governed processes require instead the setting in place of supportive institutions that facilitate the peaceful resolution of long-suppressed conflicts, the acquisition of new skills to govern in a modern age, and the management of valuable resources in an ever-widening global economy.

As one begins unpacking the concept of community as Agrawal and Gibson challenge us to do, the importance of addressing other issues becomes apparent. The puzzle of the effect within a community of the identification of groups of individuals by gender and in other ways is always present. Ruth Meinzen-Dick and Margreet Zwarteveen illustrate that concepts of gender are intricately mixed with concepts of community. When community is seen as imposing traditional values and ways of life on members, then the presence of community can be viewed as itself oppressive for women. If, on the other hand, community is viewed as a protection against the inequality fostered by market relations, then community may be a mechanism for shielding women against unfair practices and exploitation. If we are to have a reasonable discourse concerning the role of women in development, we simply must have a clearer set of concepts than the muddied ones we have inherited. We are further along in this enterprise as a result of the work of these authors.

The chapter by Hsain Ilahiane deepens our understanding of complex communities that are characterized by substantial internal inequalities and yet manage resources sustainably over long periods of time. Sara Singleton's work undermines a different aspect of the mythic notion of community. She shows how communities may not be territorially based and in so doing reinforces Tania Murray Li's account of the importance of relationships of members of one community with those of others and with governmental agencies at multiple levels.

The chapter by Bettina Ng'weno on land tenure in Kenya illustrates dramatically the complexity of traditional communities and some of the added complexity that occurs when colonial powers attempt to impose notions of land tenure coming from Western traditions. Strategic individuals in all communities can take advantage of conflicting legal systems to make claims under the set of rules that leaves them most advantaged. Simply presuming that one can impose a new system on an already complex system and straighten everything out within a short time is another example of the naiveté of contemporary public policy. Colonial efforts in Africa were in most cases continued by the newly independent national governments. They too have been mired in overly simplistic concepts of community and land tenure.

Tania Murray Li helps us understand better the puzzle of how communities form. Instead of accepting the prevalent assumption that communities are natural entities based on common kinship, language, and customs, Li stresses that the boundaries of communities may be delineated and strengthened by the relationships established between members of one community and members in others. Market and state are not the antithesis of communities but are rather overlapping, interacting, formative processes in and of themselves. As Li points out, involving communities effectively in conservation will tend to increase the level of involvement of state and market in local community affairs rather than decrease it. Indeed, policies based on the notion of isolated communities apart from the market and the state are likely to generate counterproductive processes.

After reading the chapters of this volume, one has to agree with Agrawal and Gibson that the role of community in expanding the strategies for achieving conservation is better understood by "focusing on the multiple interests and actors within communities, on the process of how these actors influence decision-making, and on the internal and external institutions that shape the decision-making process" (Agrawal and Gibson, this volume, p. 2). One can only hope that these foci will be adopted by scholars and policymakers in future efforts to study these processes and to improve them through public policies.

Acknowledgments

All books require sustained cooperation and often much patience. Our collaborators had both in good measure as this volume moved from a set of informal conversations and ideas toward this final product. We want to thank our colleagues for their support and understanding during this long—seemingly unending—but ultimately rewarding process.

This book originated as the contributors to this volume, both individually and jointly, began to question the approach of community-based conservation that has blossomed in recent years. While discussions about institutional solutions to resource management dilemmas included only markets and states, advocates of communities as a third way rarely had to specify what they really meant by such an approach. But regardless of our own advocacy for community empowerment, we believe that as policies shift in favor of communities it is necessary to analyze the idea of community-based conservation more critically. In a very immediate sense, then, this book is a response to the changing terms of the debate on institutions and environmental conservation. We are grateful to those who engaged in this debate; we hope this volume engages their ideas at least partially.

We want to acknowledge invaluable comments and suggestions from friends who have given freely of their intellect and time during the making of this volume. Many thanks to colleagues who have read or commented on parts of the manuscript or chapters: Julie Greenberg, Courtney Jung, Fabrice Lehoucq, Donald Moore, Elinor Ostrom, Vincent Ostrom, Kimberly Pfeifer, Jesse Ribot, Amy Poteete, Kent Redford, Steven Sanderson, Suzana Sawyer, Marianne Schmink, K. Sivaramakrishnan, Ajay Skaria, Leslie Thiele, and George Varughese. We also thank Patty Zielinski for her eagle eye and deft editorial hand in the preparation of this manuscript.

Some chapters in this book have had earlier incarnations. Chapter 1 owes much to an earlier version in *World Development*. It was first written as a longer article commissioned for the Conservation and Development Forum at the University of Florida. The *Journal of Theoretical Politics* published a different version of Sara Singleton's chapter, and an earlier version of Ruth Meinzen-Dick and Margreet Zwarteveen's chapter appeared in *Agriculture and Human Values*. We would like to thank Sage Publications and Kluwer Academic Publishers, respectively, for permission to use materials from the versions of papers they published.

Arun Agrawal would like to acknowledge the research time made available by support from the Workshop in Political Theory and Policy Analysis at Indiana University during 1996–97. Support under the MacArthur Foundation (Grant # 96-42825-WER) and the National Science Foundation (Grant # SBR 9905443) has also been available to Arun Agrawal over the period he has worked on this manuscript. Clark C. Gibson acknowledges the support of the Ford Foundation (Grant # 950-1160), and support from the National Science Foundation (Grant # SBR 9521918) to the Center for the Study of Institutions, Population, and Environmental Change at Indiana University during this same period.

Communities and the Environment

Introduction

ARUN AGRAWAL
CLARK C. GIBSON

The Role of Community in Natural Resource Conservation

THE POOR CONSERVATION outcomes that followed decades of intrusive resource management strategies and planned development have forced policymakers and scholars to reconsider the role of community in resource use and conservation. In a break from previous work on development, which considered communities to be a hindrance to progressive social change, current writing champions the role of community in bringing about decentralization, meaningful participation, cultural autonomy, and conservation (Chambers and McBeth 1992; Chitere 1994; Etzioni 1996). According to a recent survey carried out by the Food and Agriculture Organization (FAO 1999), more than fifty countries report that they pursue partnerships with local communities in an effort to better protect their forests. But despite its recent popularity, the concept of community rarely receives the attention or analysis it needs from those concerned with resource use and management.

In this volume we seek to redress this omission by investigating "community" in work concerning resource conservation and management.[1] Communities are complex entities containing individuals differentiated by status, political and economic power, religion and social prestige, and intentions. Although some may operate harmoniously, others do not. Some see nature or the environment as something to be protected; others care only for nature's short-term use. Some have effective traditional norms; others have few. Some community members seek refuge from the government and market; others quickly embrace both. And sometimes communities come into existence only as a result of their interactions with governments and markets.

This chapter begins by exploring the conceptual origins of the community, especially as it relates to writings on resource use. The ensuing analysis reveals that three aspects of community are most important to those who advocate a positive role for communities in resource management—community as a small spatial unit, as a homogeneous social structure, and as shared norms. The chapter argues that community is better examined in the context of conservation by focusing on the multiple interests and actors within communities, on the process of how these actors influence decision-making, and on the internal and external institutions that shape the decision-making process. A focus on institutions rather than on community is likely to be more fruitful for those interested in community-based natural resource management. The chapter suggests that research and policy move away from universalist claims either for or against community. Instead, community-based conservation initiatives must be founded on images of community that recognize their internal differences and processes, their relations with external actors, and the institutions that affect both. The final section reviews how the contributors to this volume explore these themes.

Community in History

An understanding of the current widespread preoccupation with community requires an understanding of at least some history of the concept's use. Such a history shows the ways in which "community" has moved in and out of fashion, and prompts caution in accepting community as a panacea for problems concerning the conservation of natural resources.

Current perceptions of community appear strongly linked to analyses of nineteenth- and early-twentieth-century scholars attempting to understand the portentous transformations that rocked their world.[2] The source of these changes was thought to lie in the economic sphere—industrialization, monetization, and production to satisfy material needs. Sir Henry Maine, for example, saw the world moving from relationships based on status, kin networks, and joint property to one based on contract, territory, and individual rights.[3] Maine's underlying image of societal evolution influenced Tönnies's formulation of *Gesellschaft* and *Gemeinschaft*, or community and society.[4] Tönnies's view of community as an organic whole continues to color present conceptions to a significant degree, and accounts for some of the attraction community holds for many conservationists.

Most of these scholars of social change highlighted the disappearance of community and its replacement by other forms of social organization. Their theories of classification, in this sense, were also theories of evolution.[5] For Marx and Engels, Spencer and Comte, and even for Weber and Durkheim, society moved along an evolutionary path. Status, tradition, charisma, and religion would increasingly give way to equality, modernity, rationality, and a scientific temper. This theorization of social change automatically pits community against the market, since marketization and urbanization erode community.

Modernization theorists shared this evolutionary view. Under the strong influence of Parsonian structuralism, they characterized whole societies using the evolutionary labels "underdeveloped," "developing," and "developed." The dichotomous pattern variables of Parsons were presumed to describe not only existing realities and directions of historical change, but also the desirability of movement in that direction.[6] Analytical categories representing discontinuous social states overshadowed the real processes of historical change.

While scholars of social change generally accepted the ongoing nature and irreversibility of change, they differed in their judgments regarding the benefits of progress and the desirability of traditional community. A strong correlation exists between those who view progress positively and community negatively: Marx, Spencer, and the early Durkheim saw ongoing social changes as liberating humanity from the coercive and limiting world of the past, from the "idiocy of rural life," that community, in part, embodied. The same is true of most modernization theorists.[7] Other scholars with less sanguine views about the benefits of progress did not abandon community altogether. Writers like Tönnies, the later Durkheim, and Dewey did not see any utopia at the end of the social changes they described. Instead of liberation from the tyranny of custom, they saw "progress" dissolving the ties that anchor humans to their milieu, providing a sense of selfhood and belonging. Writers during this period and after made impossible searches for the community that they believed had existed, fully formed, just prior to the disruptive set of social changes they experienced.

Community and Conservation

Like more general works on community, the history of community in conservation is also a history of revisionism. Images of pristine ecosystems and innocent primitives yielded over time to views of despoiling communities out of balance with nature, mostly due to the double-pronged intrusion of the state and the market. A recuperative project on behalf of the indigenous and the local (community) has attempted to rescue community. But the rescue project has itself come under attack by new anthropological and historical research suggesting that communities may not, after all, be so friendly to the environment. The practical and policy implications that accompany these changing images are immense.

The basic elements of earlier policy and scholarly writings about local communities and their residents are familiar. "People" were an obstacle to efficient and "rational" organization of resource use.[8] A convincing logic undergirded the belief that the goals of conservation and the interests of local communities were in opposition. Conservation required protection of threatened resources: wildlife, forests, pastures, fisheries, irrigation flows, and drinking water. Members of local communities, however, rely on these resources for their fodder, fuelwood, water, and food and thus exploit them without restraint. This schematic representation, popularized by Garrett Hardin and bolstered by several theoretical metaphors that served to (mis)guide policy, provided a persuasive explanation of how resource degradation and depletion took place.[9]

Empirical evidence about the context within which most rural communities are located helped prop up the view. The population of many rural areas in tropical countries has grown rapidly, even with out-migration to cities.[10] Demographic growth, it was argued, could only increase consumption pressures. Penetration by market forces, which linked local systems of resource use to a larger network of demand, further increased the pressure on natural resources.[11] At the same time, many believed that poorly articulated and enforced property rights arrangements provided disincentives for individuals to protect resources.

These factors implied that even if people had successfully managed resources in some harmonious past, that past was long gone. Instead, the way to effective conservation was through the heavy hand of the state or through the equally heavy, if less visible, hand of the market and private property rights. Such ideas supported conservation policies that aimed to exclude locals. National parks and other protected areas are the most obvious result of this thinking. International conservation agencies backed many of these policies.[12]

While many of these beliefs persist,[13] most of the current ideas about the community's role in conservation have changed radically: Communities are now the locus of conservationist thinking.[14] International agencies such as the World Bank, IDRC, SIDA, CIDA, Worldwide Fund for Nature, Conservation International, the Nature Conservancy, the Ford Foundation, the MacArthur Foundation, and USAID have all "found" community. They direct enormous sums of money and effort toward community-based conservation and resource management programs and policies. A flood of scholarly papers and policy-centric reports also feature community-based management (e.g., Arnold 1990; Clugston and Rogers 1995; Dei 1992; Douglass 1992; Perry and Dixon 1986; Raju et al. 1993; Robinson 1995). Exemplifying the swing toward community, a recent collection of essays on community-based conservation tells us, "Communities down the millennia have developed elaborate rituals and practices to limit off take levels, restrict access to critical resources, and distribute harvests" (Western and Wright 1994, 1).[15]

A host of other more specific factors have aided advocates of community-based conservation. The past several decades of planned development and top-down conservation practices have made one fact amply clear: The capacity of states to coerce their citizens into unpopular development and conservation programs is limited. These limits are seen starkly when state actors attempt to discipline resource users.[16] Where resources such as fodder, fuelwood, fish, and wildlife are intrinsic to everyday livelihood and household budgets, even well-funded coercive conservation generally fails. Faulty design, inefficient implementation, and corrupt organizations have played an equally important role in the poor outcomes associated with state-centered policies. Combined with local intransigence and lack of livelihood alternatives, this mix of factors has pushed most enforced conservation projects into spectacular failures. In their review of twenty-three conservation and development programs, Wells and Brandon (1992) argue that the weaknesses of state-centric policy mean few options other than community-based conservation exist.[17]

Some contextual factors have also focused the attention of conservationists on community. With the spread of democratic political structures and the increasing insistence on participation, unrepresentative development and conservation projects have become as unattractive as they are impractical.[18] The increasing prominence of indigenous and ethnic claims about the stewardship role of native populations in relation to nature (Clay 1988; Redford and Mansour 1996) assists those who advocate a central role for community.[19] In addition, NGOs at various political levels have helped to amplify the voices of local, indigenous, and community groups (Borda 1985; Borghese 1987; Bratton 1989a).

The recognition of the limits of the state and the emphasis on popular participation came roughly at the same time that new revisionist ecological research began to question the two other main planks of coercive conservation. The first was that pristine environments untouched by human hands had existed until the very recent past. The second was the belief that indigenous and other local communities had been relatively isolated in the past (and therefore used their resources sustainably). Questioning these two beliefs has thrown the romantic image of the "Ecologically Noble Savage" into disarray (Redford 1990).[20]

Historical ecologists emphasize that environments have histories from which humans cannot be excluded. A categorization of landscapes as either natural or human-influenced is a false dichotomy, since humans have modified ecosystems greatly for millennia. Many of the more recent studies that question the notion of "virgin forests" received at least part of their inspiration from Darrell Posey's work on the forest islands of the Kayapo in Brazil (1984, 1985).[21] Denevan (1992) argues that most forests are, in fact, anthropogenic. An increasing number of scholars have marshaled evidence about how humans manipulate biodiversity and influence the species composition and structure of forests around them (Alcorn 1981; Bailey and Headland 1991; Balee 1992, 1994; Brookfield and Padoch 1994; Conklin 1957; Hart and Hart 1986; McDade 1993; Posey and Balee 1989; Roosevelt 1989). The intentional clearing of central African forests for cultivation may have begun more than five thousand years ago (Clist 1989; Phillipson 1985). And traditional swidden agriculture, like small-scale disturbances in the forest, can enhance biodiversity (Bailey 1990, 1996; Park 1992; Sponsel 1992; Sponsel et al. 1996; Yoon 1993).[22]

Such studies undermine arguments that portray communities only as despoilers of natural resources. If humans have shaped and used their environments in sustainable ways for thousands of years, it may be possible to establish partnerships that accomplish the same results today. Indeed, as anthropologists begin to pay greater attention to the historical experiences of "people without history" (Wolf 1982), it has become increasingly obvious that if local communities in the past had used resources without destroying them, they had done so even as they remained in contact with other peoples. Such contacts contributed to survival and helped to conserve resources by allowing foragers, hunter-gatherers, and pastoralists to get starches and other foods from farmers and traders.[23]

In addition to empirical and historical works that have helped resurrect community and local participation in conservation, a choice-theoretic foundation for the role of community in conservation has become available as well. Scholarly research on common property has shown communities to be successful and sustainable alternatives to state and private management of resources. Scholarship regarding the commons (Berkes 1989; Bromley et al. 1992; McCay and Acheson 1989; McKean 1992; Ostrom 1990, 1992; Peters 1994; Wade 1987) has highlighted the important time- and place-specific knowledge that members of local communities possess and the institutional arrangements they forge to achieve successful, local-level resource management.

In light of the significant symbolic, theoretical, and intellectual resources available to advocates of community, it is somewhat surprising that claims on behalf of community-based conservation often retain a rather simple quality. One such form such claims assume is that "communities" have a long-term need for the renewable resources near which they live, and they possess more knowledge about these resources than other potential actors. They are, therefore, the best managers of resources.[24] Some refinements to this view can be found: If communities are not involved in the active management of their natural resources, they will use resources destructively (Sponsel et al. 1996; Western and Wright 1994). Still other work includes the notion of interests, in addition to that of needs: Since it is in the interest of a community to protect its resources, it will.[25]

In its prescriptive form, this thesis of community-based conservation and resource management uses new beliefs about the suitability of communities to suggest policy recommendations. The implicit assumption behind these recommendations is that communities have incentives to use resources unsustainably when they are not involved in resource management. If communities are involved in conservation, the benefits they receive will create incentives for them to become good stewards of resources (if only the state and the market would get out of the way).[26]

This vision of community—as the centerpiece of conservation and resource management—is attractive. It permits the easy contestation of dominant narratives that favor state control or privatization of resources and their management (Li 1996). Such positive, generalized representations of community make available "points of leverage in ongoing processes of negotiation" (1996, 505, 509).[27] But such representations of community ignore the critical interests and processes within communities, and between communities and other social actors. Ultimately, such representations can undermine their advocates' long-term goal of increasing the role of community in natural resource management.

What Makes Community?

The vision of small, integrated communities using locally evolved norms and rules to manage resources sustainably and equitably is powerful. But because it views community as a unified, organic whole, this vision fails to attend to differences within communities, and ignores how these differences affect resource management outcomes, local politics, and strategic interactions within communities, as well as the possibility of layered alliances that can span multiple levels of politics. Attention to these details is critical if policy changes on behalf of community are to lead to outcomes that are sustainable and equitable.

Although current writings on community-based conservation assert that community is central to renewable resource management, they seldom devote much attention to analyzing the concept of community, or explaining precisely how community affects outcomes.[28] Some authors refuse to elaborate on what it might mean, preferring to let readers infer its contours in the descriptions of specific cases (for example, Western and Wright 1994). However, most studies in the conservation field refer to a bundle of concepts related to space, size, composition, interactions, interests, and objectives. Much of this literature sees community in three ways: as a spatial unit, as a social structure, and as a set of shared norms. It is on the basis of one or a combination of these three ideas that most of the advocacy for community rests. But these conceptions fail to explain the cause of these features or articulate their effect on natural resource use. They offer, therefore, a weak foundation upon which to base policy.

COMMUNITY AS A SMALL SPATIAL UNIT

Small size and territorial affiliation have been proxies for community since the very beginnings of writings on the subject. Tönnies, for example, saw Gemeinschaft as existing in villages, and characterized it by "intimate, private, and exclusive living together" (cited in Bender 1978, 17). Such closeness was impossible in large cities, and impractical if not impossible to achieve at a distance. Increased mobility and larger settlements that accompanied urbanization and industrialization, it was believed, weaken communal bonds naturally found in small villages. These two aspects of community—smallness (of both area and numbers of individuals) and territorial attachment—also mark many current writings on community-in-conservation. Instead of examining and drawing out the possible connections of shared space and small size with the political processes of local conservation, they tend to assume a link between the territorial conception of community and successful resource management.[29]

The popularity of this view of community can be traced, at least in part, to the fact that the renewable resources that communities use, manage, and sometimes protect are themselves usually located near territorially fixed homes and settlements. If top-down programs to protect resources failed because of the inability of governments to exercise authority at a distance, the reasoning goes, then decentralization of authority to those social formations that are located near the resource might work better. There may be other contributing factors at work. Members of small groups sharing the same geographical space are more likely to interact with each other more often. Such regular, more frequent interactions can lower the costs of making collective decisions. These two aspects of community—fewer individuals and shared small spaces—may also contribute to group distinctiveness. Because of continuing interactions among members over time, territorially circumscribed communities might also be able to develop specific ways of managing the resources near which they are located. These advantages have led some policymakers and analysts to define strictly the size of "communities" that should be participating in community-based resource programs.[30]

But because many small, territorially contained groups do not protect or manage resources well, and because some mobile, transitional groups manage them efficiently, important processes are at work that are not captured by spatial location alone (Agrawal 1999). Indeed, the territorial attachment of small groups may make them inappropriate managers for particular resources because the geographical spread of the resource (large watersheds, forests, lakes, etc.) could be larger than a small community could ever hope to control. Consequently, it becomes important to consider the negotiations and politics to which common spatial location and small size might contribute.

The bounded and stationary character of terrestrial resources such as forests and pastures does not imply a consequent ease in their allocation to particular spatial communities—a piece of forest or pasture for every community. Because more than one community (in the spatial sense) may be located near a given patch of forest or pasture, and because the members of each would have an interest in the resources nominally belonging to the other community, spatial bases for allocating resource management rights can prove untenable. For fugitive resources such as wildlife and fish, an added dimension of complexity might be introduced (Naughton-Treves and Sanderson 1995). The literature on community-based conservation also often elides the thorny question of densities: Does the success of a conservation practice depend on the density of individuals per hectare of land, per hectare of productive land, or per hectare of a certain natural resource? (Matzke and Nabane 1996). Focusing on a community's shared space and small numbers alone, therefore, is necessarily incomplete and possibly misleading to analyze local-level management of resources.

COMMUNITY AS A HOMOGENEOUS SOCIAL STRUCTURE

Much of the rhetorical weight of community comes from papering over the differences that might prevail within actually existing communities. Indeed, the feature of community receiving the greatest attention in its construction as a social artifact is its homogeneous composition. Typically, observers assume communities to be groups of similarly endowed (in terms of assets and incomes), relatively homogeneous households who possess common characteristics in relation to ethnicity, religion, caste, or language. The relationship proceeds both ways since ethnic, religious, or linguistic homogeneity is often presumed to lead to community as well. Such homogeneity is assumed to further cooperative solutions, reduce hierarchical and conflictual interactions, and promote better resource management. Outside the community conflicts prevail; within, harmony reigns.[31]

The notion that a community is homogeneous meshes well with beliefs about its spatial boundaries. In the rural areas of poorer countries (the sites where most advocates of community-based resource management locate their analyses and projects), people living within the same location may indeed hold similar occupations, depend on the same resources, use the same language, and belong to the same ethnic or religious group. These similarities may facilitate regular interactions among group members.

Even if members of a group are similar in several respects, however, it is not clear at what point the label "homogeneous" can be applied, nor is it clear that these shared characteristics are critical to conservation. Because all human groups are stratified to some extent or the other, it becomes important to analyze the degree of homogeneity and those dimensions of it that are important to resource conservation. Few studies, however, wrestle with the difficulty of operationalizing what social homogeneity might be.[32] Most studies, when they do focus on the social composition of a community rather than assuming it to be homogeneous, indicate intentionally or unintentionally that within the same group (e.g., Masai, or pastoralist, or women), multiple axes of differentiation exist.[33] Recent studies of resource use at the local level have recognized the salience of intracommunity conflicts (Agrawal 1994a; Gibson and Marks 1995; Ilahaine 1995; Madzudzo and Dzingirai 1995; Moore 1996a, 1996b). And yet even highly differentiated communities may be able to take steps to use local resources sustainably (e.g., Agrawal 1994b). These studies show that there is no easy correspondence between social homogeneity and sustainable resource use.

COMMUNITY AS COMMON INTERESTS AND SHARED NORMS

The concept of community as shared norms and common interests depends strongly upon the perceptions of its members; in this sense all communities are imagined communities. This imagined sense of community attracts scholars of conservation to community. And it is this notion of community that is supposed to grow out of common location, small size, homogeneous composition, and/or shared characteristics. As Ascher puts it, community exists among individuals who share "*common* interests and *common* identification . . . growing out of shared characteristics" (1995, 83). Common and shared interests rather than individual and selfish interests make successful resource management more likely. In a community, "individuals give up some of their individuality to behave as a single entity to accomplish goals" (Kiss 1990, 9).

Internalized norms of behavior among members of communities can guide resource management outcomes in desired directions. Community as shared norms is itself an outcome of interactions and processes that take place within communities, often in relation to those perceived as outsiders. But community as shared norms also has an independent positive effect on resource use and conservation.

Shared community-level norms can promote conservation in two different ways. First, norms may specifically prohibit some actions. In many villages in semiarid western Rajasthan, for example, existing norms impede villagers from cutting *khejri* trees (*Prosopis cineraria*), especially when these trees are present in the local *oran*, a common area set aside for grazing, and often dedicated to a religious deity.[34] In the same region, the Bishnois have strong norms against the killing of wild animal species such as deer. Carolyn Cook (1996, 279–282) details how the Amung-me in Irian Jaya protect certain groves of trees as sacred, and a marsupial (*amat*) that plays a role in the propagation of the Pandanus trees. Mishra (1994) explains that women belonging to the Juang and Saora tribal communities in Orissa follow strong norms about the timing and season for collecting nontimber forest products. Other examples of "conservationist" norms also exist.[35]

Second, it is possible that the existence of communal norms will promote cooperative decision-making within the community. If members of a community believe in shared identities and common experiences, they also may be willing to cooperate over more formal decisions to manage and conserve resources. The presence of community-level norms can facilitate resource management by preventing certain behaviors, or encouraging others (Coleman 1990).

Although community as shared norms, especially when such norms are concerned with the management of resources or conservation, may be the hope of conservationists, the extent to which norms aid conservation needs to be questioned.[36] At a minimum, current research indicates that conservationist norms cannot be equated with particular identities such as "woman," or "the indigenous."[37] Norms, in fact, may be a significant part of the problem to a conservationist if a norm promotes exploitation (posing an enormous obstacle for those interested in community-based conservation).[38] For example, as a result of land laws in the early colonial periods of many countries in Latin

America, there is a strong norm that holds that land is useful only when it is cleared of trees and used for agriculture.[39] In many parts of Africa, wildlife is considered a threat to crops and human lives, not a resource to be conserved (Marks 1984; Naughton-Treves 1997). Further, norms cannot be taken as a set of beliefs that communities hold, never to give up. They come into being in relation to particular contextual factors, and even when they are codified and written, they do not remain static.[40] Just because some small social groups hold conservationist norms today, this does not mean that they will not necessarily hold them in the future.

Those who conceptualize community as shared norms may fail to recognize the difficulties this position poses for conservation. Unlike the factors of community size, composition, and links to a specific territorial space, which all can be directly influenced through external intervention, community as shared understandings is probably the least amenable to such manipulation. Conservationist norms cannot be easily introduced into a community by external actors (although the current emphasis on participation and conservation by state actors means that at least the attempt is being made in many locations).[41] Indeed, we hardly know which strategies successfully alter the norms people hold about conservation, especially when the resources in question are a critical part of the family income.

Actors, Processes, and Institutions

To summarize, advocates of community-based conservation forward a conceptualization of communities as territorially fixed, small, and homogeneous. These characteristics supposedly foster the interactions among members that promote desirable collective decisions. While certain types and levels of these characteristics might facilitate collective action, few studies demonstrate that this collective action is necessarily connected with conservation behavior. Most important, few social scientists or policymakers have systematically tested these propositions in the field. In fact, some community characteristics considered important to collective action may actually thwart conservation efforts. Small-sized groups may be unable to defend their resources in the face of strong external threats, or be unable to manage resources if they are spread over large areas. Strongly held norms may support exploitative behavior, or be resistant to outside attempts at their modification.

To be more accurate in our efforts to depict communities and their relationship with their natural resources—and thus to be more relevant to policymaking—we argue that greater attention should be focused on three critical aspects of communities: the multiple actors with multiple interests that make up communities, the processes through which these actors interrelate, and, especially, the institutional arrangements that structure their interactions. These three proposed foci for the study of community-based conservation allow for a better understanding of the factors critical to the success or failure of efforts aimed at local-level conservation.

MULTIPLE INTERESTS AND ACTORS

A growing number of studies that explore natural resource management at the local level do not find communities comprising just one group of individuals who possess similar endowments or goals. Instead, they find many subgroups, and within subgroups they find individuals with varying preferences for resource use and distribution. These authors bring to light the politics of the local: Economic elites may vie with religious elites; chiefs may battle with their advisors; women may contest the rights of their husbands; the politically marginalized may dispute the acts of the politically dominant. Recognizing and working with the multiplicity of actors and interests is crucial for those advocating community-based programs. Such recognition indicates that empowering local actors to use and manage their natural resources is more than the decentralization of authority over natural resources from the central government to "a" community. The far more challenging task is to understand patterns of difference within communities.[42]

Recognizing that multiple actors exist at the local level is a useful step forward because it forces researchers to consider their different and dynamic interests.[43] A more acute understanding of community in conservation can be founded only by understanding that actors within communities seek their own interests in conservation programs, and that these interests may change as new opportunities emerge.

LOCAL-LEVEL PROCESSES

Within communities, individuals negotiate the use, management, and conservation of resources. They attempt to implement the agreed-upon rules resulting from their negotiations. And they try to resolve disputes that arise in the processes of implementation of the interpretation of rules. These three types of local interactions are irreducibly influenced by the existing distribution of power and the structure of incentives within a given social group.[44] Because the exercise of power and incentive-oriented behavior are variable over time and space, and because all groups have members who can be strategic in their behavior, planned conservation efforts can never address all contingencies completely.

Analyses of only local-level phenomena are insufficient to explain interactions at the local level. All local interactions take place within the context of larger social forces. Attempts by governments to implement community-based conservation and specific projects of nongovernment organizations that seek to involve communities are examples of directed influence on local-level conservation. Such initiatives bring into the local context those larger political forces that generated the programs. Other pressures—changes in prices of different resources, development assistance, demographic shifts, technological innovations, institutional arrangements at different levels—also impinge on local interactions.[45]

Local interactions may also prompt responses from macro-level actors. Local reactions to conservation programs can lead to modifications in the shape of these programs. Thus, although it is convenient to talk about the community and the state, or about the local and the external, they are linked together in ways that might make it difficult to identify the precise line where local conservation begins and the external (that helps construct the local) ends.

INSTITUTIONAL ARRANGEMENTS

Institutions can be seen as sets of formal and informal rules and norms that shape interactions of humans with others and nature.[46] They constrain some activities and facilitate others; without them, social interactions would be impossible (Bates 1989; North 1990). Institutions promote stability of expectations *ex ante*, and consistency in actions, *ex post*. They contrast with uncertain political interactions among unequally placed actors, and unpredictable processes in which performances of social actors do not follow any necessary script. Strategic actors may attempt to bypass the constraints of existing institutions, and create new institutions that match their interests. But institutions remain the primary mechanisms available to mediate, soften, attenuate, structure, mold, accentuate, and facilitate particular outcomes and actions (Agrawal 1995b; Alston, Eggertsson, and North 1996; Ensminger 1992; Gibson 1999). This holds whether change is radical, moderate, or incremental.

When actors do not share goals for conserving resources and are unequally powerful, as is likely the case in most empirical situations, institutions are significant for two reasons. On one hand, they denote some of the power relations (Foucault 1983, 222, 224) that define the interactions among actors who created the institutions; on the other, they also help to structure the interactions that take place around resources. Once formed, institutions exercise effects that are independent of the forces that constituted them. Institutions can change because of constant challenges to their form by the actions of individuals whose behavior they are supposed to influence. No actual behavior conforms precisely to a given institutional arrangement. Everyday performances of individuals around conservation goals possess the potential to reshape formal and informal institutions. Institutions can also change when they are explicitly renegotiated by actors. Institutions should be understood, therefore, as provisional agreements on how to accomplish tasks. Rather than setting the terms of interactions among parties with varying objectives, they help the behavior of actors congeal along particular courses.

Studying Community

The authors of this volume's remaining chapters employ this general framework of actors, processes, and institutions to explore more deeply particular cases of communities and natural resources management. While analyzing the shortcomings of the conventional view both theoretically and empirically, the authors also investigate three of the most important issues confronting the research and practice of local-level conservation efforts: ethnicity, gender, and community-state relations. The geographical range of these chapters, and their focus on land as well as water-based resources, indicates that their arguments are relevant to many different places and localities. Especially germane are concerns about social and economic stratification within communities, the local and translocal factors that contribute to the formation of communities, and the role of new and old institutions that help to bind communities together.

The chapters in this book collectively emphasize that in the rush to embrace a notion of community as being harmonious and homogeneous, critical issues of gender relations, ethnic negotiations, and community-state-market interactions have been relegated to the background. In so doing, they join important new research that also emphasizes the need not to accept community uncritically. The objective of such research that underlines differences within communities and the differentiated relations of community actors with those in other communities, states, and markets is not to deny the benefits of transferring political authority to locally based actors. Certainly the processes of state construction and consolidation tended to marginalize local actors for much of the 1960s and 1970s. But as the authors in this volume demonstrate, it is not enough to pose the community against the state and elide differences within communities if the objective is to reclaim some voice for the marginalized in the management of renewable resources such as forests, fisheries, irrigation waters, and pastures. If communities are viewed as units, and insufficient attention is devoted to politics within communities, the shifting of power to community actors can have the pernicious effect of allowing powerful elite within a community to consolidate their own positions (Agrawal 1999; Gibson 1999).

The chapters in this volume marshal empirical evidence to substantiate some of the major themes evoked in this introduction, and often further the theoretical arguments we broach. Melanie Hughes McDermott investigates the ways that states can create community at the local level. In her study of Palawan, the Philippines, McDermott demonstrates how the national government assumed that communities were homogeneous, spatially fixed, and lived harmoniously with nature. On the basis of these assumptions, the government created policies to foment community-based conservation. A community that could prove that it had occupied a specific area since "time immemorial" could apply to the government for a Certificate of Ancestral Domain, which would entitle the community to the legal right to use the land, as well as the duty to enforce environmental laws. But this definition of community had little to do with the reality in Palawan, which was marked by various migrating or partially displaced ethnic groups, occupying spaces with fluid boundaries, and possessing little interest in environmental protection for its own sake. Given the legal incentives, these groups mobilized and reinvented themselves as a strategy to keep more recent migrants out of nearby lands. McDermott's fascinating analysis not only reveals the difficulty of maintaining a belief in the mythic community, but also demonstrates that groups will use outsiders' beliefs strategically to create institutions that advance their own interests. In highlighting these processes, McDermott draws a parallel with the account that Bettina Ng'weno later provides about the selective deployment of inheritance laws by the Digo.

Ruth Meinzen-Dick and Margreet Zwarteveen directly confront the community-based conservation movement for its lack of attention to intra-community differences, especially across gender lines. The authors indicate that scholars and development practitioners have not systematically considered the linkages between gender relations and communities, or to the role of women in community management of resources. But differences within communities do not fall only along class or ethnic lines. They argue that existing studies tend to focus on the interhousehold gender issues. But even within households, gender differences are important. Using examples from women's roles and activities regarding water resources in South Asia, the authors examine how informal and formal membership criteria, the costs and benefits of participating in community organizations, and informal participation shape the contours of women's roles in water resource management. Meinzen-Dick and Zwarteveen end their study with a persuasive argument for the focus on gender as a primary concern of community-based natural resource management.

Hsain Ilahiane's study of local irrigation systems in the Ziz Valley of Morocco focuses on inequalities that many communities harbor. He demonstrates that although traditional management institutions can successfully distribute and protect resources over a long period of time, such institutions do not have to be either egalitarian or benign. The politics of ethnic institutions in this community help explain why a minority group controls access to water in a desert region. Arabs and Berbers enjoy greater decision-making power over and thus access to water for agriculture, in spite of the fact that the Haratine ethnic group forms 82 percent of the community. But institutions that reinforce status and religious hierarchy keep the Haratine as predominantly laborers who own a small minority of the land. Far from the egalitarian mythic community, inhabitants of this part of Morocco experience a highly stratified society of rank and status, which manifests itself in water management.

Bettina Ng'weno explores how locals determine what community membership means in the context of access to land resources, especially in disputes during inheritance. Members of the same Digo community apply different systems of law—traditional, Muslim, and Western—according to how they perform in increasing an individual's access to land. These conflicts at the local level not only demonstrate the fallacy of assuming a homogeneous community, but also illustrate that community members are involved in their own dynamic processes of self-definition and can reach out to external actors and institutions. Indeed, Ng'weno's analysis also demonstrates the political and contingent nature of categories such as "traditional" and "Western." Such changes are even threatening a shift among the Digo from matrilineal to patrilineal institutions to govern natural resources.

Sara Singleton discusses the role of community in the evolution of a highly sophisticated set of institutions that currently govern Pacific Northwest salmon fisheries. As the result of a 1974 federal court decision, twenty Native American tribes, several state and federal agencies, and an international regulatory panel comanage this complex transboundary resource system. There are both shared and competing interests between government agencies and the tribes, and both between and within different tribal communities. Initially a highly conflictual process, today the comanagement regime proceeds fairly smoothly, incorporating a system of checks and balances between tribal and nontribal agencies that results in a more balanced and environmentally sustainable set of institutions than either set of actors would be likely to produce on their own. The chapter also investigates the process by which tribal communities have wrestled with distributional conflicts and the institutions they have created to manage such conflicts, while at the same time maintaining their capacity to act collectively in the context of bargaining with external regulatory agencies. Thus the chapter demonstrates how both conflict and cooperation are regular features in relationships between community members and between communities.

Tania Murray Li's chapter furthers some of the critical work begun and carried through by the earlier studies in the volume. She argues that advocacy for community-based resource management has assumed a boundary separating communities from markets and states, placing hopes in the "subsistence orientation" and "autonomy" of villagers. These are assumptions she subjects to critical scrutiny through a wide-ranging review of the literature, and through a detailed study in Central Sulawesi, Indonesia. Li argues that while it is fraught with definitional ambiguity, the concept of community requires boundary work before it can be used. Central to Li's study is community's relation to various boundaries, but not necessarily those drawn on maps. Instead she approaches boundaries as related to particular constellations of social and political relations. These relations generally contain strands that include interactions with markets and states as well as with individuals. Li claims that both the old and the new communities literature ignore this possible interrelationship and, instead, see markets and states as outside the community. Li applies her ideas about boundaries and the connectedness of state, market, and community to an analysis of the Lauje people of the Sulawesi hills. She finds that the Lauje have little notion of themselves as a community in any sense, and in fact argues that without outside forces people will not perceive themselves as communities, a notion at odds with the idea of the mythic community. Indeed, the Lauje have just begun to coalesce in an effort to get development assistance from the state, something they had never done before. Again, Li's account resonates with themes in the chapters by Singleton and McDermott about the importance of community-outsider relationships in the production of community.

In the volume's concluding chapter, Bonnie McCay argues that "romancing the commons" has occupied a central place in how many view the relationship between community and conservation. McCay claims that this romantic alternative has routinely cropped up in even the better studies of communities and conservation, and has consequently led analyses to many inappropriate dichotomies: local actors versus governments, traditional knowledge versus modern knowledge, and premodern environmental harmony versus modern environmental disaster (for a more detailed critique of such dichotomization in environmental analyses, see Agrawal and Sivaramakrishnan 2000).

McCay also urges those interested in environmental change to remain open to all of its possible causes. To bring only an economist's property rights perspective, to see only the political ecologist's view of nonlocal influences, or to adopt the romanticized version of the community as critiqued in this volume, unnecessarily limits the exploration of environmental change. More often than not, these narrow perspectives miss crucial variables. McCay prescribes theoretically informed empirical research rather than dichotomies and disciplinary blinders that ignore realities on the ground.

Conclusion

To analyze community-based conservation, this chapter began by casting a critical historical eye at the notion of community. Current works on community borrow extensively, if unconsciously, from past writings. Visions of community as an organic whole, as small and territorially fixed, as under siege and eroding, or as standing in opposition to markets and states, can be traced directly to writings from the nineteenth and the early twentieth centuries. A longer-term perspective on community prompts caution before one embraces it as a general answer to conservation-related woes.

An analysis of the perceptions of community in the literature on conservation reveals strong oscillations over time in the recognition and value it has been accorded. The current valorization of community should be viewed in the context of a general loss of faith in progress and future utopias. It also stems from the disillusionment of conservationists with two other gross concepts: the state and the market. In addition, revisionist historical ecological research and contributions from the scholars of the commons have also played a role in bringing community to the fore.

Given the potential benefits of locally based resource management, the celebration of community is a move in the right direction. But the implications of community as conservation agent are little analyzed in most writings on community-based conservation. Indeed, the existing literature on community-based conservation reveals a widespread preoccupation with what might be called the mythic community: small, integrated groups using locally evolved norms to manage resources sustainably and equitably.

Such characteristics capture the realities of few, if any, existing communities. The vision of the mythic community fails to attend to differences within communities. It ignores how differences affect processes around conservation, the differential access of actors within communities to various channels of influence, and the possibility of layered alliances spanning multiple levels of politics. Small, territorially attached, and relatively homogeneous communities, where they exist, might find it easy to make decisions collectively. They would still find it difficult, however, to withstand external threats (even from other community groups competing for access to the same resources), or to manage resources that have a wide geographical spread. A focus on the shared norms of community is also incomplete, because norms may not prevent over-exploitation of resources, and they are scarcely amenable to change through external interventions.

The authors in this volume propose a shift in emphasis away from the usual assumptions about communities: small size, territorial fixity, group homogeneity, and shared understandings and identities. Instead, we suggest a stronger focus on the divergent interests of multiple actors within communi-ties, the processes through which these interests emerge and through which various actors interact with each other, and the institutions that influence the outcomes of political processes.

As governments and nongovernmental organizations seek new solutions to the challenges of natural resource overexploitation, the studies in this vol-ume could not be more timely. Community now enjoys a relatively unchal-lenged role. Perhaps this uncontested vision of community was essential if any advocacy for community was to enjoy some policy success. But for commu-nity-based conservation to achieve lasting success, it is necessary for even the strongest supporters of community to examine thoughtfully the potential weaknesses in the conceptions of community they tend to deploy. Only with the critical examination of the kind found in this book can we move toward a more enduring future for individuals, communities, and resources.

Notes

1. Throughout the article we use the terms "conservation," "resource use," and "resource management" interchangeably; renewable resources such as forests, pas-tures, wildlife, and fish have been, are being, and will always be used by people; those who wish to conserve must incorporate use and management in their strate-gies (Robinson and Redford 1991, 3).
2. The quick review that follows pays little attention to the earliest scholars of com-munity such as the Greek philosophers. For an introduction to these writings, see Booth (1994). The ensuing discussion on community is strongly influenced by Bender (1978) and Gusfield (1978).
3. Maine's work (1871, 1905) was focused primarily on issues of law and political economy, including a comparative study of property in village communities. But the distinctions he drew equally influenced the understanding of social changes related to urbanization and modernization.
4. We note that "community" and "society" are not exact, but only close translations of Gemeinschaft and Gesellschaft.
5. For an introduction to how classical theories of cyclical change in Europe gave way to evolutionary beliefs in progress during the nineteenth century, see Cowen and Shenton (1995).
6. Parsons expanded the Gemeinschaft/Gesellschaft dichotomy into four parallel dimensions (Bender 1978, 21; Parsons 1951, 1960; Parsons and Shils 1962). These

comprised: affectivity versus affective neutrality; particularism versus universalism; ascription versus achievement; and diffuseness versus specificity. Initially, Parsons included a fifth, collectivity-orientation versus self-orientation. Parsons (1966) shows his interest in applying his pattern variables to social systems.

7. Writing to address concerns about the direction of change in the newly emerging nations of the so-called Third World, these theorists argued against particularistic affiliations of kinship, religion, and ethnicity. These arguments were also explicit arguments against traditional community. Lerner (1962), perhaps, provides the classic statement on the apathy, fatalism, passivity, and static nature of traditional communities. But he is certainly not alone. Almond and Verba (1963), Black (1967), Deutsch (1961), Geertz (1963), and Shils (1962) wrote influential studies of modernization, forming the viewing lens for an entire generation of scholars.

8. See, for example, Eckholm (1976). Ives and Messerli (1989) present a discussion of some of the literature, especially in the Himalayan context.

9. See Ostrom (1990) for a discussion of how the metaphors of the "Prisoner's Dilemma" and the "Logic of Collective Action" have been important in shaping understandings about the (im)possibility of cooperation.

10. Given the large literature on the negative impact of population growth on resource conservation, it is perhaps unnecessary to refer to it at length. For some general statements, see Meffe et al. (1993), Myers (1991), and essays in the journal *Population and Environment*. Dissenting views are available in Lappé and Schurman (1989), and Simon (1990). Arizpe et al. (1994) provide a thoughtful summary.

11. For a critical review of some of the literature on overpopulation and market pressures, and an emphasis on institutions in the context of resource management, see Agrawal and Yadama (1997).

12. See Ascher (1995), Fairhead and Leach (1994), and Gibson and Marks (1995) for discussions of examples and brief reviews of the relevant literature.

13. Although new beliefs have entered the picture, not all who think about the role of community in resource use have begun to subscribe to new views. The result is a complex mosaic of notions about how villages or other nonurban groups may be connected to the resources upon which they depend. The ensuing lines on community in conservation attempt to pick on the most important beliefs that depart from earlier themes.

14. An enormous outpouring of literature bears witness. See Bhatt (1990), Ghai (1993), Gurung (1992), and Lowry and Donahue (1994). See also Wisner (1990) for a review.

15. Scholars in developed countries have also argued for the importance of community in resource management. See Huntsinger and McCaffrey (1995) for a study of the state against the Yurok in the United States, and Hoban and Cook (1988) for a critique of the conservation provision of the U.S. Farm Bill of 1985 for its inadequate involvement of local communities.

16. A number of works are available that point to the inadequacies of state-centric policy in general. See, for example, Bates (1989) and Repetto and Gillis (1988).

17. Ecologists have also underscored the limits of the state in protecting resources. Even if states had the power to enforce perfectly, some ecologists argue that protected areas are often too small to maintain valued biological diversity (Newmark 1995, 1996).

18. A number of writings have focused on the importance of participation for sustainable democratization. Many of them have also highlighted the (potential) role of nongovernmental organizations in the process (Bratton 1989b; Clark 1991; Fernandes 1987; Kothari 1984; Warren 1992). The fall 1996 special issue of *Cultural*

Survival Quarterly edited by Pauline Peters contains a number of useful essays on the role of participation in conservation and development.

19. Agrawal (1995a) questions the possibility of separating indigenous forms of knowledge from Western or scientific forms while stressing the political significance of claims on behalf of the indigenous.

20. On the subject of the "Ecologically Noble Savage," see also Alvard (1993).

21. Anderson and Posey (1989) present a later work on the same group of Indians. For a strong critique of Posey's work, see Parker (1993).

22. A significant body of research argues against indigenous peoples being natural conservationists (Alcorn 1993; Edgerton 1992; Hames 1991; Parker 1993; Rambo 1985; Redford and Stearman 1993; Robinson and Redford 1991). But as Sponsel et al. (1996, 23) conclude after an extensive survey, there is relatively widespread agreement that values, knowledge, and skills of indigenous peoples and many local communities "can be of considerable practical value."

23. See Fox (1969), Morris (1977), and Parker (1909) for early arguments highlighting contacts between local groups and "outsiders." Bailey et al. (1989) and Wilmsen (1989) presented similar arguments more recently.

24. For two examples of this view, see Lynch and Talbott (1995) and Poffenberger (1990). Often the last part of the claim is probabilistically modified: "Communities are likely to prove the best managers."

25. McNeely (1996, xvii). See also the various issues of the influential Indian news magazine *Down to Earth*, published by the Center for Science and Environment, New Delhi.

26. See the various chapters in Western and Wright (1994) for an elaboration of this perspective, and Gibson and Marks (1995) for a critique.

27. Zerner's (1994) essay on *sasi*, a highly variable body of practices linked to religious beliefs and cultural beliefs about nature in Indonesia's Maluku islands, also makes the same point. Current images of sasi depict it as a body of customary environmental low promoting sustainable development. Sasi has, thus, emerged as a site and a resource for social activists to contest an oppressive, extractive political economy. In sasi, the rhetoric of local environmental management can be united with culturally distinctive communities. The result is an unusually potent political metaphor. See also Baines (1991) for a similar argument in relation to assertions on the basis on traditional rights in the Solomon Islands.

28. One exception can be found in Singleton and Taylor (1992, 315). They conceive of community as implying a set of people with some shared beliefs, with stable membership, who expect to interact in the future, and whose relations are direct (unmediated), and over multiple issues. Significantly, they do not include shared space, size, or social composition, a concern of many other writers, in their discussion.

29. See, for example, Donovan (1994), Hill and Press (1994), and Poffenberger (1994). The point is not that links between group size and the emergence of community are nonexistent. It is, rather, that such links, if present, require substantial attention and institutionalization if they are to become a foundation for community-based conservation.

30. For example, Marshall Murphree refers to the "optimal" size for communities (around ninety families) for revenue-sharing schemes incorporated within the CAMPFIRE wildlife program in Zimbabwe (Murphree 1993). See also Agrawal and Goyal (1998) for a game-theoretical argument about the relationship between group size and successful collective action in the context of resource management by village residents.

31. Such difficult-to-believe notions of community, in part, become possible owing to the conventional separation of market, state, and community from each other, and

the erosion of community that is presumed to proceed apace when external forces impinge upon it.

32. Taylor (1982) uses anthropological and historical sources to provide an extensive survey of hierarchy and stratification within even supposedly egalitarian communities. See also Rae (1981) and Sen (1992) for related arguments about the nature and existence of inequality.

33. See Western (1994), whose study of the Amboseli National Reserve shows, even though this is not a focus of the study, the differences within the putative community of "Masai." Agrawal (1999) and Robbins (1996) point to stratification within raika pastoralist groups who see themselves as distinct from landowners within their villages.

34. For similar proscriptions against cutting particular tree species, see Dorm-Adzobu and Veit (1991) and Matowanyika (1989).

35. See, for example, Nikijuluw (1994) for a discussion of sasi and Petuanang, which influence harvests of fish; and Rajasekaran and Warren (1994) for a discussion of sacred forests among the Malaiyala Gounder in the Kolli hills in India.

36. Michael Dove demonstrates how developers, planners, academics, and bureaucrats working with the Kantu of Kalimantan incorporated their own desires, hopes, and fears into the construction of a local "community" (Dove 1982).

37. The history of massive deforestation that occurred even prior to industrialization, and recent empirical literature that shows wasteful practices among indigenous groups, show that "the indigenous" cannot be identified with a conservation ethic. See Abrams et al. (1996) for a review of evidence in the case of the early Mayans; Fairservis (1975) for the Harappan civilization; and Meilleur (1996) and Steadman (1989) for Polynesia.

38. Western and Wright (1994) broach this idea in their first chapter. See also the discussion in Wells and Brandon (1992), who point out that sometimes communities may not be as effective as state officials in protecting resources or ensuring conservation.

39. Tully (1994) presents a clear argument about how Western theories of property, which provided the justification for taking over lands from Native Americans, were founded on the idea of land as being best used for agricultural purposes.

40. For insightful discussions of how tradition may often be only recently created but may change through politicized memory into a timeless, unchanging tradition, see Hobsbawm and Ranger (1983). For related work on how the past may be constituted in the present, or may exert a strong influence in shaping contemporary regimes of conservation, see Saberwal (1996) and Sivaramakrishnan (1995). In various forms these points are also being made in several recent writings on community, but rarely together. For some representative works, see Anderson and Grove (1989), Baviskar (1995), Fairhead and Leach (1996), and Sivaramakrishnan (1996).

41. For example, staff from the Game Department of Northern Rhodesia had a publicity van that traveled in rural areas trying to foment values for conservation in the early 1950s. Poaching rates remained unaffected.

42. Those who have worked with community-based projects in the field recognize this multiactor reality, and are forced to deal with complex webs of interests on a daily basis. It is curious that this reality has not found its way into those papers and studies that advocate community-based conservation. Michael Watts (1995, 60) approvingly cites Terry Eagleton's concern (1990, 88) about the attention to difference, as if "we have far too little variety, few social classes, that we should strive to generate 'two or three new bourgeoisies and a fresh clutch of aristocracies.' " Eagleton's worry about too many different groups is explicable, perhaps,

as the worry about not being able to carry out neat Marxist or rational choice analyses.

43. See, for example, Agrawal (1994b, 1995b).

44. The reverse also holds true. Power is visible only when it is put into action—its workings cannot be imagined or understood outside of the trace it leaves on processes. See Foucault (1983, 219–220).

45. Indeed, the list of the possible political-economic factors that impact upon processes at the local level can be increased several times without redundancy. See Sanderson (1994) and the other essays in Meyer and Turner (1994) that examine land use and cover change more generally.

46. See Bates (1983), Riker (1980), and Shepsle (1989). We define institutions in keeping with the large literature on the subject. But we underline that institutions in the shape of informal norms are difficult if not impossible to change in desired directions through external intervention.

Bibliography

Abrams, Elliot, AnnCorine Freter, David Rue, and John Wingard. 1996. "The Role of Deforestation in the Collapse of the Late Classic Copan Maya State." In *Tropical Deforestation: The Human Dimension*, ed. Leslie E. Sponsel, Thomas N. Headland, and Robert C. Bailey, 55–75. New York: Columbia University Press.

Agrawal, Arun. 1994a. "Rules, Rule-Making and Rule-Breaking: Examining the Fit between Rule Systems and Resource Use." In *Rules, Games, and Common-Pool Resources*, ed. Elinor Ostrom, Roy Gardner, and James Walker, 267–282. Ann Arbor: University of Michigan Press.

————. 1994b. "I Don't Need It But You Can't Have It: Politics on the Commons." *Pastoral Development Network* 36a (July): 36–55.

————. 1995a. "Dismantling the Divide between Indigenous and Scientific Knowledge." *Development and Change* 26:413–439.

————. 1995b. "Institutions for Disadvantaged Groups." Paper prepared for the Department of Policy Coordination and Sustainable Development, United Nations. Mimeo.

————. 1999. *Greener Pastures: Politics, Markets, and Community among a Migrant Pastoral People*. Durham, N.C.: Duke University Press.

Agrawal, Arun, and Sanjeev Goyal. 1998. "Group Size and Collective Action: Forest Councils of Kumaon, India." New Haven, Conn.: Department of Political Science, Yale University. Mimeo.

Agrawal, Arun, and K. Sivaramakrishnan, eds. 2000. *Agrarian Environments: Resources, Representation, and Rule in India*. Durham, N.C.: Duke University Press.

Agrawal, Arun, and Guatam Yadama. 1997. "How Do Local Institutions Mediate Market and Population Pressures on Resources? Forest *Panchayats* in Kumaon, India." *Development and Change* 28(3):435–465.

Alcorn, Janis. 1981. "Huastec Noncrop Resource Management: Implications for Prehistoric Rain Forest Management." *Human Ecology* 9:395–417.

————. 1993. "Indigenous Peoples and Conservation." *Conservation Biology* 7(2): 424–426.

Almond, Gabriel A., and Sidney Verba. 1963. *The Civic Culture: Political Attitudes and Democracy in Five Nations*. Princeton: Princeton University Press.

Alston, Lee J., Thrainn Eggertsson, and Douglass C. North, eds. 1996. *Empirical Studies in Institutional Change*. Cambridge, U.K.: Cambridge University Press.

Alvard, Michael S. 1993. "Testing the 'Ecologically Noble Savage' Hypothesis: Interspecific Prey Choice by Piro Hunters of Amazonian Peru." *Human Ecology* 21:355–387.

Anderson, Anthony, and Darrell Posey. 1989. "Management of a Tropical Scrub Savanna by the Gorotire Kayapo of Brazil." *Advances in Economic Botany* 7:159–173.

Anderson, David, and Richard Grove. 1989. *Conservation in Africa: People, Policies and Practice.* Cambridge, U.K.: Cambridge University Press.

Arizpe, Lourdes, M. Priscilla Stone, and David Major, eds. 1994. *Population and Environment: Rethinking the Debate.* Boulder, Colo.: Westview.

Arnold, J.E.M. 1990. "Social Forestry and Communal Management in India." *Social Forestry Network Paper* 11b. London: Overseas Development Institute.

Ascher, William. 1995. *Communities and Sustainable Forestry in Developing Countries.* San Francisco: Institute for Contemporary Studies Press.

Bailey, Robert C. 1990. "Exciting Opportunities in Tropical Rain Forest: A Reply to Townsend." *American Anthropologist* 92(3):747–748.

———. 1996. "Promoting Biodiversity and Empowering Local People in Central African Forests." In *Tropical Deforestation: The Human Dimension,* ed. Leslie E. Sponsel, Thomas N. Headland, and Robert C. Bailey, 316–341. New York: Columbia University Press.

Bailey, Robert C., et al. 1989. "Hunting and Gathering in the Tropical Rain Forest: Is it Possible?" *American Anthropologist* 91:59–82.

Bailey, Robert C., and Thomas Headland. 1991. "The Tropical Rain Forest: Is It a Productive Environment for Human Foragers?" *Human Ecology* 19(2):261–285.

Baines, Graham. 1991. "Asserting Traditional Rights: Community Conservation in Solomon Islands." *Cultural Survival Quarterly* 15(2):49–51.

Balee, William. 1992. "People of the Fallow: A Historical Ecology of Foraging in Lowland South America." In *Conservation of Neotropical Forests,* ed. Kent Redford and C. Padoch, 35–57. New York: Columbia University Press.

———. 1994. *Footprints of the Forest: Ka'apor Ethnobotany—The Historical Ecology of Plant Utilization by an Amazonian People.* New York: Columbia University Press.

Bates, Robert H. 1983. *Essays in the Political Economy of Tropical Africa.* Berkeley: University of California Press.

———. 1989. *Beyond the Miracle of the Market.* Cambridge, U.K.: Cambridge University Press.

Baviskar, Amita. 1995. *In the Belly of the River: Tribal Conflicts over Development in the Narmada Valley.* Delhi: Oxford University Press.

Bender, Thomas. 1978. *Community and Social Change in America.* Baltimore, Md.: Johns Hopkins University Press.

Berkes, Fikret, ed. 1989. *Common Property Resources: Ecology and Community-Based Sustainable Development.* London: Belhaven Press.

Bhatt, Chandi Prasad. 1990. "The Chipko Andolan: Forest Conservation Based on People's Power." *Environment and Urbanization* 2:7–18.

Black, Cyril. 1967. *The Dynamics of Modernization.* New York: Harper.

Booth, W. James. 1994. "On the Idea of the Moral Economy." *American Political Science Review* 88:653–667.

Borda, F., ed. 1985. *The Challenge of Social Change.* London: Sage.

Borghese, Elena. 1987. "Third World Development: The Role of Non-governmental Organizations." *OECD Observer,* No. 145.

Bratton, Michael. 1989a. "The Politics of Government-NGO Relations in Africa." *World Development* 17(4):569–587.

———. 1989b. "Beyond the State: Civil Society and Associational Life in Africa." *World Politics* 41(3):407–430.

Bromley, Daniel W., et al., eds. 1992. *Making the Commons Work: Theory, Practice and Policy.* San Francisco: Institute for Contemporary Studies Press.

Brookfield, H., and C. Padoch. 1994. "Appreciating Agrodiversity: A Look at the Dynamism and Diversity of Indigenous Farming Practices." *Environment* 36(5): 6–11, 37–45.

Chambers, Robert E., and Mark K. McBeth. 1992. "Community Encouragement: Returning to the Basis for Community Development." *Journal of the Community Development Society* 23(2):20–38.

Chitere, Orieko Preston, ed. 1994. *Community Development: Its Conceptions and Practice with Emphasis on Africa.* Nairobi: Gideon S. Were Press.

Clark, John. 1991. *Democratizing Development: The Role of Voluntary Organizations.* West Hartford, Conn.: Kumarian Press.

Clay, Jason, ed. 1988. *Indigenous Peoples and Tropical Forests: Models of Land Use and Management from Latin America.* Report # 27. Cambridge, Mass.: Cultural Survival.

Clist, N. 1989. "Archaeology in Gabon, 1886–1988." *African Archaeological Review* 7:59–95.

Clugston, Richard M., and Thomas J. Rogers. 1995. "Sustainable Livelihoods in North America." *Development* 3 (Sept.): 60–63.

Coleman, James S. 1990. *Foundations of Social Theory.* Cambridge, Mass.: Harvard University Press.

Conklin, Harold. 1957. *Hanunoo Agriculture.* Rome, Italy: United Nations.

Cook, Carolyn. 1996. "The Divided Island of New Guinea: People, Development and Deforestation." In *Tropical Deforestation: The Human Dimension,* ed. Leslie E. Sponsel, Thomas N. Headland, and Robert C. Bailey, 253–271. New York: Columbia University Press.

Cowen, Michael, and Robert Shenton. 1995. "The Invention of Development." In *Powers of Development,* ed. Jonathan Crush, 27–43. New York: Routledge.

Dei, George J. S. 1992. "A Forest Beyond the Trees: Tree Cutting in Rural Ghana." *Human Ecology* 20(1):57–88.

Denevan, William M. 1992. "The Pristine Myth: The Landscape of the Americas in 1492." *Annals of the Association of American Geographers* 82(3):369–385.

Deutsch, Karl. 1961. "Social Mobilization and Political Development." *American Political Science Review* 53(3):493–514.

Donovan, Richard. 1994. "BOSCOSA: Forest Conservation and Management through Local Institutions (Costa Rica)." In *Natural Connection: Perspectives in Community-Based Conservation,* ed. David Western and R. Michael Wright, 215–233. Washington, D.C.: Island Press.

Dorm-Adzobu, Clement, and Peter G. Veit. 1991. *Religious Beliefs and Environmental Protection: The Malshegu Sacred Grove in Northern Ghana.* Nairobi: World Resources Institute.

Douglass, Mike. 1992. "The Political Economy of Urban Poverty and Environmental Management in Asia: Access, Empowerment and Community Based Alternatives." *Environment and Urbanization* 4(2):9–32.

Dove, M. 1982. "The Myth of the 'Communal' Longhouse in Rural Development." In *Too Rapid Rural Development,* ed. C. MacAndrews and L. S. Chin, 14–78. Athens: Ohio State University Press.

Eagleton, Terry. 1990. "Defending the Free World." In *Socialist Register,* ed. R. Miliband and L. Panitch. London: Macmillan.

Eckholm, Eric. 1976. *Losing Ground: Environmental Stress and World Food Prospects.* New York: W. W. Norton.

Edgerton, Robert. 1992. *Sick Societies: Challenging the Myth of Primitive Harmony*. New York: Free Press.

Ensminger, Jean. 1992. *Making a Market: The Institutional Transformation of an African Society*. Cambridge, U.K.: Cambridge University Press.

Etzioni, Amitai. 1996. "Positive Aspects of Community and the Dangers of Fragmentation." *Development and Change* 27:301–314.

Fairhead, James, and Melissa Leach. 1994. "Contested Forests: Modern Conservation and Historical Land Use in Guinea's Ziama Reserve." *African Affairs* 93:481–512.

———. 1996. *Misreading the African Landscape: Society and Ecology in a Forest Savannah Mosaic*. Cambridge, U.K.: Cambridge University Press.

Fairservis, Walter, Jr. 1975. *The Roots of Ancient India*. Chicago: University of Chicago Press.

FAO (Food and Agriculture Organization). 1999. "Status and Progress in the Implementation of National Forest Programmes." Outcome of an FAO worldwide survey. Rome, Italy: FAO. Mimeo.

Fernandes, Aloysius. 1987. "NGOs in South Asia: People's Participation and Partnership." *World Development* 15 (supplement): 39–49.

Foucault, Michel. 1983. "The Subject and Power." In *Michel Foucault: Beyond Structuralism and Hermeneutics*, ed. Hubert L. Dreyfus and Paul Rabinow, 208–226. Chicago: University of Chicago Press.

Fox, Richard. 1969. "'Professional Primitives': Hunters and Gatherers of Nuclear South Asia." *Man in India* 49:139–160.

Geertz, Clifford, ed. 1963. *Old Societies and New States: The Quest for Modernity in Asia and Africa*. New York: Free Press of Glencoe.

Ghai, Dharam. 1993. "Conservation, Livelihood and Democracy: Social Dynamics of Environmental Change in Africa." *Osterreichische Zeitschrift fur Soziologie* 18: 56–75.

Gibson, Clark. 1999. *Politicians and Poachers: The Political Economy of Wildlife Policy in Africa*. Cambridge, U.K.: Cambridge University Press.

Gibson, Clark, and Stuart Marks. 1995. "Transforming Rural Hunters into Conservationists: An Assessment of Community-Based Wildlife Management Programs in Africa." *World Development* 23:941–957.

Gurung, Barun. 1992. "Towards Sustainable Development: A Case in the Eastern Himalayas." *Futures* 24:907–916.

Gusfield, Joseph R. 1978. *Community: A Critical Response*. New York: Harper and Row.

Hames, Raymond. 1991. "Wildlife Conservation in Tribal Societies." In *Biodiversity: Culture, Conservation and Ecodevelopment*, ed. Margery L. Oldfield and Janis B. Alcorn, 172–199. Boulder, Colo.: Westview.

Hart, Terese, and John Hart. 1986. "The Ecological Basis of Hunter-Gatherer Subsistence in African Rain Forests: The Mbuti of Eastern Zaire." *Human Ecology* 14(1):29–56.

Hill, M. A., and A. J. Press. 1994. "Kakadu National Park: An Australian Experience in Comanagement." In *Natural Connections: Perspectives in Community-Based Conservation*, ed. David Western and R. Michael Wright, 135–160. Washington, D.C.: Island Press.

Hoban, Thomas J., and Maurice G. Cook. 1988. "Challenge of Conservation." *Forum for Applied Research and Public Policy* 3:100–102.

Hobsbawm, Eric, and Terence Ranger. 1983. *The Invention of Tradition*. Cambridge, U.K.: Cambridge University Press.

Huntsinger, Lynn, and Sarah McCaffrey. 1995. "A Forest for the Trees: Forest Management and the Yurok Environment." *American Indian Culture and Research Journal* 19:155–192.

Ilahaine, Hsain. 1995. "Common Property, Ethnicity, and Social Exploitation in the Ziz Valley, Southeast Morocco." Paper presented at the IASCP conference.

Ives, J. D., and B. Messerli. 1989. *The Himalayan Dilemma: Reconciling Development and Conservation*. London: Routledge.

Kiss, Agnes, ed. 1990. *Living with Wildlife: Wildlife Resource Management with Local Participation in Africa*. Washington, D.C.: World Bank.

Kothari, Rajni. 1984. "Environment and Alternative Development." *Alternatives* 5:427–475.

Lappé, Frances Moore, and Rachel Schurman. 1989. *Taking Population Seriously*. London: Earthscan.

Lerner, Daniel. 1962. *The Passing of Traditional Society: Modernizing the Middle East*. Glencoe, Ill.: Free Press.

Li, Tania Murray. 1996. "Images of Community: Discourse and Strategy in Property Relations." *Development and Change* 27(3):501–528.

Lowry, Alma, and Timothy P. Donahue. 1994. "Parks, Politics, and Pluralism: The Demise of National Parks in Togo." *Society and Natural Resources* 7:321–329.

Lynch, Owen J., and Kirk Talbott. 1995. *Balancing Acts: Community-Based Forest Management and National Law in Asia and the Pacific*. Washington, D.C.: World Resources Institute.

McCay, Bonnie J., and James Acheson, eds. 1989. *The Question of the Commons: The Culture and Ecology of Communal Resources*. Tucson: University of Arizona Press.

McDade, Lucinda, ed. 1993. *La Selva: Ecology and Natural History of a Neotropical Rainforest*. Chicago: University of Chicago Press.

McKean, Margaret A. 1992. "Success on the Commons: A Comparative Examination of Institutions for Common Property Resource Management." *Journal of Theoretical Politics* 4(3):247–282.

McNeely, Jeffrey A. 1996. "Foreword." In *Tropical Deforestation: The Human Dimension*, ed. Leslie Sponsel, Thomas N. Headland, and Robert C. Bailey, xix–xxi. New York: Columbia University Press.

Madzudzo, E., and Y. Dzingirai. 1995. "A Comparative Study of the Implications of Ethnicity on CAMPFIRE in Bulilimamangwe and Binga." Centre for Applied Social Sciences Working Paper. Harare: University of Zimbabwe.

Maine, Henry. 1871. *Village Communities in the East and the West*. New York: Holt and Company.

———. 1905. *Ancient Law*. London: Murray.

Marks, S. 1984. *The Imperial Lion: Human Dimensions of Wildlife Management in Central Africa*. Boulder, Colo.: Westview Press.

Matowanyika, J.Z.Z. 1989. "Cast Out of Eden: Peasants vs. Wildlife Policy in Savanna Africa." *Alternatives* 16(1):30–35.

Matzke, Gordon Edwin, and Nontokozo Nabane. 1996. "Outcomes of a Community-Controlled Wildlife Program in a Zambezi Valley Community." *Human Ecology* 24(1):65–85.

Meffe, G., A. Ehrlich, and D. Ehrenfeld. 1993. "Human Population Control: The Missing Agenda." *Conservation Biology* 7(1):1–3.

Meilleur, Brien A. 1996. "Forests and Polynesian Adaptations." In *Tropical Deforestation: The Human Dimension*, ed. Leslie E. Sponsel, Thomas N. Headland, and Robert C. Bailey, 76–94. New York: Columbia University Press.

Meyer, William B., and B. L. Turner II, eds. 1994. *Changes in Land Use and Land Cover: A Global Perspective*. Cambridge, U.K.: Cambridge University Press.

Mishra, Smita. 1994. "Women's Indigenous Knowledge of Forest Management in Orissa (India)." *Indigenous Knowledge and Development Monitor* 2(3).

Moore, Donald. 1996a. "A River Runs Through It: Environmental History and the

Politics of Community in Zimbabwe's Eastern Highlands." Working Paper Series, Center for Applied Social Sciences, University of Zimbabwe, and Program for Land and Agrarian Studies, University of Western Cape, South Africa.

——. 1996b. "Marxism, Culture and Politics Ecology: Environmental Struggles in Zimbabwe's Eastern Highlands." In *Liberation Ecologies: Environment, Development, Social Movements*, ed. Richard Peet and Michael Watts. New York: Routledge.

Morris, Brian. 1977. "Tappers, Trappers and the Hill Pandaram (South India)." *Anthropos* 72:225–241.

Murphree, Marshall W. 1993. *Communities as Resource Management Institutions*. London: International Institute for Environment and Development.

Myers, Norman. 1991. "The World's Forests and Human Populations: The Environmental Interconnections." In *Resources, Environment, and Population: Present Knowledge, Future Options*, ed. K. Davis and M. Bernstam, 237–251. New York: Oxford University Press.

Naughton-Treves, Lisa. 1997. "Wildlife versus Farmers: Vulnerable Places and People Around Kibale National Park, Uganda." *Geographical Review* 87(1):462–488.

Naughton-Treves, Lisa, and Steven Sanderson. 1995. "Property, Politics and Wildlife Conservation." *World Development* 23(8):1265–1275.

Newmark, W. D. 1995. "Extinction of Mammal Population in Western North American National Parks." *Conservation Biology* 9(3):512–526.

——. 1996. "Insularization of Tanzanian Parks and the Local Extinction of Large Mammals." *Conservation Biology* 10(6):1549–1556.

Nikijuluw, Viktor. 1994. "Indigenous Fisheries Resource Management in the Maluku Islands." *Indigenous Knowledge and Development Monitor* 2(2):7–10.

North, Douglass. 1990. *Institutions, Institutional Change, and Economic Performance*. Cambridge, U.K.: Cambridge University Press.

Ostrom, Elinor. 1990. *Governing the Commons: The Evolution of Institutions for Collective Action*. New York: Cambridge University Press.

——. 1992. *Crafting Institutions for Self-Governing Irrigation Systems*. San Francisco: Institute for Contemporary Studies Press.

Park, Chris. 1992. *Tropical Rainforests*. New York: Routledge.

Parker, Eugene. 1993. "Fact and Fiction in Amazonia: The Case of the Apete." *American Anthropologist* 95:715–723.

Parker, H. 1909. *Ancient Ceylon: An Account of the Aborigines and a Part of the Early Civilization*. London: Luzac.

Parsons, Talcott. 1951. *The Social System*. New York: Free Press.

——. 1960. "Pattern Variables Revisited: A Response to Robert Dubin." *American Sociological Review* 25:467–483.

——. 1966. *Societies: Evolutionary and Comparative Perspectives*. Englewood Cliffs, N.J.: Prentice-Hall.

Parsons, Talcott, and Edward Shils. 1962. *Toward a General Theory of Action*. New York: Harper.

Perry, James A., and Robert K. Dixon. 1986. "An Interdisciplinary Approach to Community Resource Management: Preliminary Field Test in Thailand." *Journal of Developing Areas* 21(1):31–47.

Peters, Pauline. 1994. *Dividing the Commons: Politics, Policy and Culture in Botswana*. Charlottesville: University of Virginia Press.

——, ed. 1996. "Who's Local Here: The Politics of Participation in Development." *Cultural Survival Quarterly* 20(3):1–5 (special issue).

Phillipson, D. 1985. *African Archaeology*. Cambridge, U.K.: Cambridge University Press.

Poffenberger, Mark, ed. 1990. *Keepers of the Forest: Land Management Alternatives in Southeast Asia*. West Hartford, Conn.: Kumarian.

————. 1994. "The Resurgence of Community Forest Management in Eastern India." In *Natural Connections. Perspectives in Community-Based Conservation*, ed. David Western and R. Michael Wright, 53–79. Washington, D.C.: Island Press.

Posey, Darrell. 1984. "A Preliminary Report on Diversified Management of Tropical Forest by the Kayapo Indians of the Brazilian Amazon." *Advances in Economic Botany* 1:112–126.

————. 1985. "Indigenous Management of Tropical Forest Ecosystems: The Case of the Kayapo Indians of the Brazilian Amazon." *Agroforestry Systems* 3:139–158.

Posey, Darrell, and W. Balee, eds. 1989. *Resource Management in Amazonia: Indigenous and Folk Strategies*. Bronx, N.Y.: New York Botanical Garden.

Rae, Douglas. 1981. *Equalities*. Cambridge, U.K.: Cambridge University Press.

Rajasekaran, B., and D. M. Warren. 1994. "IK for Socioeconomic Development and Biodiversity Conservation: The Kolli Hills." *Indigenous Knowledge and Development Monitor* 2(2):15–19.

Raju, G., Raju Vaghela, and Manju S. Raju. 1993. *Development of People's Institutions for Management of Forests*. Ahmedabad, India: Viksat, Nehru Foundation for Development.

Rambo, Terry. 1985. *Primitive Polluters: Semang Impact on the Malaysian Tropical Rain Forest Ecosystem*. Ann Arbor: Museum of Anthropology, University of Michigan.

Redford, Kent. 1990. "The Ecologically Noble Savage." *Cultural Survival Quarterly* 15(1):46–48.

Redford, Kent, and Jane Mansour, eds. 1996. *Traditional Peoples and Biodiversity Conservation in Large Tropical Landscapes*. Arlington, Va.: The Nature Conservancy, Latin America and Caribbean Division.

Redford, Kent, and Allyn Stearman. 1993. "On Common Ground: Response to Alcorn." *Conservation Biology* 7(2):427–428.

Repetto, Robert, and M. Gillis. 1988. *Public Policies and the Misuse of Forest Resources*. Cambridge, U.K.: Cambridge University Press.

Riker, William. 1980. "Implications for the Disequilibrium of Majority Rule for the Study of Institutions." *American Political Science Review* 74:432–447.

Robbins, Paul. 1996. "Nomadization in Western Rajasthan: An Institutional and Economic Perspective." Mimeo.

Robinson, John G., and Kent Redford, eds. 1991. *Neotropical Wildlife Use and Conservation*. Chicago: University of Chicago Press.

Robinson, Mike. 1995. "Towards a New Paradigm of Community Development." *Community Development Journal* 30(1):21–30.

Roosevelt, Anna. 1989. "Resource Management in Amazonia Before the Conquest: Beyond Ethnographic Projection." *Advances in Economic Botany* 7:30–62.

Saberwal, Vasant. 1996. "You Can't Grow Timber and Goats in the Same Patch of Forest: Grazing Policy Formulation in Himachal Pradesh, India, 1865–1960." Prepared for presentation at the workshop on Agrarian Environments: Resources, Representations and Rule in India, Program in Agrarian Studies, 2–4 May 1997,Yale University, New Haven, Conn.

Sanderson, Steven. 1994. "Political-Economic Institutions." In *Changes in Land Use and Land Cover: A Global Perspective*, ed. William B. Meyer and B. L. Turner II, 329–356. Cambridge, U.K.: Cambridge University Press.

Sen, Amartya. 1992. *Inequality Reexamined*. Cambridge, U.K.: Cambridge University Press.

Shepsle, Kenneth. 1989. "Studying Institutions: Some Lessons from the Rational Choice Approach." *Journal of Theoretical Politics* 1:131–149.

Shils, Edward. 1962. *Political Development in the New States*. The Hague: Mouton.

Simon, Julian. 1990. *Population Matters: People, Resources, Environment and Integration.* New Brunswick, N.J.: Transaction Publishers.

Singleton, Sara, and Michael Taylor. 1992. "Common Property, Collective Action and Community." *Journal of Theoretical Politics* 4(3):309–324.

Sivaramakrishnan, K. 1995. "Colonialism and Forestry in India: Imagining the Past in Present." *Comparative Studies in Society and History* 37(1):3–40.

———. 1996. "Forests, Politics and Governance in Bengal, 1794–1994." Vols. 1 & 2. Ph.D. dissertation, Yale University.

Sponsel, Leslie E. 1992. "The Environmental History of Amazonia: Natural and Human Disturbances and the Ecological Transition." In *Changing Tropical Forests,* ed. Harold Steen and Richard Tucker, 233–251. Durham, N.C.: Forest History Society.

Sponsel, Leslie E., Thomas N. Headland, and Robert C. Bailey, eds. 1996. *Tropical Deforestation: The Human Dimension.* New York: Columbia University Press.

Steadman, David. 1989. "Extinction of Birds in Eastern Polynesia: A Review of the Record, and Comparison with Other Island Groups." *Journal of Archaeological Science* 16:175–205.

Taylor, Michael. 1982. *Community, Anarchy and Liberty.* Cambridge, U.K.: Cambridge University Press.

Tully, James. 1994. "Aboriginal Property and Western Theory: Recovering Middle Ground." *Social Philosophy and Policy* 11(2):153–180.

Wade, Robert. 1987. *Village Republics: Economic Conditions for Collective Action.* Cambridge, U.K.: Cambridge University Press.

Warren, Mark. 1992. "Democratic Theory and Self-Transformation." *American Political Science Review* 86(1):8–23.

Watts, Michael. 1995. "A New Deal in Emotions: Theory and Practice and the Crisis of Development." In *Power of Development,* ed. Jonathan Crush, 44–62. London: Routledge.

Wells, Michael, and Katrina Brandon. 1992. *People and Parks: Linking Protected Area Management with Local Communities.* Washington, D.C.: World Bank, World Wildlife Fund, and United StatesAgency for International Development.

Western, David. 1994. "Ecosystem Conservation and Rural Development." In *Natural Connections. Perspectives in Community-Based Conservation,* ed. David Western and R. Michael Wright, 15–52. Washington, D.C.: Island Press.

Western, David, and R. Michael Wright, eds. 1994. *Natural Connections: Perspectives in Community-Based Conservation.* Washington, D.C.: Island Press.

Wilmsen, Edwin. 1989. *Land Filled with Flies: A Political Economy of the Kalahari.* Chicago: University of Chicago Press.

Wisner, Ben. 1990. "Harvest of Sustainability: Recent Books on Environmental Management." *Journal of Development Studies* 26:335–341.

Wolf, Eric. 1982. *Europe and the People without History.* Berkeley: University of California Press.

Yoon, Carol. 1993. "Rain Forests Seen as Shaped by Human Hand." *New York Times,* July 27, pp. C1, C10.

Zerner, Charles. 1994. "Through a Green Lens: The Construction of Customary Environmental Law and Community in Indonesia's Maluku Islands." *Law and Society Review* 28(5):1079–1122.

Chapter 1   Invoking Community

MELANIE HUGHES MCDERMOTT

Indigenous People
and Ancestral Domain
in Palawan,
the Philippines

"COMMUNITY-BASED FOREST MANAGEMENT" has been proclaimed as official policy of the Philippine government.[1] One of the mechanisms for implementing this approach was formulated in 1993 as the Certificate of Ancestral Domain Claim (CADC). This administrative instrument grants indigenous groups conditional rights within newly mapped boundaries of ancestral land for which they can demonstrate occupation since "time immemorial."[2] This policy is based upon a model of an indigenous community that is homogeneous, that is territorially and socially bounded, and that has always existed in an ecologically harmonious balance. This codification of community fixes its spatial and temporal dimensions and ignores its internal divisions, rendering it ahistorical and apolitical—and therefore amenable to external political control. Although it represents an important step forward in indigenous peoples' struggles, the policy fails to bring about the reallocation of resource control (i.e., power) necessary to achieve stated objectives of social justice and environmental protection.

A brief review of the political context and evolution of Philippine land and forest policy indicates that the new "community-based" trend does not significantly deviate from the historical pattern of perpetuating state control over land and natural resources and their allotment to powerful interests. The task is then to analyze the specific language of the CADC policy to examine how and why the state constructs "community" in the way it does, and to consider why "indigenous" communities might have been chosen as the particular subjects.

The second part of this chapter presents a case study of one community indigenous to the island province of Palawan.[3] When the characteristics of this community are matched against those of the state-invented image of community, several discrepancies emerge. First, the state's image clearly fails to account for differences within the community with regard to interests, access to external resources, and influence over political decision-making. Second, the community lacks the posited capacity to engage in collective action, particularly to regulate resource use by outsiders. Finally, the policy is based on the misconception that the historic relationship between the community and its environment was based on a culturally maintained balance, rather than on exclusive use and de facto control. However, even the correction of these deficiencies would not be sufficient to achieve policy goals in this case. Rather, an effective ancestral domain policy would provide local people with control over local resources and open channels of access to necessary extralocal resources, in particular, political influence and capital.

The struggle to obtain and maintain the CADC, however, may be catalyzing the development of "community capacity" (Kusel and Fortmann 1991). Significantly, the CADC has also provided symbolic resources. The indigenous people of Palawan have used the new meanings of indigenous identity and ancestral domain emerging out of national and local debates over the CADC to make strategic alliances that have yielded political and material resources. In the process, they have raised the local and national profile of the struggle for indigenous peoples' rights.

Community as Constructed by the State

EVOLUTION OF CADC AND "COMMUNITY-BASED" RESOURCE POLICIES

The Certificate of Ancestral Domain Claim represents an apparently radical step by the Philippine government toward recognizing indigenous people's claims on land and resources that had heretofore been controlled exclusively by the state. But the extent to which the CADC represents a truly radical shift is contestable. First, the CADC instrument was developed and approved not because there was a sea-change at the highest levels of the natural resource bureaucracy or among its political masters, but because of a convergence of efforts on the parts of an internal bureaucratic faction, external supporters, and foreign-funded consultants. Not surprisingly then, almost as soon as the CADC policy was passed, it was assailed by legal challenges and constrained by contradictory government issuances. Second, the CADC in fact fails to devolve practical resource control to local communities. Nonetheless, indigenous peoples and their advocates have been using the CADC to their strategic advantage in advancing their struggles for self-determination and in pushing for a more adequate governmental response to their demands.

In order to understand the conception of community constructed by the Certificate of Ancestral Domain Claim (CADC) instrument, it is necessary to review how this policy and its precedents evolved in response to changing legal, political, and economic contexts. The CADC instrument is one in a series of policy issuances and programs that the Department of Environment and Natural Resources (DENR) has attempted to integrate under the unifying theme of "community-based forest management," declared the national forest policy in 1995. In contrast, twenty years previously, the Revised Forestry Code, P.D. 705 (still in effect), pronounced all forest residents illegal squatters on public land. Now these same communities are being tasked with forest stewardship. What changed in the intervening two decades?

With respect to the nation's forests, the most striking change is their decline. Estimated at 90 percent in precolonial times, Philippine forest cover had declined to roughly 20 percent by 1988 (Kummer 1992; World Bank 1989). By this time the Philippines had become a net importer of timber (DENR 1995), after having been one of the world's largest exporters from the 1920s to 1960s (Broad 1993). It would appear that both the resource to be managed and the potential profits have been grossly diminished—and with them the opportunity costs of sharing management with communities or any other party. At the same time, the population in communities available for the job has burgeoned. The earliest reliable estimate of the number of people residing (illegally) within "public forest land" put the figure at over 14.4 million in 1980 (Cruz, Zosa-Feranil, et al. 1988)—estimated to have reached 24 million by 1995[4] out of the national population of 68.5 million (NSO 1995).

Both the formally illegal occupation of public lands by millions of citizens and the policies perpetuating the issue can be seen as colonial legacies. The Spanish conquest bequeathed the Philippines a legal concept known as the Regalian Doctrine, asserting that all land and resources that the Crown (or its successor, the State) has not privately granted or sold remain under its dominion. While the validity of this interpretation has been challenged by some legal authorities (see A. B. Gatmaytan 1992; Royo 1988), the principle of state ownership of all untitled land and resources was adopted by the U.S. colonial administration and is today enshrined in the Philippine Constitution

(1987, art. XII, sec. 1 and 2). In a continuation of U.S. policy, access to public lands and all natural resources is granted only by means of a system of leases, concessions, permits, and "production-sharing agreements," currently administered by the DENR. This is mandated by the 1975 Revised Forestry Code (P.D. 705), which includes among "forest" lands all untitled lands of slope 18 percent or over (regardless of the presence or absence of forest cover). The occupation of the 53 percent (DENR 1995) of the nation's land area constituting its "public forest land" was thereby criminalized (A. B. Gatmaytan 1992; Lynch and Talbott 1988).

By the 1980s it had become clear that the state had neither the capability nor the political mandate to evict millions of upland dwellers. At the same time, government was manifestly failing to check the troubling rate of deforestation. Although upland farming remained a favorite target of blame for this destruction, the state did not wish to interdict migration to the uplands, a critical safety valve against explosions of discontent over the skewed distribution of power, wealth, and land in the lowlands—as had occurred in the post–World War II Huk rebellion (Kerkvliet 1977). The DENR acknowledged that without any tenurial security, upland farmers had little incentive to use sustainable methods or to improve their land. Moreover, the successors to the Huks, the communist New People's Army and Muslim separatist insurgents, were finding support in their upland home bases among the landless.

In response to these pressures, the Integrated Social Forestry Program was initiated in 1982.[5] This was the first of a series of programs allowing individuals or registered communities to obtain a form of conditional leasehold within public forest land in return for a commitment to its protection and improvement (e.g., by planting trees). The DENR releases land for this purpose, however, only after the timber is gone. In return, the DENR expects to obtain a cheap labor force for upland reforestation and forest protection, to stabilize upland encroachment, to increase the productivity of upland agriculture, and to quiet potential dissent.

The Philippine government has also reaped a rich harvest of foreign aid that finances a plethora of programmatic solutions designed by the DENR to meet these objectives. Each of these programs is mandated by a unique policy instrument, many of which have created unique tenurial instruments. This proliferation of policy issuances reflects the fact that each has been sponsored under separate, multimillion-dollar international development aid agreements with different donors and lending institutions.[6] Impoverished rural households, it would seem, are good foreign exchange earners.

Prior to 1992, none of these policies made a distinction between recent migrants to public forest lands and the ethnic groups indigenous to them. The

Spanish and U.S. colonial administrations invented the ethnic and spatial division of the native population of the Philippines into a Christian, nominally Western majority residing in the lowlands, and a "non-Christian," "tribal" minority originating in (or having retreated to) the uplands (Hirtz 1998; Scott 1982). Preserving the colonial logic, the Philippines' post-Marcos 1987 Constitution conferred a special status to "indigenous cultural communities." In addition to their cultural distinctiveness, then, indigenous groups are characterized as being necessarily associated into communities. Indeed, beginning in the first years of American administration with the creation of civil reservations, the various administrative and legislative attempts to make special provisions with regard to public lands for "tribal" Filipinos have almost all been made explicitly in favor of communities (de Guzman 1992; Gatmaytan 1989).

By the 1970s, after centuries of retreat and episodic struggles to retain territory, indigenous peoples began seeking alliances with guerrillas, religious organizations, and other nongovernmental groups. They sought to resist the state's appropriation of their homelands through the construction of dams, the granting of timber and mining concessions, and military attempts to flush out rebels. After the 1986 "People Power" revolution that overthrew the Marcos dictatorship, nongovernmental organizations (NGOs) proliferated. Many were led by former dissidents, human rights lawyers, and indigenous rights advocates, some of whom received appointments to government agencies or foreign-funded consultancies. These individuals were in a good position to influence the Constitutional Commission and the Department of Environment and Natural Resources in favor of indigenous people. Meanwhile the demands of newly formed indigenous people's organizations were crystallizing around recognition of ancestral domain. As a result, the 1987 Constitution promises (art. XII, sec. 5): "The State . . . shall protect the rights of indigenous cultural communities to their ancestral lands. . . . The Congress may provide for the applicability of customary laws governing property rights or relations in determining the ownership and extent of ancestral domains."

Concurrent with seeking legislative remedy, advocates for indigenous people have pursued alternative strategies that focus on the administrative powers of the DENR.[7] After 1986, newly appointed human rights lawyers worked both inside the bureaucracy in alliance with sympathetic agency staff, and outside it with their NGO colleagues who were aligned with indigenous people's organizations and supported by certain project consultants and foreign organizations.[8] This informal coalition was able to bring about the insertion of conditionalities addressing the concerns of indigenous communities into international loans. Significantly, "action to recognize and protect ancestral domain rights," reflected in "performance indicators," was made an objective for the release of loan "tranches" of the five-year, multimillion-dollar USAID-funded Natural Resources Management Program (NRMP 1990). A team of NRMP consultants, composed of indigenous rights lawyers and advocates, working with allies within the DENR, drafted the Department Administrative Order No. 2, series 1993 (hereafter DAO 2), which establishes the Certificate of Ancestral Domain Claim (CADC).

While the state is constitutionally prohibited from granting ownership over public land and resources to any party, the DAO 2 stipulates a process through which an "indigenous cultural community" can delineate, document, and gain "recognition" of its "claim" to territory in the form of a certificate, or CADC. While the precise nature of the resource rights the CADC bestows upon recipients remains a matter of debate, the DAO 2 does specify the nature of the communities that may qualify. In order to avail itself of the limited tenurial security that the CADC offers, an applicant group must meet the standard and supply the proofs expected of an "indigenous cultural community." In this sense, the state may create community in two ways: first, by defining what constitutes community and thereby creating the incentive for groups of coresidents to define themselves in that way, and second, by indirectly catalyzing the formation of community capacity through local pursuit and implementation of the policy.

CONCEPTIONS OF COMMUNITY IN THE CADC

A close examination of the administrative order (DAO 2) that established the CADC reveals the way in which it rests upon a particular notion of what constitutes a community. The DAO 2 further assumes that particular features characterize indigenous communities in a way that qualifies them as deserving of special rights to resources and as capable of managing those resources sustainably.

DAO 2 (art. I, sec. 1) opens by stating: "It is the policy of the DENR to preserve and maintain the integrity of ancestral domains and ensure recognition of the customs and traditions of the indigenous cultural communities."

It then adopts the following definitions (art. I, sec. 3):

> *Indigenous Cultural Communities*—a homogenous society [sic] identified by self-ascription and ascription by others, who have continuously lived as a community on communally bounded and defined territory, sharing common bonds of language, customs, traditions and other distinctive cultural traits, and who, through resistance to the political, social and cultural inroads of colonization, became historically differentiated from the majority of Filipinos.

Ancestral domain—refers to all land and natural resources occupied or possessed by indigenous cultural communities . . . in accordance with their customs and traditions since time immemorial.

These statements reflect the conception that indigenous communities are fixed, homogeneous groups occupying delimited territories since some unspecified time in the past. Furthermore, in this conception, the boundaries of this territory have been communally established.

In order to obtain a CADC, the applicant must submit "proof of claims [that] include the testimony of elders and other documents directly or indirectly attesting to the possession or occupation of the area since time immemorial." These documents may include: "sketch maps, pictures of old improvements, burial grounds, sacred places, traditional land marks, and communal forest and hunting grounds; as well as written accounts of the community's history, customs, political institutions, place names in local dialect, anthropological data, and genealogical surveys" (art. III, sec. 5).

A CADC assumes that the individuals currently residing within the domain in question are descendants of an unbroken line that has lived and died within this same space. The effects of their residence, agriculture and forest management activities, the location of graves and the sacredness of particular places ought to be visible (indeed, clearly indicated in photographs). While a community's management of natural resources is expected to have produced permanent "improvements," it is also asserted to be uniquely "indigenous," "sustainable," "ecologically sound," and "traditional" (art. I, sec. 1).

Finally, the DAO 2 makes a number of assertions about the nature of a community's political institutions and processes. The administrative order posits that strong, representative, and accountable leaders head the CADC-holding communities. If leaders are able to speak with one voice, it follows that the same interests must either be held by all, that the community must cede all authority to its leaders, or that an equitable process exists for forging a consensus or selecting among competing interests: "Unless otherwise specified by the indigenous cultural community concerned, the indigenous organizational and leadership systems such as, but not limited to, Council of Elders or bodies of similar nature existing in the community, shall be recognized as the decision-making and managing body within the domain" (art. VI, sec. 2).

Some of the decisions the community may be called upon to make include: boundary delineation, preparation of a "comprehensive management plan," executing a "memorandum of agreement," and "transferring responsibility over [critical watershed] areas" to other parties. While it is implied that, in general, leaders follow indigenous principles for reaching decisions, two other processes are specified for specific kinds of decisions. "A majority of their acknowledged leaders" may make and sign a written decision approving land transfers (art. IX, sec. 1). In another case, in order to permit resource exploitation by outsiders, it would be necessary to obtain the "collective consent in writing of the community expressed through public hearings and consultations with them" (art. IV, sec. 4). It is not specified how this will be achieved despite high illiteracy rates, nor who will conduct these consultations or how they will conclude whose voices reach what consensus.

WHAT RIGHTS DOES THE CADC GIVE COMMUNITIES?

The CADC grants communities the rights "to occupy, cultivate, and utilize the land and all natural resources found therein . . . to benefit and to share the profits . . . to claim ownership of all improvements" (art. VII, sec. 1). They are also given "the right to negotiate the terms and conditions for the exploitation of natural resources in the area." Their objective in doing so, however, is given: "for the purpose of ensuring the observance of . . . environmental protection . . . measures pursuant to national and customary laws." Existing forest product concessions held by other parties within CADC areas will be allowed to expire without renewal (unless explicitly permitted by "the community"). In return, the CADC-holders agree to take on responsibilities, which include: "establish and activate indigenous practices or culturally-founded strategies to protect, conserve and develop the natural resources . . . restore, preserve and maintain a balanced ecology" (art. VII, sec. 1). In other words, DENR grants beneficiary communities rights to protect and improve resources, rather than to exploit them.

Just in case the assumption of traditional ecological virtue might be violated, the DAO 2 provides that utilization rights are "subject to existing laws, rules, and regulations" (art. VII, sec. 1) and that areas "which are found to be necessary for critical watersheds" and other matters of "National Interest . . . shall be maintained, managed, protected from encroachment" (art IX, sec. 1). Moreover, "the DENR reserves the right to regulate the cutting or harvesting of timber crops . . . should it discover . . . that the manner by which the timber and other minor [sic] products are cut or harvested may lead to the destruction of the forest cover" (art IX, sec. 2).

This restriction points to a crucial area of ambiguity in the DAO 2 that became the subject of legal challenges and fierce contention both inside and outside the DENR. The debate fully emerged only after a number of CADCs had been issued and it had come to wider attention that potentially vast areas, indeed much of the nation's remaining forest resource, could be subject to

;tral domain claims. Positions were split in at least four ways. Several rad-indigenous peoples federations opposed the CADC outright on the grounds that it represents a mere "claim" and thus confirms the principle of state ownership of ancestral domain. A faction of CADC supporters claimed that the DAO 2 as a legal instrument grants CADC-holders the rights to extract and market forest resources. At the other end of the spectrum, others insisted that the CADC merely represents a "claim," and therefore recipient communities must submit an application (with the requisite technical inventories, fees, etc.) for the usual licenses. Finally, the DENR's DAO 34 of 1996 marked a compromise position. This new order established guidelines that a CADC-holding community must follow in the preparation of an "Ancestral Domain Management Plan."[9] DAO 34 states that this plan shall be sufficient for the exercise of "sustainable traditional resource rights," which include the use of "areas of economic . . . value in accordance with their indigenous knowledge, belief systems, and practices" (art. III, sec. 8; art. I, sec. 2). Other forms of resource utilization, however, will require the community to follow standard procedures to obtain standard licenses. The administrative order does not resolve the question of whether "traditional resource rights" include the commercial trade of forest products, a centuries-old source of income for many indigenous groups. Since the DENR has not established any new procedures for its local offices to grant transport documents and other requirements on the basis of a domain management plan, communities have gained no practical rights to earn money.

THE ROLE AND INTENTIONS OF STATE AGENCIES

The inconsistencies and gaps in DENR policy implementation may reflect not so much conceptual confusion as the fact that there are multiple factions within the bureaucracy that represent various interests, legal opinions, and patrons among politicians and donors. Indeed, the lack of clarity in DENR's administrative orders regarding indigenous community rights and their implementation may serve the function of appearing to resolve these debates and to address advocates' demands—without devolving effective new rights to communities.

This lack of clarity, together with the evidence from the case of Kayasan, suggests that the DAO 2 created an ideal-type of "indigenous cultural community" and its claims in an attempt to serve various interests simultaneously. It also suggests that when we look for the role of the state, or one of its agencies, in inventing community we should expect to find multiple functions, functionaries, and interests.

Why would the elements of the state use a particular statute (the DAO 2)

to construct community in a particular way? Why might the DENR have chosen to mandate community as the recipient of the "recognition" of indigenous
peoples' claims? Why might "indigenous cultural community" have been
defined in the way DAO 2 does?

The DENR's policy shift toward community-based resource management
serves several objectives. These can be grouped in three sets: (1) improving
the welfare of uplanders and defusing social conflict, (2) protecting the forest
and containing upland encroachment, and (3) maintaining state ownership
and control over forest land and resources.

The objective of meeting social needs and preventing conflict can be met
only by tacitly keeping open the safety valve for lowland out-migration
(which the state lacks the capacity to shut in any event), while taking steps
toward meeting uplanders' demands for tenurial security (Eder and Fernandez
1996; Lynch and Talbott 1988). When the claims of one set of uplanders,
namely the indigenous people, are regularized, their demands for tenurial
security are partly met while the government continues to maintain control.

Why were indigenous communities selected for this purpose? First, there
is the Constitutional promise "to protect the rights of indigenous cultural
communities to their ancestral lands" (art. XII, sec. 5). As the fact that this
provision made it into the 1987 Constitution reflects, national advocates,
allies within the state, and international supporters back the demands of
indigenous people for land rights. In addition, the state-constructed image of
an "indigenous cultural community" epitomizes the qualities of an ideal community: timeless, homogeneous, cohesive, self-regulating, adhering to common values, socially and environmentally sustainable . . . and poor and
powerless. The state, through the agency of the DENR, maintains control by
creating this standard for indigenous community status, serving as the arbiter
of applicants' attainment of such status, verifying (or registering) "proofs" of
ancestral domain, accepting domain management plans, and/or issuing
resource utilization permits. Furthermore, by assuming ecological virtue as a
component of this status and by effectively restricting resource use to "traditional" (i.e., subsistence) uses, the state maintains control over the forests as
well as protecting them against potential abuse.

If the CADC is an indirect exchange between the DENR and indigenous
people, the DENR gets quite a bargain. The grant of limited resource rights to
marginalized indigenous communities rests upon the expectation of their
inability to extract significant quantities—or to compete with commercial
interests.[10] Should a community succeed in its extractive efforts to the point at
which it affects the resource base, or if it constrains the efforts of elites and
corporations to extract from the same, the DENR has reserved for itself the

power to intervene. Regulatory provisions of DAO 2 provide the mechanisms for intervention after the CADC is issued. Moreover, the CADC process provides no mechanism for challenging preexisting conflicts between ancestral domains and competing uses, such as industrial plantations or pasture leases (A. B. Gatmaytan 1992; G.[A.]B. Gatmaytan 1996, 26). Even more significantly, when ancestral domains sit on top of valuable, foreign-exchange-earning and foreign-investment-attracting resources, such as mineral deposits, other statutes, such as the Mining Act of 1995 (R.A. 7942, a law), overrule DAO 2 (a mere departmental order).[11] This is of more than academic interest to the DENR and national politicians, given the great degree of overlap between the area of potential ancestral claims and that of the nation's remaining untapped forest and mineral resources.

In return for "recognizing" the boundaries of "ancestral domain claims" and granting limited resource use priorities, CADC-holders provide the state with free forest protection services and limit their claims. The DENR expects that the indigenous community will discourage forest encroachment by keeping out migrant farmers, policing itself, and settling down. Settlement and mapping of groups that have historically resisted or avoided state influence facilitates their control by the state and reduces the area they can utilize (Vandergeest and Peluso 1995).[12] Finally, the characterization of certain communities as "indigenous" may serve to divide marginalized rural people—and thereby mute their demands against the state.

It would, however, be unfair to imply that the ideal-type "indigenous cultural community" was constructed in the way it was by DAO 2 solely to limit resource claims. Indeed, the authors of the DAO 2 genuinely attempted to consult indigenous groups and to ally themselves with them. One potential objective they may have had for defining communities as cohesive units represented by traditional political institutions could be to strengthen such features through the processes of implementing the CADC. As the case study indicates, these processes can catalyze community organizing at the local level. Moreover, the goal of local self-determination demands that as large a scope as possible be left for internal decision-making, whether its appearance to outsiders is equitable or otherwise. As a case in point, while the CADC recognizes a communal land claim, it does not assume exclusively communal tenurial systems. Rather, the "allocation of lands within any ancestral domain claim" to individuals and families "shall be left to the community" (art. V, sec. 1). Unfortunate experiences with allocating land to individuals, which have resulted in their sale at unfavorable terms (e.g., through Integrated Social Forestry), have led to the promotion of community-based instruments. Finally, much of the language incorporated in the DAO 2 was drawn from that of indigenous groups and their advocates themselves. Indigenous peoples often do define themselves as communities with a historic attachment to a land base, which they manage in accord with ecological values and which they do not perceive as an individually owned commodity. However, the crucial flaw in the state's definition of community is its fixity; it fails to reflect the dynamism of both the community itself and of its relationship to the land. Hence, the opportunity provided by the CADC is double edged: By articulating its identity as an "indigenous cultural community" and mapping it on the ground, a group may establish its claims to resources, but at the same time it cedes to the state the power to impose the form of that identity and the manner of recognizing its claims.

The real question then becomes: Does the CADC provide strategic gains to indigenous peoples in their nationwide and local struggles? Given political and legal constraints, the CADC does provide a degree of territorial protection for indigenous groups as they continue their quest for more robust tenurial security. The mere fact that over 100 indigenous "communities" have sought to avail of the CADC opportunity indicates their position. At this local level, as well as in national campaigns, the CADC has allowed indigenous groups to make strategic alliances that have attracted political and capital resources (e.g., international donor and advocate pressure on the DENR and project capital for CADC implementation). The struggle for the CADC has raised the national and local profile of indigenous people's demands for land and resource rights. In fact, this struggle itself may have generated new resources in the forms of new meanings for contested concepts such as "community," "indigenous," and "rights." Both the policy (DAO 2) and the implementing instrument (CADC) can be viewed as the product of struggles for resource allocation through social contestation over meaning (Berry 1989; Li 1996). In the final analysis, however, the real struggles over what a community is, and what a CADC means, what rights and opportunities it offers, are fought out on the ground in particular locations—as described in the case of Kayasan.

The Case of Kayasan

In the CADC policy, three misrepresentations of community have caused particular difficulties in practice. First, this concept of community overlooks the existence of multiple interests within the community and how their unequal access to power and resources affects the outcome of the political decision-making the CADC entails and hence the distribution of its benefits. Second, lack of community capacity constrains the local ability to respond collectively to the challenges of surmounting the obstacles to making a CADC work. Finally, and most significantly, the DAO 2 misconstrues the relationship between the community and its territory, or environment. Rather than coexisting in a timeless balance, the community and its environment exist in a dynamic, changing relationship that responds, among other things, to external constraints (e.g., land loss) and opportunities (e.g., trade). The historic sustainability of forest resource management by indigenous communities was not based on some harmonious balance, but rather on its exclusive use.[13] In some areas, communities fought to maintain territorial boundaries (e.g., in the Cordillera). In the case of Kayasan, however, isolation provided for autonomous use. Throughout the Philippine hinterlands, rural residents must compete for resources with new migrants and elite and corporate interests. Under these conditions, the maintenance of exclusive use of a territory is possible only with the devolution to the local level of: the authority and capacity (power) to exclude others from extracting resources, as well as the authority and capacity to use those resources for a sufficient livelihood. The Kayasan case demonstrates that in this instance, while CADC gives the local group the authority to exclude, it has not (yet) generated the capacity or necessary support to do so; furthermore, the CADC does not give adequate authority for resource exploitation, nor has it (yet) provided access to the necessary capacity—organizational competence, capital, and political influence—for the community to succeed on its own.

I contrast Kayasan with the ideal-type of a community imagined in the DAO 2. For each set of community characteristics I examine the consequences for CADC implementation of this contrast. The most significant factors militating against achieving CADC policy objectives are not the shortcomings of Kayasan as a community, but the failure of the policy to change relationships of resource access and control.

INTRODUCING KAYASAN

Loosely incorporating fifty-six scattered households in 1995, Kayasan lies within the boundaries of Puerto Princesa City, the capital of Palawan. This island province lies in the extreme southwest of the Philippines, close to Borneo (see Figure 1-1). The steep terrain of Kayasan, situated on the upper reaches of the Babuyan River, is swathed in a patchwork of green, punctured by upward-jutting white limestone cliffs. Dark green primary mixed dipterocarp rain forest forms the high-elevation background, contrasting with patches of swidden clearings, regenerating swidden fallow forests, and, where the river valley flattens out, the light green and brown quilted squares of rice-paddy fields.

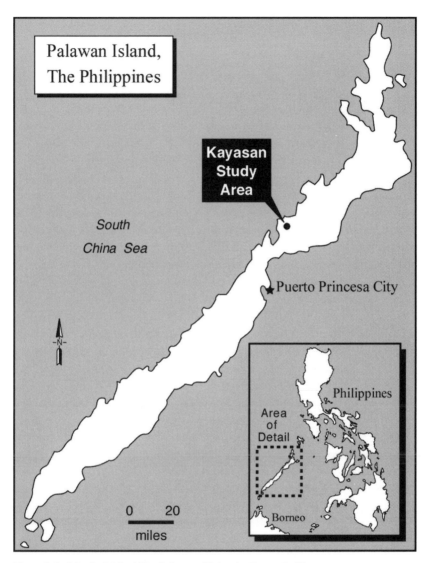

Figure 1-1. Map by Michael Siegel, Rutgers University Geography Department.

The residents of Kayasan identify its original name-givers as their more or less distant ancestors. They explain that the name Kayasan derives from a legendary threat made against these ancestors by marauding Muslims who raided the coastal areas of Palawan from before the sixteenth up to the nineteenth centuries (Fox 1982; Ocampo 1996).[14] This estab-lishes a central fact: There is a historic association with this place by a group of people who define themselves in opposition to a threatening out-side world.

KAYASAN VERSUS THE CADC'S "COMMUNITY":
DIFFERENCES AND CONSEQUENCES

The DAO 2 states that the community is bounded and homogeneous, and it has continuously lived in a communally bounded and defined territory.

The Kayasan Certificate of Ancestral Domain Claim is one of the few that have been granted in the name of two "indigenous cultural communities": Batak and Tagbanua. The Batak are a so-called Negrito ethnolinguistic group today comprising several hundred people who have pursued a "multidimensional livelihood strategy" based on shifting cultivation and the hunting, gathering, and trade of forest products for hundreds of years (Eder 1987). James Eder writes that the Batak "once lived in small, mobile, family groups . . . isolated by land from other indigenous tribal groups on Palawan and by the Sulu Sea from all but occasional contact with Filipino and Muslim peoples," and places Kayasan within the southernmost reaches of their historic homeland (1987; 1997, 4).

If indeed the Batak were historically isolated, this would cast into doubt the antiquity of the Tagbanua claim. The Tagbanua, who do not display the Batak's Negrito physical characteristics, speak a closely related but distinct language. Today they are generally more educated and acculturated, and their livelihood system is similar to that of the Batak, although their material and ritual life has always been centered around the cultivation of rice to a much greater degree. The center of their population, which follows a more settled and nucleated residence pattern, is considerably to the south and west of that of the Batak. The ethnographic map drawn by Robert Fox (1982) in the 1950s shows the northernmost extreme of the Tagbanua domain falling short of Kayasan, although reaching up to the coast due west. Local informants also indicate that the "time immemorial" occupation of Kayasan by the Tagbanua extends back at most to the post–World War II years. While many informants have asserted that the Tagbanua range has always extended even farther north along the coast, the consensus seems to be that Tagbanua did not settle in the Babuyan interior nor mix with the Batak before the past few decades.[15]

Although all are agreed that the Tagbanua are relatively recent arrivals to the area, no one has openly remarked upon any discrepancy associated with their inclusion in the CADC. This fact is probably attributable to several factors. Although intermarriage was rare as recently as twenty years ago, in 1995 Tagbanua and Batak mixed couples headed 23.6 percent of the households, while 25.5 percent are dual Tagbanua and only 5.5 percent are dual Batak.[16] There are recent arrivals among both the Batak and the Tagbanua, some of the latter having preceded some of the former. Indeed, among the adult generation, only nine Batak or Tagbanua and one migrant, all of whom were under age thirty-five, were born within the CADC. That so many of the currently resident "indigenous" people of Kayasan came from other watersheds reflects the fact that in 1975 Kayasan was the site of the second of two compulsory government resettlement schemes that attempted to relocate the entire Batak population. A number of Batak had previously escaped upriver to Kayasan from the location of the nearby 1969 attempt. The earlier settlement had included both Batak and Tagbanua, while the later one at Kayasan, intended exclusively for the Batak, soon incorporated spontaneous Tagbanua arrivals.[17]

Given the evident fact that the CADC-holding community is not bounded with respect to membership, but rather has been entered and exited over time, what then of the territory in question? Extensive questioning failed to uncover a set of tenurial rules corresponding to community-level regulation of land and resource access, such as are documented for numerous indigenous groups in nearby Borneo.[18] Some elders averred that new arrivals ought to seek out a local leader to inform him that they would like to make a swidden or collect forest products. However, there is no question of then being denied access (family-held swidden fallows being excepted), "*basta katutubo sila,*" that is, "just as long as they're an indigenous person." Despite this lack of functional boundaries, there appeared to be unanimity on the location of the historic boundaries demarcating the territory on the map submitted for the CADC application.[19] The boundaries of the ancestral domain correspond to the high ridges demarcating the upper portion of the Babuyan River watershed on the north, east, and south, and on the west, to a widening of the river valley, bisected by a road and abutting a neighboring, Tagbanua CADC. This roughly eight-thousand-hectare region is dissected into numerous, named places marked by detailed natural features and local history. It appears then, that Kayasan is a geographic region bounded by well-known landscape features across which people and their claims move. Ethnic identity, which encompasses people coming from a much wider territory, provides the basis for legitimate access to land and resources within the Kayasan territory. While historically this identity might have been limited to fellow Batak (a positive ascription), today it has expanded to incorporate the Tagbanua, or all *katutubo* (defined in opposition to migrants).[20] The latter are dubbed *dayuhan*, or foreigners, regardless of birthplace.

The local perception of community appears to be based on ethnic identity and the associated shared norms, in contrast to territory and birthplace, as the CADC postulates. Furthermore, it is clearly not the case that the territorial boundaries mapped by the CADC have been occupied by a delimited group of people since "time immemorial"—unless the area incorporated were much enlarged. In Kayasan (as almost anywhere under modern conditions), even given its reduced extent, "ancestral domain" inevitably incorporates migrant residents, and thereby necessarily violates the assumption of social homogeneity.

The principal axis differentiating the Kayasan community is that of "indigenous" versus "migrant" (katutubo versus dayuhan). The influx of migrants provides the driving motivation for the katutubo of Kayasan to define themselves as a community and to establish and defend its boundaries. Indigenous people have historically mediated the access of others to the forest—by physically occupying the forest interior, locating and bringing out forest products, clearing the forest for swidden cultivation—and thereby transforming the landscape. In Kayasan, it was the Batak who first cleared the primary forest for agriculture—a much more labor-intensive process than in secondary forest. Then the Tagbanua arrived, often capitalizing on this accumulated labor by displacing or marrying the Batak, expanding the area of forest fallow, and initiating the establishment of rice paddies (a technology learned by imitating migrants). Migrants then expropriated the labor of indigenous farmers in the form of improved land, which they acquired by either unchallenged assertion, intimidation, trickery, purchase (usually at unfavorable terms), "borrowing," or intermarriage. This pattern is evident in the spatial distribution of farms and fields in Kayasan—swiddens of Batak families scattered far upriver, Tagbanua and mixed Batak-Tagbanua swiddens and houses clustered farther downstream, and migrant and mixed katutubo-migrant swiddens, houses, and paddy fields approaching the road.

The lines of economic differentiation correspond closely with those of ethnic difference. While no one in Kayasan is prosperous, in comparison with the indigenes, migrant farmers control more land, including more irrigated rice fields and fruit trees, own draft animals and agricultural tools, and have better access to credit. Among the indigenes, a few Tagbanua are better off than the rest, among whom the Batak form the most impoverished stratum.

CONSEQUENCES FOR CADC: LACK OF BOUNDEDNESS AND HOMOGENEITY. In Kayasan, the social boundaries of community membership are not fixed; the latter are permeable to claims made on the basis of indigenous identity, stronger if bolstered by kin ties. In particular, the lack of any cultural precedent for excluding kin from access to land, or any other katutubo from access to forest products, is problematic for CADC management.

While the differences in interests and cultural traits between Batak and Tagbanua are relatively slight, the gap between them and the migrants (a few of whom had been resident for over thirty years) is a major one. The migrants have been excluded from all CADC-related activities: The katutubo express a fundamental mistrust of migrants and a fear that they would dominate any group process. Although migrants grumble, they have not actively opposed the CADC, since they don't see any benefit and little potential threat. Neither have they honored CADC terms, however, as they continue to buy and sell land and bypass the local tribal association in the forest products trade.

Since CADC implementation has yet to change resource access in the forest products trade, the better-off Tagbanua group have not seized any new advantage over the poorer katutubo. Rather, as described below, they continue to exploit the minor edge they hold by virtue of their connections to concessionaires and capital.

The community is guided by strong, representative and accountable "traditional" leaders; communal decisions are made through "traditional political institutions" by an equitable process.

In the past, Batak lived and moved in bands composed of a shifting group of several related families. They generally acknowledged the leadership of an elder man, but his opinions, while respected, could be countered and the disputant was free to leave the group (Eder 1987). Fox (1982) describes an elaborate system of traditional councils and customary law for Tagbanua living several river valleys south about fifty years ago. Although a very few of these offices are still filled by Kayasan elders today, they, like their forebears, deal with matters limited to either religious ritual or the adjudication of social disputes (such as those arising over insults, divorce, and adultery). In contrast, the indigenous people of Kayasan insist that any issues over land that arise among them are "talked out" by the immediate parties involved (while conflicts with migrants are taken, if contested, to local government officials, the courts, and/or NGOs). The practice of consulting elders and reaching face-to-face consensus appears to function as a viable political institution for some matters—although when consensus appears unlikely on others, open discussion is impossible and the result is inaction. Moreover, for the past several decades, the most active political institutions have not been the traditional ones, but rather those organized into new (and sometimes competing) associations by various governmental and nongovernmental agencies.

CONSEQUENCES FOR CADC: FLAWS IN COMMUNITY LEADERSHIP. The most recent of these new organizations, SATRIKA (the Tribal Association of Kayasan), was established in 1991 as the local member association of a provincial federation NATRIPAL (the United Tribes of Palawan). SATRIKA's elected president, who was not a traditional elder, was the most active in pursuing the CADC application, despite the disbelief of many members. Yet he was ultimately discredited because he mishandled funds and allowed his nonresident kin to exploit the local forest product collectors. This has damaged attempts to achieve CADC objectives and pursue NGO-supported projects by demobilizing the most committed leader, and has only heightened the tendency of the community to fragment along kin-based factional lines, resulting in inaction in the face of any controversial decisions and projects.

The community as an entity manages the natural resources in the ancestral domain, and does so in a sustainable and ecologically sound manner; "traditional" (i.e., subsistence) resource rights are sufficient for a sustainable livelihood.

There is no precedent for any decisions made with respect to resource use on a communitywide scale. The question of the ecological sustainability of indigenous swidden cultivation and forest product collection practice never arose under historic conditions of low population density and diverse economic strategies. Making this evaluation under present conditions of increasing competition for land and forest product extraction, together with growing expectations and indebtedness, is a much more complex proposition. There is no doubt that the indigenous folk of Kayasan retain an impressive repository of knowledge about their environment and its effective management (Eder 1987, 1997; McDermott 1994). Many Batak in particular express an affinity for the forest and view their access to it as a privilege granted by the spirits. While the depth of these folk beliefs varies with age and education, Batak and Tagbanua alike express dismay at the profligate practices of the migrant rattan and resin collectors and some predict eventual resource exhaustion if current behavior persists. While shared norms prohibit this behavior and most local katutubo eschew it, there is no precedent for restraining it by means of social sanctions—for it is the spirits, not people, who punish "ecological misbehavior" (Eder 1997, 28).

The forest-based economy of the indigenous people of Palawan has involved international trade in forest products for at least eight centuries.[21] Among these products, rattan and almaciga resin constitute the chief sources of cash income in Kayasan today. The longevity of this economy self-evidently demonstrates its sustainability under historic conditions; the continuing association of indigenous peoples with old-growth forests and high biodiversity occurs in Kayasan as throughout the rest of the Philippines. Historical evidence thus clearly refutes the limitation of "traditional resource rights" to subsistence resource use potentially imposed by the CADC implementation guidelines (DAO 34 s. 1996).

However, in their struggle to compete with uncontrolled extraction by migrants, indigenous residents of Kayasan participate in an overall pattern of forest product extraction that is unsustainable.

CONSEQUENCES FOR CADC: ECOLOGICAL SUSTAINABILITY AND NONSUBSISTENCE RESOURCE USE. The mismatch here is not with respect to attributes of community, but rather with conditions of control. It is not relevant whether indigenous people retain the knowledge and institutions to maintain sustainable resource management under past conditions. Instead, the issue is what controls must be devolved to allow residents to restrain extraction to sustainable levels under present economic and demographic conditions. The CADC gamble is that indigenous people will supply the motivation, and that the CADC will supply sufficient means, to transform these conditions. While the motivation seems certain, the lack of resource exploitation rights granted by the CADC, together with the lack of trading capital, render the reestablishment of sustainable conditions most uncertain.

IS THE CADC PROCESS CREATING COMMUNITY?

Its apparent failure to match up to many of the community characteristics posited by DAO 2 suggests that perhaps Kayasan should not be considered a community at all. From another perspective, we might consider whether and how the Batak and Tagbanua understand themselves to form a community, or social unit of sorts.

While Kayasan folk understand the Spanish-Tagalog borrowing *komunidad*, they have no equivalent expression in their own languages. The Batak have a word for an extended family grouping, but for no larger unit. Batak and Tagbanua both identify themselves and others as being *taga* X, or "from" a particular place, the specificity of which depends on the context. Place is the key to association; it includes not only place of birth and place of residence, but places where a family has buried its dead and has established land claims—that is, swidden fallows and cultivated fruit trees. The local landscape—every bend in the river, every rock outcropping, every overgrown mango tree—is replete with named markers of local history. The affective ties and historical association between the local people and the land are evident to any perceptive observer. Note, however, that the physical markers thereof are generally not visible, contrary to the expectation implied by the "proofs" required in

CADC applications. Local custom does not involve placing permanent markers, even on graves, and the luxuriance and speed of tropical forest regrowth soon obscure material evidence of past settlement or cultivation.

As a consequence of mobility, the network of kin ties extends across boundaries of place of origin or residence. Batak and Tagbanua seem to recognize a continuum of degrees of association—one that is not crosscut by the boundaries of community in any particular place. In recent years, this continuum appears to have extended further. Externally generated opportunities predating the CADC have created incentives for attaining the "community" level of association. For example, local government incorporated Kayasan as a subunit and, for a time, provided a school. NATRIPAL, the tribal federation, brokered the formation of SATRIKA as its local member association in Kayasan—in competition with the government-sponsored tribal council and another NGO-organized group. The net effect of these outside interventions in creating a sense of community is difficult to ascertain. The more significant, pre-CADC ingredient in forging a common, though not seamless, Batak-Tagbanua katutubo identity was the perception of common oppression, marginality, and external threat. The opportunity to apply for a government certification provided the incentive to express a single, shared identity that encompasses both Batak and Tagbanua—in a single claim to land (the CADC) and, in the process, to community.

In other, practical respects CADC processes have catalyzed the development of community capacity. The process of application required a number of communitywide activities, such as participatory community sketch-mapping, consulting elders, documenting communal memory, surveying the boundary, passing resolutions, and hosting government and NGO visitors. It is perhaps too early to say whether or not the need to maintain the CADC will continue to foster collective action to defend common boundaries.

CONSEQUENCES FOR CADC: RESOURCE CONTROL

The factors constraining efforts in Kayasan to achieve CADC objectives have less to do with deficiencies in its qualities of community and more to do with lack of change in relations of resource access and control. The state's objectives as articulated in the DAO 2 are to protect tenure over ancestral domain, provide equitable resource access, and "to ensure the sustainable development of natural resources" (art. I, sec. 2). Major objectives sought by the people of Kayasan through their CADC are to gain resource access (forest product licenses and shifting cultivation rights) and to keep migrants out. Changes in the distribution of resource access and benefits would indicate their success in attaining these objectives. An evaluation of how these changes have affected resource management practices and thereby the environment will demonstrate the degree of success in achieving the governmental objectives of forest protection and "sustainable development." The evidence indicates that the failure of the state to devolve control over resources poses a critical constraint in reaching these goals.

Access to productive resources has not thus far changed as a result of CADC implementation in Kayasan. There are two major categories of natural resources upon which indigenous residents depend and in search of which migrants are drawn to Kayasan: forest products and land. The following section outlines changes in resource access, management practices, and indicative environmental impacts for these two resource types. Finally, I consider the extent to which the CADC has provided access to symbolic resources that may be wielded in material struggles.

LAND: ACCESS, MANAGEMENT, AND ENVIRONMENTAL STATUS. The indigenous residents of Kayasan have achieved little success in excluding migrant settlers. Within two years following the CADC boundary survey several migrant families illegally bought and sold land within the CADC and five new migrant households established farms.[22] Furthermore, within this period, fourteen Tagbanua families arrived (although two households lasted less than one year). Of this group, six had previously farmed within Kayasan. The remainder joined previously resident relatives, who initially housed them and loaned them land for their first harvest. Thus, indigenous values favoring kin, together with the CADC's possible magnet effect, may mitigate against the exclusion of migrants necessary for sustaining a shifting cultivation-based agriculture within a limited territory.

The trends in land resource management appear to continue as before CADC implementation. Swidden plots are being made closer to the road and to an increasingly discernible village center. Older forest is not being cleared; fallow periods are decreasing, as are yields. Those with access to inputs and surplus labor, disproportionately migrants and migrant-Tagbanua households, are investing in their land, converting flat land to paddy fields or planting cash-crop trees. As a consequence, land is taken out of the swidden regeneration cycle, so that forest conversion becomes more permanent. However, since the area under swidden is decreasing in favor of other agricultural land uses, the overall rate of forest conversion is declining.

FOREST PRODUCTS: ACCESS, MANAGEMENT, AND ENVIRONMENTAL STATUS. There are two major commercial forest products harvested in Kayasan: rattan (cane) and almaciga resin (also called Manila copal).[23] External resources, namely political influence and capital, are required to gain access to these forest resources. Legal access is still regulated through the concession system: For each product a separate license is required from the local DENR office. The application process is involved and expensive—especially due to the emoluments required to grease the bureaucratic wheels.

The provisions of DAO 2 have not been implemented in Palawan, and it will take political influence to get it done. Provincial and local DENR officers often do not understand these provisions, are highly skeptical, and have not received operational instructions for implementing them. Provincial and local governments have also balked at implementing DAO 2. The political battle over almaciga concessions provides a case in point. The DAO 2 clearly states that upon issuance of a CADC, existing concessions will be allowed to expire, but will not be renewed (an annual requirement for almaciga). Yet when the concessionaires, mostly provincial elites, rose up in arms, the governor of Palawan responded by granting a one-year renewal of all almaciga concessions.[24] This outraged the tribal association (SATRIKA) in Kayasan, which produced a resolution of protest, backed by NGOs and the Palawan tribal federation (NATRIPAL).

The struggle to gain legal access to forest products via the CADC's Ancestral Domain Management Plan has not yet yielded results. It took over a year after the CADC award to draft this plan, since people of Kayasan are dependent on the assistance of NGOs to express their "indigenous knowledge" in the required format. Furthermore, given the controversy, confusion, and resistance prevalent within DENR, and the confusion and resistance prevailing at lower bureaucratic levels, NGO supporters advised against relying on the domain management plan to guarantee promised rights. Rather, the strategy has been to work within the old system, applying for individual concessions for each resource, following the old boundaries (which cross-cut the ancestral domain).

While SATRIKA did not succeed in winning its own concessions, even if it were to do so, the struggle for resource control would be just beginning. The requirements for operating capital for a concession are quite onerous. In addition to the business expenses (such as transporting costs) and the various DENR fees (both legal and extralegal), operators must supply credit advances to players at each level in the grossly undercapitalized forest products trade. Collectors obtain the provisions for their harvesting trips (and often other needs) on credit from middlemen, who in turn are in debt to higher-level middlemen, the concessionaire (who may lack independent capital), the "financier," and/or the buyers. Thus, any attempt to regulate extraction would be severely constrained—no one at any position in the chain of trade is in a position to stint, since each player is in debt to the one above him. If this would be true of control exercised from any level, how much more so from the proposed community level, where not only power is the least, but so too is the room for maneuver. Here, maintaining the caloric buffer against starvation provides the ultimate constraint.

In 1990, a neighboring NATRIPAL-member local association obtained a special rattan concession for indigenous communities that incorporated Kayasan. This concession was controlled by José, the brother-in-law of Rufino (later the first president of SATRIKA).[25] José ran his concession in a manner very unpopular in Kayasan—not only did he pay very low prices, but residents feared their resource would be depleted if José continued the illegal practice of letting his concession papers out for a royalty and inviting in migrant middlemen and cutters. José proved himself to be resourceful in obtaining credit and cutting deals. He talked Rufino into one such arrangement—which ended in the issue of a warrant for Rufino's arrest for theft. The financier who brought the charges offered not to press the case as long as Rufino and José sold Kayasan rattan exclusively to her—and he was thereby able to control the resource, its price, and any profits. Although DENR offered to approve a separate concession for SATRIKA, no one had the nerve to defy José. NGO supporters provided an alternative credit source for rattan trading, but the scheme foundered for a number of reasons, reflecting the lack of community capacity. When José eventually appropriated SATRIKA's NGO-financed rattan, no one stood up to stop him.

The consequences for resource management of the external control of the rattan trade in Kayasan are predictable. Rattan (and profits) continue to be extracted at uncontrolled rates from across the CADC border. While recovery is still possible if extraction is slowed, if it is not, commercial extinction will occur as it has elsewhere in Palawan. In the case of almaciga, concessionaires and their middlemen see their time running out and have been pushing for resin extraction at even higher and less sustainable levels. Almaciga trees are dying from excessive tapping, for which the katutubo blame the migrants.

SYMBOLIC RESOURCES: TOOLS TO GAIN MATERIAL ADVANTAGE. As we have seen, whatever form policy takes in Manila, it is reinterpreted and reworked in the process of local contestation. The national debate that yielded the DAO 2 centered on struggles over meaning and negotiations over identity ("indigenous cultural community") and its entitlements ("ancestral domain") (Berry 1993; Moore 1993). The people of Kayasan and their larger political alliance, NATRIPAL, are now struggling to give these concepts meaning in Palawan. "Ancestral domain" has been redefined, for instrumental purposes, as the English abbreviation CADC. They are trying to wield the symbolic resource provided by a state-endorsed certificate to convince migrants and middlemen, local DENR staff and Palawan's politicians, that they have special rights to control resources in Kayasan.

Even if CADC implementation falls short of what the DAO 2 specifies, the people of Kayasan will have gained if their hand has been strengthened in their struggle for resource control. The CADC may serve as another tool in their "practical political economy" (Chambers 1983, cited in Li 1996). To some extent this has occurred. For example, the adjacent National Park has conceded some territory and backed off enforcement on the basis of CADC-bolstered claims. SATRIKA ultimately succeeded in making several independent almaciga trades. In addition, the CADC has made it possible for NATRIPAL and advocates to raise the debate over the forest product concession system to level of the provincial government. This debate and these voices have also been part of pushing indigenous peoples' rights higher on the national agenda. However, when it comes to the crucial micropolitical level, on the ground, where katutubo must face off against migrant farmers, rattan cutters, almaciga middlemen, and the like—they lack confidence. They lack confidence, they say, because the migrants "don't believe in" the CADC. Local government officials and DENR rangers, who are all migrants, are uninformed and unsupportive, if not hostile. In this context, people in Kayasan are asking for additional forms of state legitimation that the people with whom they contend recognize, such as concession papers and DENR deputization to apprehend forest law violators.

The picture is mixed. The struggle continues. The term "CADC" is now in the vocabulary of a widening circle. Probably the most significant resources leveraged through CADC processes are the strategic alliances that have been made. Investing in these social networks has in turn yielded political, organizational, and financial resources. Many of Kayasan's external social networks pass through NATRIPAL. This Tagbanua-run organization early on sought allies among urban-based NGOs—both the national offices that lobbied for DAO 2 and the Palawan-based organizations that facilitated the CADC applications of member associations. These assisting NGOs have steered CADC applications through a morass of bureaucratic requirements and have fought defensive battles with resistant local governments and DENR officers. They have also brought in international support, including funds. Since the start of the local campaign in Palawan to push through CADC applications (of which Kayasan was the first), NATRIPAL has attracted almost one million U.S. dollars to support forest-enterprise-based approaches to conservation and development—for which CADCs are meant to supply the necessary tenurial-security ingredient. Kayasan was selected to be a field site for one of these projects.[26] From 1994 through 1997, NATRIPAL had channeled in excess of $12,000 in U.S. dollars in investment into Kayasan (this figure does not include trading loans).

The people of Kayasan have parlayed the symbolic resource of indigenous identity into material and political resources by building and drawing upon social networks (Berry 1993). While these resources provide grounds for hope in Kayasan, there have been few concrete gains since the CADC was awarded. Lack of access to and control over resources has been shown to be a key constraint. However, we also find that, even when access is gained, capital and connections are not enough; local capacities are tested. In the end, community—or at least the ability to stand up to outsiders and to work together for a common goal—matters.

Conclusion and Policy Implications

The case of Kayasan paints a complex picture. While it bears at least a family resemblance to the idealized portrait of a community embodied in the DAO 2, significant differences exist. Three have emerged as pivotal in Kayasan. First, Kayasan is not homogeneous with respect to differentials of interest, role in decision-making, and access to resources, among other parameters. Second, the capacity of Kayasan to engage in collective action (e.g., to defend boundaries or operate a concession) is limited and has been developed only partially by the potentially community-building processes involved in acquiring and maintaining a CADC. Third, in the past the people of Kayasan "managed" their environment through a relationship of exclusive control; the fact that these conditions no longer apply means that the capacity to maintain environmental balance must not be assumed.

Community remains a problematic concept. It is used to refer both to actual associations of people and to an ideal that people hold about them or toward which they may strive. It is not surprising, then, that when policies are designed on the basis of the postulated existence of communities, policymakers may conflate the reality and the ideal. Policy based on misleading analysis is unlikely to succeed. A better grounds for developing policy lies in the examination of how people gain access to resources and control others' access in terms of internal (among coresidents) and external (supralocal) social relations. Shifts in social relations of resource access can change patterns of resource use and hence the environment; changing resource access can also transform the social distribution of benefits resulting from that resource use. Therefore, if policy is aimed at modifying resource use (e.g., toward protecting the environment) and achieving social amelioration, it follows that its targets ought to be aimed at changing access to productive resources.

The CADC does not do that. In order to control forest resource extraction and land use, the people of Kayasan need to be given the means to control others' access. Even if the CADC is fully implemented and in fact changes formal tenure arrangements, this would not be sufficient to change cross-cutting relationships of power. It is the power inequities bound up in relations of political influence and debt, for example, which may impose the decisive constraints on what locals may accomplish. To succeed both in excluding others and in profiting from their own resource use, Kayasan residents will need additional resources—financial (e.g., trading capital), political (a strong lobbying presence), and symbolic (state legitimation of their enforcement efforts). Furthermore, the people of Kayasan will need to overcome internal divisions and a history of domination by outsiders to act together to defend their boundaries and to cooperate in forest-based livelihood enterprises. They need to act like a community.

Unfortunately, the administrative order that created the CADC presumes the existence of community capacity rather than providing means to develop it. Neither Kayasan nor any other CADC-holder is typical of "indigenous cultural communities" throughout the Philippines. Yet the CADC policy fails to take this diversity into account. An improved ancestral domain policy would assume little about the nature of particular indigenous communities, but rather would institute a process for building upon the local institutions that already exist. Either directly, by cooperating with NGOs, or simply by providing opportunities and resources, state agencies may assist in the strengthening and adaptation of local institutions toward the development of community capacity. However, the government must first provide for the measured devolution of resource access and control to localities and back it up with legitimation and defensive support—"capacity" means nothing if there is no means or discretion with which to exercise it. Furthermore, state agencies must monitor the impact of this devolution on weaker members and provide them with routes of appeal and redress. Finally, environmental standards and limitations on resource extraction should be forthrightly set, rather than based on the historically inaccurate and socially unjust assumption of an exclusively subsistence livelihood.

Notes

1. This was pronounced by President Fidel A. Ramos in Executive Order No. 263, dated 19 July 1995.
2. Despite its ambiguity in the Philippine context, I use the word "indigenous" out of deference to its choice by local and national activists. The Philippines has no colonial settler-descended population; rather, the *mestizo* (Spanish-Chinese-"native") elite represent only a thin veneer on the dominant ethnolinguistic groups (e.g., Tagalog, Ilocano). These historically lowland-dwelling groups are indigenous to the Philippines, although many have migrated from their original population centers.
3. This study is based on fieldwork conducted in the community of Kayasan, the provincial capital, and Manila. I first served as a project consultant in Palawan for three months in 1993 and then conducted dissertation research over eleven months in 1995, two months in 1996, and two weeks in 1997. The period under analysis ends in March 1997. A shorter version of this chapter first appeared in *Pilipinas* (McDermott 1999). A much more extensive discussion of this and related themes can be found in McDermott (2000).

    This research was assisted by grants from the Fulbright-Hays Doctoral Dissertation Research Abroad Program, the National Science Foundation and the Joint Committee on Southeast Asia of the Social Science Research Council and the American Council of Learned Societies with funds provided by the Andrew W. Mellon Foundation, the Ford Foundation, and the Henry Luce Foundation.
4. Cruz, personal communication, cited in Lynch and Talbott 1995, 58.
5. Letter of Instruction No. 1260 (1982); Ministry Administrative Order No. 48, series 1982; Department Administrative Order No. 97, series 1988 (Gatmaytan 1989).
6. To name only those programs specified in the implementing order of E.O. 263 (DAO 29 s. 1996), these include: the Integrated Social Forestry Program (ISF), Upland Development Project, Forest Land Management Program, Community Forestry Program (CFP), Low Income Upland Community Project, Regional Resources Management Project, Integrated Rainforest Management Project, Forestry Sector Project, Coastal Environment Program, and the CADC. For example, ISF created the Certificate of Forest Stewardship and the Certificate of Communal Forest Stewardship; the CFP created the Community Forestry Management Agreement; the FLMP (or Contract Reforestation) created the Forest Land Management Agreement; and the Natural Resource Management Program (NRMP) created the CADC. ISF and the Forest Land Management Program have been primarily funded by the Asian Development Bank, and the NRMP was funded by USAID.
7. Beginning in 1988, a series of Congressional bills were filed that aimed to implement the constitutional provision for Ancestral Domain. This effort continued nearly annually until 1997, when Republic Act 8371, or the Indigenous People's Rights Act, astounded many by passing. (This law was still under challenge in the courts three years later.)
8. The most influential consultants were working under the NRMP, described below. The Philippine Development Forum, in Washington, D.C., was prominent among these foreign organizations.
9. It took over three years before ADMP guidelines were approved, under DAO 34 s. 1996, and another year before the first, pilot ADMP was signed. In the meantime, a different division of the DENR had obtained approval for DAO 29 s. 1996 (see

above), providing for the ADMP-CBFM, an alternative plan that confers a different, commercially oriented set of rights and responsibilities.

10. If the national battle to gain commercial rights through the CADC and local struggles to gain access to capital are lost, then the instrument that was intended to guarantee communities resource rights may instead guarantee their marginality.

11. Indeed, the passage of the Mining Act of 1995, which is even more prejudicial to community interests than its predecessor, and the continued promotion of corporate-oriented licenses, such as the Industrial Forest Management Agreement (DAO 42 s. 1991), call into question the sincerity of the state's "community-based forest management" policy.

12. Pursuit of the CADC as an instrument may decrease the land area indigenous communities are effectively able to demand in other respects as well. Many communities lack the capacity and support to undertake the long bureaucratic process—into which opponents (such as migrant-dominated local governments) can introduce obstacles. Areas subject to existing DENR-certified competing uses may be ruled out. Many groups are unwilling to reduce their demands to a process of appealing to the state for "recognition" of a "claim" within "public land" to what they consider to be land that they themselves own. Some militant activists consider the CADC to be a sellout and a distraction that focuses efforts on delineation that would better be put toward more substantive goals (Gatmaytan 1996).

13. This does not necessarily mean that such communities have no mechanisms for internal regulation of resource use, but rather that (a) such principles should not be assumed in every case, and (b) they will not be sufficient if outsiders are not excluded.

14. These "Moro" pirates demanded that the people of Kayasan surrender their abundant rice harvest or else the pirates would scrape the skin off their lower legs—as in to *kayasan* a stem of rattan by removing its outer bark with a bush knife.

15. The very nature of "the Tagbanua," as with most any ethnolinguistic category, is problematic. Several subgroups are distinguished, some of which are identified with the Batak (Eder 1987; Fox 1982).

16. The figures cited in this section are based on a 100 percent household survey I conducted in Kayasan in 1995. A household was defined as a residential unit, with the exception of four single males who had no homes of their own. Migrants headed 40 percent of households, and mixed migrant-indigenous households comprised 5.5 percent of the total.

17. This ill-fated scheme was perpetrated by Manuel Elizalde, the head of PANAMIN (Presidential Assistance on National Minorities) under Marcos (Eder 1987).

18. Cf. Appell 1971; Freeman 1970; Geddes 1966.

19. The only debates over the boundaries did not concern their historic location, but rather whether or not to concede area to the adjacent National Park or rattan concession.

20. While the literal meaning of the Tagalog word *katutubo* is "sprung from the same place," it is used in Kayasan, as elsewhere, to indicate what used to be referred to as "tribal" or "non-Christian" people.

21. Eder 1987; Fox 1982; Hutterer 1977; Kress 1977.

22. The CADC boundary was surveyed in February 1995, and the certificate was granted one year later.

23. The source of this resin is an exudate from a tree of the higher elevation primary forests, *Agathis celebica* (Koord.)Bl. This species also has appeared in the literature as *Agathis philippinensis* Warb. (e.g., Callo 1995) and *Agathis dammara* (Lambert) L. C. Rich (e.g., Conelly 1985).

24. Although granting concessions is supposed to be a DENR prerogative, a special

law for Palawan (RA 7611, 1992) has created a provincial committee with special authority, the Palawan Council for Sustainable Development, and set up a bureaucratic competition between it and the DENR.

25. These names are pseudonyms.
26. USAID funded (for $0.6 million) this Biodiversity Conservation Network project (under whose auspices I first came to Kayasan, as a consultant).

Bibliography

Appell, G. N. 1971. *Observational Procedures for Land Tenure and Kin Groupings in the Cognatic Societies of Borneo.* Social Transformation and Adaptation Research Institute, Phillips, Maine.

Berry, S. 1989. "Social Institutions and Access to Resources." *Africa* 59:41–55.

———. 1993. *No Condition Is Permanent: The Social Dynamics of Agrarian Change in Sub-Saharan Africa.* Madison: University of Wisconsin Press.

Broad, R., with J. Cavanagh. 1993. *Plundering Paradise: The Struggle for the Environment in the Philippines.* Berkeley: University of California Press.

Callo, R. A. 1995. *Damage to Almaciga Resources in Puerto Princesa and Roxas, Palawan Concessions.* College, Laguna, Philippines: Ecosystems Research and Development Bureau, Department of Environment and Natural Resources.

Chambers, R. 1983. *Rural Development: Putting the Last First.* Harlow, U.K.: Longman.

Conelly, W. T. 1985. "Copal and Rattan Collecting in the Philippines." *Economic Botany* 39(1):39–48.

Cruz, C. J., et al. 1988. "Population Pressure and Migration: Implications for Upland Development in the Philippines." *Journal of Philippine Development* 15(1):15–46.

de Guzman, V. P. 1992. *Land/Resource Tenure Legal and Policy Framework.* Manila: Natural Resources Management Program.

Department of Environment and Natural Resources (DENR). 1995. *1995 Philippine Forestry Statistics.* Manila: Forest Management Bureau, DENR.

Eder, J. F. 1987. *On the Road to Tribal Extinction: Depopulation, Deculturation and Adaptive Well-Being among the Batak of the Philippines.* Berkeley: University of California Press.

———. 1997. *Batak Resource Management: Belief, Knowledge and Practice.* Gland, Switzerland and Cambridge, UK: IUCN and Gland, Switzerland: WWF-Worldwide Fund for Nature.

Eder, J. F., and J. O. Fernandez, eds. 1996. *Palawan at the Crossroads: Development and the Environment on a Philippine Frontier.* Manila: Ateneo de Manila University Press.

Fox, R. B. 1982. *Tagbanua Religion and Society* (Ph.D. diss. 1954). Manila: National Museum.

Freeman, J. D. 1970. *Report on the Iban.* London: Althone Press (rept. 1954, Her Majesty's Stationery Service).

Gatmatyan, A. B. 1992. "Land Rights and Land Tenure Situation of Indigenous Peoples in the Philippines." *Philippine Natural Resources Law Journal* 5(1):5–41.

Gatmatyan, D. B. 1989. "The Civil Reservation: The Concentration Policy as Land Acquisition Scheme." *Philippine Natural Resources Law Journal* 2(1):1–8.

———. 1992. "Ancestral Domain Recognition in the Philippines: Trends in Jurisprudence and Legislation." *Philippine Natural Resources Law Journal* 5(1): 43–90.

Gatmaytan, G. [A.] B. 1996. "Lines Across the Land: The State, Ancestral Domains Delineation and the Manobos of Agusan del Sur." *Philippines Natural Resources Law Journal* 7(1):5–34.

Geddes, W. R. 1966. *Land Dayaks of Sarawak*. New York: Ames Press (rept. 1954, Her Majesty's Stationery Service).

Hirtz, F. 1998. "The Discourse That Silences: Beneficiaries' Ambivalence Towards Redistributive Land Reform in the Philippines." *Development and Change* 29(2):247–275.

Hutterer, K. L. 1977. *Economic Exchange and Social Interaction in Southeast Asia: Perspectives from Prehistory, History and Ethnography*. Ann Arbor: Center for South and Southeast Asian Studies, University of Michigan.

Kerkvliet, B. 1977. *The Huk Rebellion: A Study of Peasant Revolt in the Philippines*. Berkeley: University of California Press.

Kress, J. H. 1977. "Contemporary and Prehistoric Subsistence Patterns on Palawan." In *Cultural-Ecological Perspectives on Southeast Asia*, ed. W. Wood, 29–47. Athens: Center for International Studies, Ohio University.

Kummer, D. M. 1992. *Deforestation in the Postwar Philippines*. Chicago: University of Chicago Press.

Kusel, J., and L. Fortmann. 1991. *Well-Being in Forest-Dependent Communities*. Prepared for the Forest and Rangeland Resources Assessment Program, California Department of Forestry and Fire Protection.

Li, T. M. 1996. "Images of Community: Discourse and Strategy in Property Relations." *Development and Change* 27:501–527.

Lynch, O. J., Jr., and K. Talbott. 1988. "Legal Responses to the Philippine Deforestation Crisis." *New York University Journal of International Law and Politics* 20(3):679–713.

———. 1995. *Balancing Acts: Community-Based Forest Management and National Law in Asia and the Pacific*. Washington, D.C.: World Resources Institute.

McDermott, M. H. 1994. Conservation Assessment Report. Annex to "Community-Based Conservation and Enterprise Program for Indigenous Communities in Palawan, Philippines," World Wildlife Fund, Tribal Filipino Apostolate, NATRIPAL and PANLIPI. Manila.

———. 1999. "Community by Default: Indigenous People and Ancestral Domain in Palawan." *Pilipinas* 33:43–56.

———. 2000. *Boundaries and Pathways: Indigenous Identity, Ancestral Domain, and Forest Use in Palawan, the Philippines*. Ph.D. dissertation, Department of Environmental Science, Policy and Management, University of California at Berkeley.

Moore, D. 1993. "Contesting Terrain in Zimbabwe's Eastern Highlands: Political Ecology, Ethnography, and Peasant Resource Struggles." *Economic Geography* 69(4): 380–401.

National Statistics Office (NSO). 1995. *Census Facts and Figures*. Manila: National Statistics Office.

Natural Resources Management Program (NRMP). 1990. *Natural Resources Management Program Assistance Approval Document*. Manila: USAID/Philippines.

Ocampo, N. S. 1996. "A History of Palawan." In *Palawan at the Crossroads: Development and the Environment on a Philippine Frontier*, ed. J. F. Eder and J. O. Fernandez. Manila: Ateneo de Manila University Press.

Royo, A. G. 1988. "Regalian Doctrine: Whither the Vested Rights?" *Philippine Natural Resources Law Journal* 1(2):1–8.

Scott, W. H. 1982. *Cracks in the Parchment Curtain*. Quezon City, Philippines: New Day Publishers.

Vandergeest, P., and N. L. Peluso. 1995. "Territorialization and State Power in Thailand." *Theory and Society* 24:385–426.

World Bank. 1989. *Philippines: Environment and Natural Resource Management Study*. Washington, D.C.: World Bank.

Chapter 2

RUTH MEINZEN-DICK
MARGREET ZWARTEVEEN

Gender Dimensions of Community Resource Management

The Case of Water Users' Associations in South Asia

THE CURRENT POLICY TREND toward devolving natural resource management responsibility from the state to communities or local user groups cuts
across countries and resource sectors. Programs such as Joint Forest Management, Irrigation Management Transfer, and Fisheries Co-Management can
all be seen as variants of attempts to establish or strengthen what is called
community-based natural resource management. What is happening in irrigation, as in other sectors, can be seen as the convergence of a number of
policy trends: decentralization, which attempts to improve the management
of natural and fiscal resources by moving both decision-making authority and
payment responsibility to lower levels of government (e.g., India's *panchayati
raj* programs);[1] privatization, which transfers ownership of resources from the
public sector to groups or individuals (including for-profit firms); and participation and democratization, which seek the involvement of citizens affected
by programs, for social goals of empowering local people as well as goals of
improving program performance.

Although devolution programs may appear to be consistent with all of
these trends, a closer examination of the motivations and reasons for adopting
such programs reveals certain inconsistencies. One strong motivation has certainly been a desire to improve the effectiveness of resource management.
This is based on evidence of the shortcomings of government management,
and a belief that local users who have the greatest stake in the resource and
interact with it on a daily basis would be more effective in its management.

But serious fiscal crises and the necessity of reducing government expenditure lie behind the most sweeping internal adoption of management transfer programs (as in Mexico's irrigation management transfer or Senegal's disengagement program). Donor pressures—either for economic reform or for participation and democratization—have clearly played a role in many cases, and are likely to continue over at least the medium term, as the World Bank and other donors push for greater stakeholder participation.

However, devolution of control over resources from the state to local organizations does not necessarily lead to greater participation and empowerment of all stakeholders. This is particularly true in highly differentiated and stratified societies. Romanticizing views of "communities" as homogeneous groups that have a strong common commitment to maintaining their local resource base, and ignoring the effects of power differences within the community on who can participate in decisions regarding management and the share of benefits, risks reinforcing inequality (Agrawal and Gibson 1999; Leach, Mearns, and Scoones 1997a; Prakash 1998).

While there may be many ways of identifying groups that are frequently marginalized, gender differences in power and influence are a recurring pattern. Women's participation has received considerable rhetoric, but less careful attention has been paid to the differences between women's and men's needs and priorities with regards to resource use, and to the barriers women face in achieving control over resources, especially within local organizations.

This chapter examines the implications of gender differences for local management of natural resources, with special reference to the management of irrigation systems in South Asia. In this context, a highly stratified social structure, as well as common patriarchal norms on the appropriate position of women, provide a clear challenge to notions of homogeneous "communities" for managing resources. The vital nature of water resources for men and women, for both irrigation and other uses, highlights what is at stake in the process of devolution of resource control. As the state transfers responsibility and rights over natural resources—forests, pastures, fisheries, or irrigation systems—to local users' organizations as representatives of the "communities," they become the gatekeepers for rights to the resource. It becomes critical to examine who within the organizations takes on the tasks, and who controls use, decision-making, and the stream of benefits. We therefore look in detail at the gender dimension of participation in water users' organizations.

The section following this introduction looks at the intrahousehold literature as a source of insight into gender differences, and links this to the need for analysis of gender in community studies. The chapter then examines the implications of gender for devolution of natural resource management

(NRM), especially irrigation. Because the outcome of devolution programs hinges on the activity of local organizations, the fourth section examines the extent and forms of women's participation in these organizations, using examples from water users' associations in South Asia. The fifth section presents evidence on the effect of gender differences in participation on the system management as a whole. The concluding section highlights policy issues and critical areas in which further understanding is needed.

Households and Communities: Beyond the "Unitary" Model

The treatment of community as a homogeneous group with common objectives parallels, in many ways, the "unitary models" of the household in economic literature. Both treat a social institution comprising multiple individuals as though it behaves as a single entity. To do this, unitary models of the household have two critical assumptions (see Alderman et al. 1995): first, that all members of the household have common objectives. This may come about because of altruism on the part of some members, who value the welfare of others in the household above their own, or through some form of coercion, or a combination of these (e.g., the "benevolent dictator"). Second, they assume pooling of all resources (which may, in turn, require monitoring and enforcement capability).

The unitary conception of the household has come under significant criticism on theoretical and empirical grounds, as findings from studies of income pooling or labor supply decisions are inconsistent with many of the model's underlying assumptions (Alderman et al. 1995). For example, a number of studies have found that women and men spend income under their control in systematically different ways, with women more likely to devote a high proportion of their income on food and health care for children (Dwyer and Bruce 1988; Guyer 1980). Thus, applying unitary concepts of the household to policy issues risks producing inappropriate policy recommendations or outcomes.

The gender analysis literature abounds in examples of how systematic, socially constructed patterns of differences between men and women affect the distribution and use of resources within households (see Haddad, Hoddinott, and Alderman 1997; Hart 1995). Agarwal (1997a) argues that leaving this analysis at the household level is incomplete, because it does not take into account the effects of the community on gender relations in the household, or vice versa.

Demonstrating the fallacy of unitary conceptions at the community level is even easier than at the household level. Although simplistic views of the "community" may assume common interests and sharing of resources (especially common property), the literature on social stratification clearly demonstrates the marked differences between subgroups (see Bendix and Lipset 1954; Dumont 1980). These differences apply not only to wealth, but also to norms. Thus, priorities for use of resources and style of management are also likely to differ (Leach, Mearns, and Scoones 1997b).[2] However, many of the analyses of stratification and intracommunity dynamics implicitly apply a unitary concept of the household, and neglect the role of gender differences.[3]

What role does gender play at the community level? The subgroups in communities are often defined along the lines of occupation, class, caste, or ethnicity. This allows a nesting of levels of actors—for example, individuals within a household, within a caste, within a locality. But gender cuts across households and other dimensions of intracommunity differentiation and hierarchy, such as class, caste, and ethnicity. Given all this complexity, it may be tempting to set aside the gender dimension, or to add "women" as a separate category, along with disadvantaged minorities, who should receive special attention. The problem with this approach is that women are not uniformly disadvantaged. Rather, gender interacts with other aspects of socioeconomic status.

As in the case of intrahousehold analysis, the case for including attention to gender differences within communities depends on the extent to which patterns of resource control, decision-making, or welfare outcomes are influenced by systematic differences between men and women. Gender relations crucially influence both the structures of property and endowment with which people enter communities, as well as the structures of reproduction that govern domestic divisions of property and labor and thereby shape people's relationships to communities. Furthermore, community organizations affect women's access to and control over resources and decision-making and welfare. Thus, whether the policy objective is to achieve more efficient and sustainable use of resources, or to promote equity and greater local participation and control, systematic power differences between men and women merit attention.

The Community: Extension of or Protection against Patriarchal Control?

Discussions and thinking about the linkages between women and communities have tended to place communities together with women and nature on one side of the equation, with society, men, and culture on the other side, as schematically represented in Table 2.1. The images that are derived from this

Table 2.1
Images Related to Women, Communities, and Nature

	Women **Nature** **Community**	**Men** **Culture** **Society**
Liberal and Marxist Western feminists Early WID scholars	Primitive nature, backwardness, traditional exploitative values and practices	Civilization, modernization, rationality, science, progressivism
WID, gender scholars Ecofeminists	Purity, environmental sustainability, altruism and sharing; holism, localism	Exploitation, aggressiveness, individualism and egoism, reductionism, universalism

bipolar view of the world are very strong and continue to pervade and structure current thinking about gender equity and environment.

How various scholars viewed the linkage between gender equity and community (often implicitly) depended on where they situated the principal site of gender struggle and exploitation, and how they analyzed the relation between patriarchy (or male domination over women) and capitalism (or development or modernization). If the family, and by extension the community, was regarded as the principal site of subordination, greater gender equality could be achieved through women's entry into the wage labor market and the public domain. On the other hand, if the family and the community were seen to offer some measure of support against oppressive class relations and forms of labor contract outside the family and the community, the proposed strategy would be to strengthen women's position within families and communities.

Early Western feminist scholars and activists supported the first view, and implicitly viewed (rural) communities as backward and traditional repositories of old-fashioned patriarchal values (see Braidotti et al. 1994; Mitchell and Oakley 1986). The image of the "modern emancipated woman" was modeled on the image of the modern successful man: an assertive individual who was not socially or economically dependent on others and whose behavior and decisions were based on rational choices. The Western feminist view of communities thus mirrored those of such scholars as Marx, Engels, and Weber and Durkheim, highlighting the virtues of marketization and urbanization and the values of equality, modernity, and rationality on which these were thought to be based. Communities had to disappear, for gender equality to occur as well as to make "rational" management of natural resources possible.

Many of the early Women in Development (WID) scholars subscribed to this set of ideas (see Bandarage 1984). Descriptions of female oppression in non-Western communities (with practices of purdah and female circumcision providing the clearest examples) were even used to demonstrate the back-wardness of these communities—using the degree of female emancipation as a yardstick of progressiveness (see also Appfel-Marglin and Simon 1994; Mohanty 1991). The basic concern of the WID school was that the benefits of modernization did not reach women, largely because women are heavily con-centrated in the household and so-called informal sectors. Fuller integration of women into the formal sectors through legal measures and changes in atti-tudes was seen as the solution. This solution can again be construed as imply-ing the need for communities to disappear to make place for the emergence of modern, equal, and independent individuals.

Later feminist, WID, and Gender and Development (GAD) scholars (for an overview see Tinker and Bramsen 1976) were more critical of models of development and modern human beings. As a consequence, the perception of the community as backward was also revisited, and gender inequality was no longer seen as merely rooted in traditional values and practices. The view of traditional communities that emerges from these writings is more positive from the perspective of women and gender equity. Communities provided women with access to community resources, and also with access to external social support systems, two factors that directly impinge on their ability to ful-fill subsistence needs outside the family (Agarwal 1990). Such ability is an important determinant of women's intrafamily bargaining power. Women were also seen to have an important role in maintaining social networks (Moser 1989) and thus in "preserving communities," which provided an important argument for more policy attention to women.

Ecofeminists have taken the positive view of the linkage between gender equality and communities one step further. Where the early feminists postu-lated that the way toward women's liberation lies in the breaking of the women-nature link, for ecofeminists this link has to be stressed and empha-sized to pave the road toward a more sustainable, humane, and equal society. Ecofeminism asserts an intrinsic closeness of women to nature, and therefore perceives women as the logical "keepers of the earth" and "guardians of the environment." Ecofeminists maintain that traditional communities lived in close harmony with nature, according to feminine principles. Colonialism and markets have broken up this harmony, often resulting in men engaging in life-destroying activities or having to migrate. The women meanwhile contin-ued to be linked to life and nature through their role as providers of suste-nance, food and water (cf. Shiva 1988, 53). Hence, for ecofeminists, in terms of environmental sustainability it is a fortunate scheme of events that women have been left out of development, because this has made it possible for them to retain their unity with nature. (See Agarwal 1992; Braidotti et al. 1994;

Jackson 1993a, 1993b; and Leach 1991 for critical reviews of the ecofeminist literature.)

Ecofeminists and "women and environment" scholars share the belief of natural resource management specialists that communities are effective in managing natural resources. Ironically, though, the resource managing communities of ecofeminists consist primarily or solely of women, whereas those of natural resource managers consist primarily of men. The idea that women are responsible for community and natural resource (particularly forests) management is probably largely based on the recognition that women are important users of these resources. Whether they also "manage" these resources partly depends on one's definition of the word "management" (Jackson 1993a, 1950). Are women still to be considered managers if management is to imply some kind of control over decision-making and planning in accordance with objectives? Or is female management "informal" and overlooked by those concerned with "formal" management of natural resources?

Whatever the answers to these questions, two important facts remain to be explained: Women in general seem to have very minimal involvement in official resource management institutions, and they have less secure access to many resources (because property rights are often vested in men). Though the representations and images of women, environment, and communities have proven useful at symbolic and political levels, they are problematic in furthering the understanding of the relationship between gender equity, communities, and environment at levels other than ideology (such as through the different work women and men do and the gender division of property and power). Neither do they address how the material and historical realities in which female and male resource managers of different classes, castes, or ethnic groups are rooted affect the ways they use and manage natural resources (cf. Agarwal 1992) or the effectiveness of natural resource management organizations. Such an understanding requires thinking across and beyond the stereotype bipolar hierarchies that automatically oppose men to women and nature to culture, and it should avoid generalized essentialist and functionalist notions of gender differences (see also Jackson 1997).

Gender, Devolution, and Natural Resource Management

The links between gender and community are much more than the subject of an abstract, academic discussion; they have direct consequences for the efficiency and sustainability of natural resources as well as for the livelihoods of people who depend on those resources. The linkages become especially relevant for policies in the context of the current emphasis on devolution of resource management, as "communities"—represented by local organizations—gain greater control over resources.

Devolution programs that vest rights or control over resource systems (including irrigation infrastructure) in local communities create (or re-create) common property resources.[4] Although there is a growing body of literature on gender and property rights (see Agarwal 1994; Lastarria-Cornhiel 1997; Meinzen-Dick et al. 1997; Rocheleau and Edmunds 1997; Zwarteveen 1997), much of the theoretical and empirical analysis has focused on gender dimensions of access to private resources. By contrast, the literature on common property resources has tended not to look at gender dimensions.[5]

Policy statements (e.g., ICWE 1992) generally use terms such as "participatory," "user-based," and "involving all stakeholders," but achieving these objectives is not so easy, especially as regards women's participation.[6] If control over resources is devolved to "traditional" institutions, these are likely to be male dominated, and reinforce existing power relations.[7] On the other hand, it is difficult to create viable new "democratic" institutions, especially those that are strong enough to manage a valuable resource over a long period. Nevertheless, if rights over resources are to be vested in local organizations, women's participation in those bodies is critical to ensuring their rights to use and manage resources.

A first and crucial condition for ensuring women's participation is the recognition of women as resource users and managers. In the context of irrigation, and with possible exception of female-headed farms, women often continue to be perceived as helpers of their husbands, and the household as a unit of common interests. Since men are seen to best represent the water-related interests and needs of the household at the level of the community, and because of the assumption of complete congruence of interests between men and women, the need for involving women in community management is not perceived to arise. In most of South Asian irrigation systems, women do use water both for productive and domestic purposes (see Zwarteveen 1994 and 1997 for a more detailed description of potential gender differences in water needs). Women also provide labor or other resources to the maintenance of irrigation systems, and they directly or indirectly benefit from the use of irrigation water. They do so mostly in their capacity as "cofarmers," working in close collaboration with their husbands to cultivate irrigated crops on their husband's (or the "family") plot. In such a situation, the nature of husband's and wife's needs for water is usually quite similar: Both want and need a supply of water that is adequate for successfully growing one or more crops a year. Differences of opinion and in preferences may nevertheless exist, regarding the timing and timeliness of water deliveries, which are based on gender divisions of tasks and responsibilities or on different crop preferences. The number of women using water for irrigation in their capacity as heads of farms is reported to be steadily increasing in most South Asian countries (see Bhattacharya and Jhansi Rani 1995). Female heads of farms may have different water needs than male farmers, either as a consequence of a reduced availability of male family labor, or because irrigated agriculture assumes a different importance in the household's livelihood strategy. Women may also use water for other purposes than irrigating the "main" crop, for instance for watering cattle or for irrigating the homestead or for domestic purposes.

It should be noted that in most irrigation situations, gender is not the primary determinant of one's access to and control of water. Access to water is often largely a function of access to land, and of the location of one's land in the irrigation system. As a consequence, women rarely share common interests as women in relation to access to water for irrigation.

The literature on common pool resource management addresses some of the implications of heterogeneity of assets, as well as heterogeneity of preferences for collective management of resources. Although this does not deal specifically with gender issues, some of the issues raised may be applicable. Baland and Platteau (1996) argue that cultural differences (in perceptions and norms) and differences in interests in a resource are detrimental to local resource management, but differences in assets or power are not necessarily a disadvantage. The negative effects of asset differences are less if the stronger members depend on the contribution of the less powerful for maintaining the infrastructure or enforcing rules, or if the links between the two sets of users are highly personalized and multidimensional. This would imply that strong differences between women and men in expectations and priorities are likely to be problematic. However, where men need women's direct or indirect contributions to resource management, it will increase women's bargaining power for getting their needs met. The multistranded linkages between women and men also mean that intrahousehold negotiations affect the outcome of natural resource management at the community level.

Evidence of Women's Participation in Resource Management Organizations

There is a long history of women's involvement in local organizations. Moser (1989) identifies participation in community managing work as part of the "triple role" of women (along with their reproductive and productive roles), and notes that this has formed the basis for many welfare approaches to women (e.g., mothers' clubs, provision of relief, or community services such as domestic water supply or health care), which treat women's organizations as an extension of their domestic roles. Other literature and efforts to organize women have focused on information and political empowerment (e.g., DAWN 1985).

The major types of women's organizations for production have been cooperatives and microcredit programs (e.g., Grameen Bank). Both of those deal with "enlarging the pie," or creating new assets. Women's participation in organizations with control over natural resources is more challenging (literally) because it deals with property rights over existing resources, and especially natural resources. Instead of creating new assets, which is a positive-sum activity for members and does not threaten the rights of nonmembers, participating in the management of resources such as forests or water can be divisive. For women, as for the poor, to claim a right to the resource and take an active role in its management therefore challenges the status quo, especially in patriarchal and highly stratified societies.

At the level of policy formulation, there seems to be widespread agreement about the need to include women in community organizations for resource management and conservation. According to the Dublin Statement on Water and the Environment, Principle No. 3, "Women play a central part in the provision, management and safeguarding of water. . . . Acceptance and implementation of this principle requires positive policies to address women's specific needs and to equip and empower women to participate at all levels in water resources programs, including decision-making and implementation, in ways defined by them" (ICWE 1992, 4).

Many projects and programs that involve the organization of community-based groups do make explicit mention of their intention to guarantee some degree of participation of women. The need to do so is theoretically justified on the basis of the idea that 1) community organizations should be democratic and representative of the interests of all members of the community, and not just a subset; and 2) community organization can be effective and efficient resource managers only if all members of the community are accountable to the organization.

In addition, the idea that women are traditionally important (or even the main) managers of natural resources (an idea generated by ecofeminists) may have an influence. In view of the considerable policy recognition of the importance of female participation in natural resource management organizations, it is likely that the number of explicit attempts at increasing or improving the involvement of women is more numerous than suggested by the available literature. Most of the mainstream literature on natural resource management (especially irrigation) does not mention gender differences (other than in the form of the occasional obligatory statements that "more attention is needed") or differentiate between male and female users. Much of what is available is in the form of project documents and so-called gray literature.

MEMBERSHIP IN WATER USERS' ORGANIZATIONS

Evidence from water users' organizations in Sri Lanka, Nepal, Pakistan, and India shows that women's participation in these organizations is much lower than men's (see Table 2.2). In all these countries there is low female participation in water users' organizations despite the high involvement of women in irrigated agriculture and agricultural decision-making. In most cases, low female participation is also in conflict with official policy statements, which almost always claim that the involvement of all farmers or water users is the ultimate objective. The few documented cases of a higher female involvement in water users' organizations either stem from women-only organizations managing groundwater pumps (Jordans and Zwarteveen 1997; van Koppen and Mahmud, 1995) or are from areas where men were not interested or were absent (Dalwai 1997; Jayasekhar, Karunakaran, and Lowdermilk 1992).

The extent of participation—by men or women—in organizations for resource management is the outcome of two factors: rules for membership, which determine eligibility to participate; and the balance of costs and benefits to be derived from involvement, which influence individuals' decisions to participate.[8] While membership criteria and incentives for participation have received attention in analyses of water users' associations generally (Meinzen-Dick et al. 1997; Ostrom 1992), there has been much less attention to gender differences in either of these critical areas (Agarwal 1997a).

Table 2.2
Female Participation in Water Users' Organizations

Country	% Female members	Membership criteria	Reference
Sri Lanka	15%	Legal ownership of irrigated land	Athukorala and Zwarteveen 1994; Kome 1997
Nepal	0%	Cultural notions regarding gender roles	Pradhan 1989; Bruins and Heijmans 1993; Zwarteveen and Neupane 1996
Pakistan	0%	Officially recognized water users on *warabandi* (irrigation rotation) lists	Bandaragoda 1997
India	6%	Legal ownership of land	Dalwai 1997; IRDAS 1993; Rao et al. 1991

FORMAL AND INFORMAL MEMBERSHIP CRITERIA

The most easily recognized gender-based barriers to participation stem from membership rules that directly or indirectly exclude women. These either stipulate that only formal right-holders to irrigated land can become members (Sri Lanka) or require head-of-household status in order to be eligible for membership, or sometimes a combination of both (Nepal). Since men tend to occupy these categories more often than women, most women are not considered eligible for membership. In the South Asian context, such formal criteria often appear to coincide with existing notions about the appropriateness of female participation in meetings. In Dry Zone irrigation systems in Sri Lanka, where legal cultivatorship is the membership criterion used, out of the limited number of women belonging to this group only very few actually do (actively) participate in the activities of the water users' organization (Kome 1997, 30).

Prevailing stereotypical ideas about the gender division of labor and about appropriate male and female behavior function as informal membership criteria. In Sri Lanka, Nepal, Pakistan, and India, ideas that only men are farmers and interested in irrigation, along with the traditional male domination in public decision-making, are factors that underlie the absence of women in water users' organizations (Bandaragoda 1997; Bruins and Heijmans 1993; Kome 1997; Zwarteveen and Neupane 1996). In addition, women are thought not to be capable of participating in meaningful ways (partly because they are illiterate), and they are assumed to be busy with other, more appropriately female activities (Bruins and Heijmans 1993; Zwarteveen and Neupane 1996). Social norms prescribing that women confine their activities to a small geographical area (homestead, village, or nearby fields) may also effectively exclude women from becoming members of water users' organizations (IRDAS 1993).

In addition to these formal and informal membership criteria, the process through which new water users' organizations are formed in management transfer programs is often gendered, partly as a result of preconceived notions of planners about who are to be considered users, and partly because of the organizing process itself. In Sri Lanka, the Irrigation Department initiated this process by contacting those farmers they already knew, whom they asked to inform and mobilize other farmers. Almost all the farmers known by the Irrigation Department were men, and very few of these men invited female farmers to participate. The fact that the first set of activities to be undertaken by the new organizations concerned rehabilitation construction work further decreased the chances for women to become involved, since construction works are considered typically male activities (Kome 1997).

Long (1989, 240) observes that "the question of non-involvement should not be interpreted to imply that nonparticipants have no influence on the constitution and outcomes. . . . On the contrary, they can, as 'backstage' actors, have a decisive influence on strategies and scenarios." In spite of not formally being members or participating in meetings, women may play other roles in organizations, or in carrying out collective action. There exist a few documented examples of such nonformal ways of female participation. Pradhan (1989) describes how in the Bhanjayang Tar Ko Kulo in the hills in Nepal, women intervened in a conflict between head- and tail-enders about canal maintenance. In the Sreeramsagar irrigation project in India, women in one village organized among themselves to remove obstructions in the canal and guard the water flow. This elicited the following comment from an old male farmer: "We have seen that nobody is bold enough to obstruct women and it has made things easy for us" (Rao, Hassan, and Shyamala 1991). A female farmer in another village in the same irrigation system played a leading role in settling water-related conflicts. In yet another village women took the initiative to help their husbands to irrigate, by allowing them to guard the canals and procure the water, while the women applied the water to the field. The *neerpaccis*, or common irrigators, in South Indian tanks are traditionally male employees of the water users' association. In several cases, women have been seen carrying out the water distribution tasks—not as neerpaccis themselves, but carrying out the work for their husbands (field observations 1994). In Sri Lanka, wives of male office-bearers often assist their husbands with administrative tasks and secretarial duties (Athukorala and Zwarteveen 1994). Women may also be asked to clean meeting areas, and to provide drinks and snacks to participants (Weerakoon 1995).

Although highly anecdotal, these examples of management-related tasks and roles of women suggest that nonformal and less recognized ways of participation in water users' organizations may prove to be a promising area of further research. This research may provide important entry points for identifying realistic ways to make water users' organizations more gender equitable, while it may also shed a new light on the determinants of the performance of organizations by uncovering management practices and decisions that have hitherto gone unnoticed.

COSTS AND BENEFITS OF PARTICIPATION

Just as membership criteria have formal and informal dimensions for men and women, so also the costs and benefits include a range of tangible as well as intangible factors that influence decisions to participate in the activities of local organizations. While the tangible factors may be easiest for outsiders to identify, other considerations can rank higher in local people's personal decisions.

Because of their high domestic and productive workloads, the opportunity cost of time to attend meetings and do other work for the organizations is different (and often higher) for women than for men. Important in this respect is that it is not as easy for women to transfer some of their responsibilities to their husbands, as it is for men to leave some of their tasks to their wives. Timing and location of meetings may also impose a higher cost on women than on men. In the Ambewela irrigation system in the hills in Sri Lanka, meetings are held at night to suit male preference. For women, it is highly unsuitable to go out after dark (Kome 1997). In another system in Sri Lanka (Parapegama), women do not like to go to the meetings of the water users' organization because they are held at the bar, and usually end up with everybody drinking liquor.[9] And, while most Sri Lankan men go to the meetings by bicycle, very few women own or ride bicycles, implying that it would take them much longer to go to meetings (Kome 1997). Similarly, formal training held away from the village or community and requiring an overnight stay imposes a higher cost (in terms of child care arrangements or family resistance) on women than on men.

Because of membership criteria and as a direct result of the process of organization, water users' organizations in South Asia have often come to be historically and socially constructed and defined as predominantly male domains. The active participation of women in water users' organizations would imply a challenge to prevailing gender norms and practices, at both the household and the community level. It would involve a revalorization of female identity and work, rejecting norms and regulations that tie women to specific roles, and it would imply that women are struggling to occupy spaces previously reserved for men. As one Sri Lankan woman tried to explain about the absence of women in the water users' organization: "Women work hard in the field. They contribute more labor to the cultivation than men. However, we never try to challenge the men. We think they should retain their position as head of household. Traditionally, a man is seen as the decision maker in the household. This is not the case in reality, but still we allow them to go to the FO [Farmers' Organization] meetings in that capacity" (Kome 1997, 14).

Also, the abilities and capacities needed for participating in organizations, and especially for office-bearer positions, may not be as easily identified with women as with men for a number of reasons. In Nepal, "Women . . . referred to their illiteracy as a reason for not attending meetings; they were afraid that they would not be able to understand what was being said and thought they would have little to contribute" (Zwarteveen and Neupane 1996, 9). Farmers (male and female) in Nepal also mentioned women's lack of negotiating skills and mobility as two factors inhibiting meaningful participation of women (Zwarteveen and Neupane 1996). On the benefits side, the prestige of participation in public forums, and especially of leadership positions in the organizations, may be valued more highly by men than by women (Agarwal 1997b; Moser 1989).

Whether women are willing to bear these costs and face these social risks will largely depend on their assessment of the effectiveness of the organizations, and of formal participation in them as a means of achieving personal objectives, as compared to other means available to them. This calculation is illustrated by comments from a woman in the Parapegama irrigation system in Sri Lanka: "I never participate in the FO meetings. If I go there I have to spend about 2 or 3 hours, but if I stay at home, I can make 200–300 beedi.[10] Therefore I do not like to go. I will ask my husband what the officers said. It is better to be a member of the Death Donation Society than to be a member of the FO.[11] The FO does not give quick benefits, we can cultivate without the FO. In addition to that, most people ignore the FO" (Kome 1997, 24).

In the Nepal Chhattis Mauja system, which is a system traditionally managed by farmers, women said that they never attended meetings of the water users' organization because the meetings offered no opportunities for them to raise their concerns and needs. Many of these women perceived stealing water to be an easier solution than what was offered by more formal channels (Zwarteveen and Neupane 1996).

In other cases, the fact that women benefit indirectly from the organizations, even without participating directly, may explain why they see no need to participate more fully and formally. In the Rajolibanda Diversion Scheme in Andhra Pradesh, India, "although women are not actively involved in the discussions and approval of the operational plan, all women are aware of it" (IRDAS 1993, 27). The women also indicated that because of the meetings, they benefited from a reduction in conflicts over water, and from information about when they would get water, which enabled them to plan their work in the house and the fields (IRDAS 1993, 28–29).

INFORMAL PARTICIPATION, OTHER DOMAINS

That female nonmembers succeed in getting their needs met indicates that not all irrigation management decisions in the community pass through the formal organization. Instead, the water users' organization can be considered one of a number of coexisting and partly overlapping "domains of interaction" (Villareal 1994) in which decisions about resource management are taken. One such domain of interaction in which women influence water-related decisions and obtain services is the household. In almost all cases reviewed, women were observed (and themselves indicated) that if they needed anything specific to be said at water users' meetings, they would either tell their husbands or try to send a male relative (often a son or son-in-law). Likewise, many women indicated that they received information about water delivery schedules and other decisions taken at water users' organization meetings through their husbands or male relatives.

When access to irrigation services is negotiated within the domain of the household, it becomes subject to the quality of the intimate relations women have with their husbands, sons and sons-in-law, or fathers. Women's success in obtaining services geared to their needs will partly depend on the extent to which their specific water needs are complementary, shared, or conflictual to those of their husbands and male relatives, and on their bargaining position in household interactions. This is consistent with Baland and Platteau's suggestion that multistranded interpersonal linkages significantly affect the outcome of local resource management.

Another important domain of interaction regarding water decisions may be the field. Many negotiations, struggles, and conflicts regarding water take place alongside the canals, and actual water distribution is often partly determined in this domain. Kome (1997) reports that in a Sri Lankan Dry Zone irrigation system, one's capacity to take water is in the first instance determined by the location of one's fields along the canals. In the second instance, water distribution follows the principle of "the survival of the fittest," reflecting existing power relations. Gender as one determinant of power also interferes in determining one's ability to obtain water. An example is provided by one woman located at the tail end, who, after having unsuccessfully tried to obtain water a number of times (at night) decided to ask her brother to divert the water for her. She assumed that other irrigators would be reluctant to prevent him from taking water, since he is a man and can better defend himself (Kome 1997). Pradhan (1989), referring to hill irrigation systems in Nepal, also mentions the ability to physically defend oneself as a factor that limits women's possibilities for taking water in times of water scarcity.

Other domains of interaction that directly or indirectly (co)determine women's access to and control of irrigation services may exist. Female networks (work groups as well as social groups) may be important, especially where male and female social networks are highly segregated. And in addition to domains, individual contacts with people (mostly men) in powerful positions (including those outside the "community," such as irrigation officials) can be a significant source of power. Female farmers in both Sri Lanka and Nepal could very clearly identify the persons they would approach in case they had water-related questions or needs (Kome 1997; Zwarteveen and Neupane 1996). Maintaining good relationships with such people through regular courtesy visits and gifts may be an important mechanism for women to secure their access to resources.

The use of indirect means to obtain water resources is consistent with women's strategies for gaining access to other resources, such as land and trees (see Lastarria-Cornhiel 1997; Meinzen-Dick et al. 1997a; Rocheleau and Edmunds 1997). But as is often the case with gender differences in property rights, gaining access through such indirect means does not provide much control over the resource, or the ability to make decisions regarding its management. Relying on connections to access the resource—whether through male relatives, officials, or others—increases women's dependence on others, whereas independent rights to resources can raise women's standing and bargaining power in both the household and community. Nevertheless, these socially nuanced means of access are critical to actual patterns of resource use, and should not be neglected in research or policies.

The extent to which women's needs are defendable in the various domains depends on their social and legal legitimacy. In the case of water needs, although the literature often refers to irrigation organizations as "water users' associations" (WUAs), they tend to include only irrigated farmers, and are concerned with water deliveries to field crops. Some of the uses of water by women, such as water used for irrigating homestead gardens or watering livestock, are likely not to be included in formal water distribution plans, and may thus not be considered legitimate in the domain of the WUA. In other domains (such as the household and field), the legitimacy of these needs may be greater, allowing women access to water for meeting these needs. In this respect it is important to realize that women may have a vested interest in not being identified as users or farmers: Claiming water as women (or mothers or domestic caretakers) may cause less resistance and be easier than claiming water as farmers.

In sum, looking at natural resource management in some South Asian countries from a gender perspective reveals that the dynamics of resource management cannot be properly understood when attention is limited to the formal organization. The evidence also suggests that the lack of visible participation of women in resource management organization cannot be construed as implying their lack of interest in the use and management of the resource, nor does it imply that women do not influence what happens within the organization. Water users' organizations are only one of a possible number of domains in which decisions about the management of water are taken. Women's access to these other domains may be easier as compared to the formal organization, while their participation in these other domains may also be more effective. However, the fact that women succeed in somehow getting their water needs accommodated does not imply that more formal participation in water users' organizations is not desirable or necessary. Access obtained through informal means is not as secure, and control over water that is not sanctioned by democratically devised rules and principles is more prone to be influenced by unequal power relations. If devolution programs are to effectively transfer rights, along with responsibility for water management, to local communities, it becomes all the more critical to examine how those rights are distributed within the communities.

Women's Participation and the Effectiveness of Organizations

The lack of participation of a large number of the users in the management of irrigation would, at least according to the theories of participatory management, imply performance weaknesses in the organization, because of weaknesses in communication, representation, democracy, and accountability, which may lead to free riding, rent-seeking, and corruption (Ostrom 1992). There is some evidence that this may indeed be the case.

In one of the few studies to address this, Zwarteveen and Neupane (1996) found that the all-male organization for the Chhattis Mauja system in Nepal faced difficulties in enforcing its rules on women. Female heads of farms in the head end of the system always took more water than their entitlements, while contributing less labor than they should. In other parts of the system, village irrigation leaders also mentioned water-stealing by women as a problem that was difficult to solve, because women were not members of the organization and thus could not be punished.

Women did not choose to steal water or shirk their duty to contribute labor to maintenance only because of opportunism. Water-stealing by women occurred partly because women had an interest in applying more water to the paddy field that would be needed for optimal crop growth. A slight increase in the ponding depth considerably decreased weed growth, and thus the time women needed to devote to weeding. As for contributing labor, rules and prevailing gender norms make it difficult for women to comply with these rules. Female labor contributions, for instance, are valued less, and there often is an official rule that stipulates that labor for emergency maintenance and maintenance of the head dam can be supplied only by men. Fear of being harassed by men, and cultural restrictions on female mobility, also impede women's ability to contribute labor (Zwarteveen and Neupane 1996). In addition, it is likely that because women never participate in meetings with other water users, they may not understand as well as male farmers how much harm they generate for those lower in the system by stealing water or by not investing in maintenance. Unlike men, head-end women are never directly confronted with tail-end farmers (both men and women) who face the consequences of their free-riding behavior.

It is when local communities see women's participation as essential that real change is likely to come (see Illo n.d.). In the case of Joint Forest Management in Nepal, Sarin (1995) reports that the exclusion of women from management organizations makes it possible for women (especially those from outside the village) to continue to gather firewood. In some communities 90 percent of the offenders are women, and male office-bearers find it difficult to stop these women, since they risk being accused of molesting them. As a result, female participation in organizations is now accepted, but not on grounds of equity, participation, or democracy—rather because women are needed to help the organization enforce its rules, or stop other women from taking firewood. The irrigation association in Chhatis Mauja has not come to this point, but the problems of enforcing rules and contributions on head-end women may yet bring about such a change.

Conclusions

Much of the more recent research on communities has as its primary purpose the demonstration of its virtues in terms of efficiency, effectiveness, and even equity in managing natural resources (Agrawal and Gibson 1999). For the most part the conceptual analysis of community resource management organizations has concentrated on the universal principles, conditions, or rules that characterize successful regimes and institutions. In the process, the analysis has largely circumvented the implications of internal differentiation or asymmetry, including the plurality of beliefs, norms, and interests involved in interactions between resource users, the effects of complex variations in culture and society, as well as wider aspects of social and political conflict relating to ownership and management of natural resources (cf. Prakash 1998).

Although some of the examples used in the literature are derived from community organizations primarily consisting of women (the Chipko movement in India and the Green Belt movements in Kenya being the most well-known examples), little systematic thought has so far been attributed to the linkages between gender relations and communities, or to the role of women in community management of resources. While studies of communities and natural resource management often ignore gender, much of the literature on gender and development limits its explorations of gender-based differences and inequities to what happens within the boundaries of the household, without looking at gender relations at the community level. Ecofeminist scholars, although recognizing the importance of women as users and managers of natural resources, tend to see women as a uniform category and assume an essentialist relation between women and nature.

The more sophisticated conceptualization of communities that allows for differences of interests and power between different members of communities, as proposed by Agrawal and Gibson in this volume, would crucially depend on a sound understanding of gender relations. Such an understanding should go beyond an analysis of intrahousehold differences and avoid the pitfalls of essentialism and populism. Rather than assuming a natural and universal closeness or link between women and nature, research and policies should question and problematize this link for every specific context.

Women's participation has received considerable rhetoric, and though quite some attention has been paid to the differences between women's and men's needs with respect to resource use, much less is known about the implications of those differences for community management in terms of both effectiveness and equity.

In setting up new institutional structures for "community" control over natural resources, devolution programs need to address gender issues and differences in power if the transfer is not to further inequalities. Just as providing for women's ownership of private property can bolster their bargaining power within the household, even if they do not always appear to exercise those rights, strengthening women's claims over common property can strengthen their position in the household and community. As users of the resource, both women and men have interests, needs, and priorities in respect to its management. As managers, women and men may have different knowledge, skills, and resources to offer. Community organizations for natural resource management will be better able to manage the resource sustainably if they tap these diverse resources. More important, if female users are not involved in setting rules for the use and maintenance of the resource, it will be difficult to ensure their compliance. Rule-setting by men only also means that work patterns come to be structured around men's physical needs and capabilities—especially their lack of child care and domestic responsibilities—making it physically more difficult for women to comply. Explicitly addressing the challenge of female participation is therefore likely to lead to better devolution policies.

Existing knowledge points to some possible ways to enhance female participation. A first step involves the definition of membership rules: Instead of allowing one member per household, both male and female members of households could be considered eligible for membership. Simply ensuring women's membership, or removing the entrance barriers for women, is important, but in itself does not guarantee women's equal and meaningful participa-

uses homogenous concept
of category, "norm"
Gender Dimensions of Resource Management in South Asia　　83

tion. Integrating women into existing organizations may not work if it implies that women have to adapt their behavior to existing rules. They may learn to win, but this will often be at the cost of bringing their different perspectives into play—as when overachieving women managers become "sociological males" (Goetz 1995). The project of "gendering" community organizations goes beyond integration: It is an inherently transformative project in that it should be oriented to routinizing gender equitable forms of social interaction and limiting the possibilities for choosing discriminatory forms of social organization. In this regard, it is important that very explicit and focused attempts to reach and mobilize female members are made early in the process of devolution. Once water users' organizations have come to be established and defined as male organizations, it will become much more difficult to remove and overcome gender barriers, biases, and inequities.

What such a transformative project entails in practice will very much depend on local specificities. It will require efforts to determine whether and how needs and interests with respect to the use and management of water are gender specific. If women have specific needs these should be publicly recognized and supported so as to increase women's visibility and social legitimacy. Because needs, and the perception of needs, are likely to be gender specific, the motivation of individual users to participate is likely to also be influenced by their gender. Women may for instance be more interested if their participation is explained and interpreted as a logical extension of their socially accepted roles as mothers and wives, whereas men may become interested if participation contributes to their perceived male roles as public decision-makers.

Although some degree of external pressure—whether from donor agencies, governments, or NGOs—or support may be essential to achieve meaningful participation of women, it is not a simple matter for external actors to prescribe a place for women in local organizations. Such interventions may be ineffective, at best, and may seem to directly contradict the objective of community control by contradicting existing structures of authority. Yet upon closer examination, most devolution programs impose many external conditions upon local management organizations: a variety of requirements for registration, auditing, bylaws, and activities if the organizations are to be recognized by the government or receive external assistance. If these can be imposed for the government's convenience, or to ensure fiscal viability or the maintenance of the resource base, interventions can also be made to ensure gender equity.

Processes and practices that lead to female exclusion are led by principles that are in most cases not made explicit. Women, and even those women who are eligible for membership, often seem to acquiesce in their own noninvolvement. This does not imply a lack of interest of women in water-related issues. Rather, it is the result of a conscious calculation of the costs and benefits of participation. The social costs and risks involved in contesting the masculine rules and norms of water users' organizations and the time costs involved in attending meetings are not balanced by the perceived benefits, especially when meetings are not very effective forums for achieving their objectives. This is especially true when organizations just start to develop, and when their aims and strengths are not yet clear.

In trying to define a legitimate place for women in natural resource management within communities, it is essential to look beyond the existing definitions of formal participation in meetings or roles, and to recognize the many ways in which women already take a role in resource management. Female roles and contributions are often not publicly appreciated, either because they are performed "behind the screens" or because their work is not seen as productive (e.g., cooking and cleaning). At present, there is relatively little documentation or analysis of this. Studies that capture the gender dimensions of collective action in natural resource management—including both formal and informal forms of participation—are a critical area for future research, if devolution programs are to achieve their aims.

People's interests and motivations to invest in resource management are to a large extent based on the interest they have in good and reliable access to the resource. In most South Asian irrigation systems, there are as many or more women with some interest in good and reliable irrigation services as there are men, although there may be gender-based differences in the precise nature of this interest. More than the nature or degree of water needs, the extent to which water users believe that participation in water users' organizations will help to satisfy their water needs is gender specific. This does not imply that all women are equally affected or disadvantaged, nor does it mean that all women will equally benefit from participation in resource management. Differences based on gender interact with other differences such as class, caste, and ethnicity, and thus must be examined along with the implications of those in the community management of natural resources.

Notes

An earlier version of this paper was presented at the International Irrigation Management Institute's Women and Water Workshop, 15–19 September 1997, and subsequently published as "Gendered Participation in Water Management: Issues and Illustrations from Water Users' Associations in South Asia," by Ruth Meinzen-Dick and Margreet Zwarteveen in *Agriculture and Human Values* 15(4):337–345 (© 1998, used with kind permission from Kluwer Academic Publishers). We wish to acknowledge the ideas and written comments provided by

Lynn Brown, Frances Cleaver, Luin Goldring, Eva Jordans, Michael Kevane, Anna Knox McCulloch, Doug Merrey, and Agnes Quisumbing.

1. The devolution of resource management to the lowest level that is consistent with efficiency is also referred to as the principle of subsidiarity.
2. One might ask why intracommunity inequality has been largely overlooked in the current enthusiasm for devolution. One reason may be that many studies documenting that communities could manage resources effectively derive from upland areas or areas where land tenure is often less permanent, and thus stratification based on unequal access to land is relatively less (but increasingly) important than in intensive agricultural areas where control over land and accumulation are more established (Peter Vandergeest, personal communication, July 9, 1997). Another reason may lie in the discursive history of the debate on the commons. The historical beginnings of the commons debate lie in an economic analysis of property rights defined along a binary axis between public and private goods (Prakash 1998).
3. For a bargaining approach with explicit gender dimensions, applied to the community level, see Carney and Watts (1991).
4. In many cases, the resources that are being vested in communities in devolution programs were originally local common property resources. The state had exerted a claim over those resources, and is now transferring them back to the communities (see Agrawal 1997b).
5. For example, only seventeen of the 529 papers presented at the International Association for the Study of Common Property meetings in 1990–1996 mention gender or women in the title or abstract.
6. Even in the domestic water supply arena, where women's roles are well recognized, Narayan (1995) found that only 17 percent of the 121 projects reviewed achieved substantial levels of female participation.
7. According to Wade (1987, 230; cited in Baland and Platteau 1996), "corporate organisations, to be effective, should be based on existing structures of authority. In practice, this means that the council will be dominated by the local elite which is a disturbing conclusion for democrats and egalitarians."
8. For a similar analysis of issues related to natural resources management in the forestry sector, see Agrawal (1997b).
9. It is not typical in Sri Lanka to use bars as meeting places for farmers' organizations. Meetings are often held at temple grounds or in community centers, which are socially accessible to women.
10. Beedis are local cigarettes. Making beedis is an attractive income-generating activity of young women with children, since they can do it at home.
11. Death Donation Societies are savings societies. In principle, savings are meant for funerals. In practice, Death Donation Societies often also provide loans for consumptive or agricultural purposes.

Bibliography

Agrawal, B. 1990. "Gender Relations and Food Security: Coping with Seasonality, Drought, and Famine in South Asia." PEW/Cornell Lecture Series on Food and Nutrition Policy: Cornell Food and Nutrition Policy Program, Cornell University.

———. 1992. "The Gender and Environment Debate: Lessons from India." *Feminist Studies* 18(1):119–157.

———. 1994. "Gender, Resistance and Land: Interlinked Struggles over Resources and Meanings in South Asia." *Journal of Peasant Studies* 22(1):81–125.

————. 1997a. *"Bargaining" and Gender Relations: Within and Beyond the Household.* FCND Discussion Paper #27. Washington, D.C.: IFPRI.

————. 1997b. "Environmental Action, Gender Equity and Women's Participation." *Development and Change* 28:1–44.

Agrawal, A., and C. Gibson. 1999. "Enchantment and Disenchantment: The Role of Community in Natural Resource Development." *World Development* 27(4): 629–649.

Alderman, H., P. Chiappori, L. Haddad, J. Hoddinott, and R. Kanbur. 1995. "Unitary versus Collective Models of the Household: Is It Time to Shift the Burden of Proof?" *World Bank Research Observer* 10(1)(Feb.): 1–19.

Appfel-Marglin, F., and S. L. Simon. 1994. "Feminist Orientalism and Development." In *Feminist Perspectives on Sustainable Development*, ed. W. Harcourt, 26–44. London : Zed Books Ltd.

Athukorala, K., and M. Zwarteveen. 1994. "Participatory Management: Who Participates?" *Economic Review* 20(6):22–25.

Baland, J., and J. P. Platteau. 1996. *Halting Degradation of Natural Resources. Is There a Role for Rural Communities?* Oxford, U.K.: Food and Agriculture Organization and Clarendon Press.

Bandarage, A. 1984. "Women in Development: Liberalism, Marxism, and Marxist-Feminism." *Development and Change* 15:495–515.

Bandaragoda, D. J. 1997. Personal email communication, August 20.

Bendix, R., and S. M. Lipset, eds. 1954. *Class, Status and Power.* Glencoe, Ill.: Free Press.

Bhattacharya, B., and G. Jhansi Rani. 1995. "Gender in Agriculture: An Asian Perspective." *Asia-Pacific Journal of Rural Development* 1:27–48.

Braidotti, R., E. Charkiewicz, S. Haüsler, and S. Wieringa. 1994. *Women, the Environment, and Sustainable Development: Toward a Theoretical Synthesis.* London: Zed Books Ltd.

Bruins, B., and A. Heijmans. 1993. *Gender Biases in Irrigation Projects. Gender Considerations in the Rehabilitation of Bauraha Irrigation System in the District of Dang, Nepal.* Kathmandu, Nepal: SNV.

Carney, J. A., and M. Watts. 1991. "Manufacturing Dissent: Work, Gender and the Politics of Meaning in a Peasant Society." *Africa* 60(2):207–241.

Dalwai, A. 1997. *Can Women do Participatory Irrigation Management (PIM)?* INPIM Newsletter 5. Washington, D.C.: World Bank.

DAWN (Development Alternatives with Women for a New Era). 1985. "Empowering Ourselves through Organizations: Types and Methods." In *DAWN, Development, Crises, and Alternative Visions: Third World Women's Perspectives*, 82–89. New Delhi: Institute of Social Studies Trust (ISST).

Dumont, L. 1980. *Homo Hierarchicus—The Caste System and Its Implications.* Complete rev. English ed. Chicago: University of Chicago Press.

Dwyer, D., and J. Bruce, eds. 1988. *A Home Divided: Women and Income in the Third World.* Stanford, Calif.: Stanford University Press.

Goetz, A. M. 1995. *The Politics of Integrating Gender to State Development Processes: Trends, Opportunities and Constraints in Bangladesh, Chile, Jamaica, Mali, Morocco, and Uganda.* Occasional Paper No. 2. Geneva: UNRISD.

Guyer, J. I. 1980. *Household Budgets and Women's Issues.* African Studies Center Working Paper 28. Boston, Mass.: Boston University Press.

Haddad, L., J. Hoddinott, and H. Alderman, eds. 1997. *Intrahousehold Resource Allocation in Developing Countries: Models, Methods, and Policy.* Baltimore, Md.: Johns Hopkins University Press.

Hart, G. 1995. "Gender and Household Dynamics: Recent Theories and Their Implications." In *Critical Issues in Asian Development: Theories, Experiences, and Policies,* ed. M. G. Quibria. Oxford, U.K.: Oxford University Press.

ICWE (International Conference on Water and the Environment). 1992. *Development Issues for the Twenty-first Century.* The Dublin Statement Report of the Conference. ICWE Conference, 26–31 January 1992, Dublin, Ireland.

Illo, J.F.I. n.d. *Women's Participation in Two Philippine Irrigation Projects.* Reprint 23 ed. Manila, Philippines: Institute of Philippine Culture.

IRDAS. 1993. *Gender Issues—A Study in Rajolibanda Diversion Scheme (RDS) (Andhra Pradesh).* Hyderabad, India: The Institute of Resource Development and Social Management (IRDAS).

Jackson, C. 1993a. "Doing What Comes Naturally? Women and Environment in Development." *World Development* 21(12):1947–1963.

———. 1993b. "Woman/Nature or Gender/History? A Critique of Ecofeminist 'Development'." *The Journal of Peasant Studies* 20(3):389–419.

———. 1997. *Gender, Irrigation and Environment: Arguing for Agency.* Paper presented to the Workshop on Women and Water, Colombo, Sri Lanka, IIMI.

Jayasekhar, L., K. Karunakaran, and M. K. Lowdermilk. 1992. "Women in Irrigation Management: A Case Study in South India." *Journal of Extension System* (India) 8:114–124.

Jordans, E. H., and M. Z. Zwarteveen. 1997. *A Well of One's Own. Gender Analysis of an Irrigation Program in Bangladesh.* Colombo, Sri Lanka: IIMI.

Kome, A. 1997. *Gender and Irrigation Management Transfer in Sri Lanka: IRMU, ID and IIMI.* Wageningen, The Netherlands: Wageningen Agricultural University.

Lastarria-Cornhiel, S. 1997. "Impact of Privatization on Gender and Property Rights in Africa." *World Development* 25(8):1317–1334.

Leach, M. 1991. "Gender and the Environment: Traps and Opportunities." Paper prepared for Development Studies Association (DSA) Conference, Swansea, 11–13 September 1991. Brighton, U.K.: University of Sussex.

Leach, M., R. Mearns, and I. Scoones. 1997a. "Challenges to Community-Based Sustainable Development: Dynamics, Entitlements, Institutions." *IDS Bulletin* 28(4):4–14.

———. 1997b. "Institutions, Consensus, and Conflict: Implications for Policy and Practice." *IDS Bulletin* 28(4):90–95.

Long, N. 1989. *Encounters at the Interface: A Perspective on Social Discontinuities in Rural Development.* Wageningen, The Netherlands: Wageningen Agricultural University.

Meinzen-Dick, R. S., L. Brown, H. Feldstein, and A. Quisumbing. 1997a. "Gender, Property Rights, and Natural Resources." *World Development* 25(8):1303–1316.

Meinzen-Dick, R. S., M. S. Mendoza, L. Sadoulet, G. Abiad-Shields and A. Subramanian. 1997b. "Sustainable Water Users' Associations: Lessons from a Literature Review." In *User Organizations for Sustainable Water Services,* ed. A. Subramanian, N. V. Jagannathan, and R. S. Meinzen-Dick, 7–87. World Bank Technical Paper no. 354. Washington, D.C.: World Bank.

Mitchell, J., and A. Oakley, eds. 1986. *What Is Feminism? A Re-examination.* New York: Pantheon Books.

Mohanty, C. T. 1991. "Under Western Eyes: Feminist Scholarship and Colonial Discourses." In *Third World Women and the Politics of Feminism,* ed. C. T. Mohanty, A. Russo, and L. Torres, 51–80. Bloomington and Indianapolis: Indiana University Press.

Moser, C.O.N. 1989. "Gender Planning in the Third World: Meeting Practical and Strategic Gender Needs." *World Development* 17(11):1799–1825.

Narayan, D. 1995. *The Contribution of People's Participation: Evidence from 121 Rural Water Supply Projects.* Environmentally Sustainable Development Occasional Paper Series no. 1. Washington, D.C.: World Bank.

Ostrom, E. 1992. *Crafting Institutions for Self-Governing Irrigation Systems*. San Francisco: Institute for Contemporary Studies Press.

Pradhan, N. C. 1989. *Gender Participation in Irrigation System Activities in the Hills of Nepal*. Proceedings of Second Annual Workshop on Women in Farming Systems, 27–29 September 1989. Rampur, Chitwan, Nepal: Institute of Agriculture and Animal Science. Kathmandu, Nepal: USAID.

Prakash, S. 1998. "Fairness, Social Capital and the Commons: The Societal Foundations of Collective Action in the Himalayas." *In Privatizing Nature. Political Struggles for the Global Commons*, ed. Michael Goldman. London: Pluto Press in association with the Transnational Institute.

Rao, S. C., T. Hassan, and C. V. Shyamala. 1991. "Role of Women in Water Management. Experiences in Sreeramsagar Project, Andhra Pradesh." Paper presented at a seminar on Men and Women Water Users in Water Management. Hyderabad, India: PMU (Production Management Unit) Indo Dutch Training Production Management Unit.

Rocheleau, D., and D. Edmunds. 1997. "Women, Men and Trees: Gender, Power, and Property in Forest and Agrarian Landscapes." *World Development* 25(8): 1351–1371.

Sarin, M. 1995. "Regenerating India's Forests: Reconciling Gender Equity with Joint Forest Management." *IDS Bulletin* 26(1):83–91.

Shiva, V. 1988. *Staying Alive: Women, Ecology and Development*. London and New Delhi: Zed Books Ltd. and Kali for Women.

Tinker, I., and M. B. Bramsen, eds. 1976. *Women and World Development: Proceedings of the World Conference of International Women's Year, 1975*. Washington, D.C.: Overseas Development Council.

van Koppen, B., and S. Mahmud. 1995. *Woman and Water-Pumps in Bangladesh: The Impacts of Participation in Irrigation Groups on Women's Status*. Wageningen, The Netherlands: Department of Irrigation and Soil and Water Conservation, Wageningen Agricultural University.

Villareal, M. 1994. "Wielding and Yielding. Power, Subordination and Gender Identity in the Context of a Mexican Development Project." Ph.D. thesis, Wageningen Agricultural University, Wageningen, The Netherlands.

Wade, R. 1987. "The Management of Common Property Resources: Finding Cooperative Solutions." *World Bank Research Observer* 2(2):219–234.

Weerakoon, P. 1995. *Gender Issues and Irrigation Management*. Study, Kalankuttyia, Mahaweli H., International Irrigation Management Institute (IIMI), Colombo, Sri Lanka. Field notes.

Zwarteveen, M. 1994. "Gender Issues, Water Issues." Working Paper #32. Colombo, Sri Lanka: International Irrigation Management Institute.

———. 1997. "Water: From Basic need to Commodity. A Discussion on Gender and Water Rights in the Context of Irrigation." *World Development* 25(8):1335–1350.

Zwarteveen, M., and N. Neupane. 1996. *Free-Riders or Victims: Women's Nonparticipation in Irrigation Management in Nepal's Chhattis Mauja Irrigation Scheme*. Research Report #7. Colombo, Sri Lanka: International Irrigation Management Institute.

The Ethnopolitics of Irrigation Management in the Ziz Oasis, Morocco

Chapter 3

HSAIN ILAHIANE

IN LIGHT OF RECENT ATTENTION to sustainability, much of the development literature stresses indigenous resource management strategies for solving the plight of the poor and vulnerable in the developing world. Much care is needed in assessing the vulnerability of the poor and advocating the rehabilitation of indigenous or homegrown institutions to protect the community from social and natural perturbations; these same institutions may act as potential barriers to any well-intentioned development effort (Arnould 1990, 10–11; Chambers 1989, 1–2). Indigenous communities are not always as homogeneous, benign, or egalitarian as the literature tends to describe them (see also Ilahiane 1999). Rather, they are often conflict-ridden entities in fierce competition over valuable but scarce natural resources: in this case traditional sources of irrigation. In the Ziz Valley, located in Southeast Morocco, irrigation management can be understood only through a historical examination of the ethnopolitical relations among social groups and the ecological relations governing the organization of, and access to, resources.

This chapter describes a locally managed and maintained small-scale irrigation system in the middle Ziz Valley oasis, with particular focus on the village of Zaouit Amelkis. The village of Zaouit Amelkis is one of the sites where the author conducted dissertation fieldwork on the relationship between ethnicity and agricultural intensification in 1994 and 1995. The Amelkis community is composed of three ethnic groups: Berbers, Arabs, and Haratine. The population of the village is 1,296, making up 193 households, 10 percent Berber, 8 percent Shurfa and Murabitin Arabs, and 82 percent Haratine. The local economy is based on irrigated subsistence agriculture, the tending of

89

date and olive trees, and livestock-raising. The farming population mainly cultivates barley, wheat, corn, alfalfa, turnips, carrots, fava beans, and various fruit trees. Dry farming or *lbur* is also practiced in rainy years for growing cereals, particularly wheat and barley, in the surrounding hills. The Amelkis village is characterized by land differentials among its ethnic groups. The entire village farming land is 163.5 hectares, 33 percent Berber, 20 percent Shurfa and Murabitin Arabs, 22 percent Haratine, 15 percent outsiders, and 10 percent mosque or *waqf* (Ilahiane 1995).

The village of Zaouit Amelkis provides a case study in which small-scale irrigation maintenance has been based on labor extortion from the low-status Haratine by the high-status Berbers and Arabs. This chapter describes: (1) the environment of the Ziz Valley, (2) the Ziz Valley's society of rank, (3) the irrigation system of the village of Zaouit Amelkis, and (4) the social organization of the Zaouit Amelkis' irrigation system.

The Environment of the Ziz Valley

To the south of the eastern High Atlas mountains, one encounters a rugged region composed of high-elevation mountains of a southwestern-southeastern slope riding over the Sillon Sud Atlassique chain, sandwiched between the Anti-Atlas and the Hammada of Meski and Guir. In the middle of these arid mountains, the Ziz Valley is the richest and most populated area (Figure 3.1). Born on the southern slopes of the Jbal Ayash (3,760 m), the Oued Ziz meanders through a 200-kilometer ribbon of olive trees, date palms, cereals, and alfalfa fields. The river, 30 to 60 meters wide and of variable depth, covers the area between upper Rich and the lowlands of Rissani. Along the Oued, myriad springs feed its course. In fall and spring, the river is subject to violent flash floods that damage property and fields. To the west of Rich, another geological cut leads to the High Atlas massif of year-round snow-capped mountains of the upper Ziz Valley reaching an elevation of 3,000 meters around the Imilchil and Zawit Sidi Hamza rural communities. To the west of Errachidia, a flat plateau dotted by the Jbal Afardou takes the eye to the little valley of Tarda in the direction of Goulmima. The Ziz drains approximately 14,125 square kilometers, a watershed with an average altitude of about 1,100 meters.

The Ziz Valley is situated in Southeast Morocco, on the edge of the Sahara Desert. Irrigated farming of cereals, olives, and dates, and livestock raising has dominated the lives of its inhabitants for more than a millennium, with pastoralism of camels, goats, and sheep in the surrounding dry hills and plateaux. The valley's livelihood is sustained by two converging rivers of the Atlas Mountains, the Ziz and the Ghris. Despite the harshness of the climate

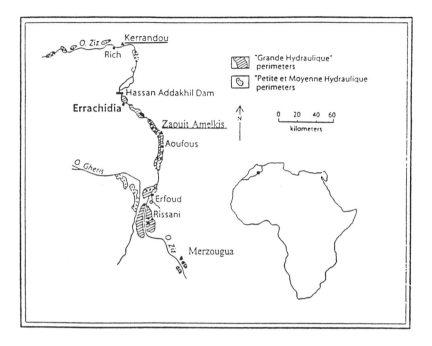

Figure 3-1. Location of the Ziz Valley, Morocco.

(aridity and low-pressure sand storms), a microclimate prevails in the oasis, and managed irrigated subsistence farming and shade provided by olive and date palm trees render the environment at the ground level less arid.

The Ziz Valley's inhabitants live in fortified villages called *ksur*. These villages are large, squared structures built of adobe, sun-baked earthen bricks and stone. As a corporate settlement formation, the *ksar* can't be separated from the palm grove, the threshing floors, the livestock grounds, the cemetery, and the olive oil press that comprise its outside spacial organization. The palm grove is the ensemble of fields and trees owned and managed by each ksar (singular form of *ksur*). The palm grove is fragmented into a myriad of parcels criss-crossed by a meticulous network of irrigation canals and ditches. Each ksar has its palm grove and its boundaries, and land belonging to the village is held in three forms of tenure: *mulk* (private land), *habous* (mosque land), and *l'assi* (infertile land).

The Ziz Valley is part of the vast and intimidating Sahara Desert. Although the harsh environment south of the High Atlas Mountains does not prohibit human habitation, the region is arid. Along with diminishing relief and elevation from north to south, average annual precipitation decreases approximately 50 millimeters with every 100 meters of descent. About 250 millimeters fall in an average of seventy days on the highest areas; fewer than twenty-five days of precipitation produce less than 50 millimeters in the far south. Dry farming is impossible in most years throughout the Errachidia province. Approximately 80 percent of the region's precipitation, mostly rain, accumulates during intense autumn (September–December) and spring (February–May) storms.

Temperatures vary from −5°C to 40°C, with an annual average daytime high of 20°C. The typical frost-free growing season begins in early March and continues well into November. Hot *chergui* winds blow out of the Sahara from the east between March and May, and scorching southwesterly *sirocco* winds bring clouds of dust and sand during the months of September and October. These winds intensify evapotranspiration and can cause widespread crop damage, especially to date and olive groves. Annual potential pan evaporation rates in the region are about 1,280 millimeters on cultivated soils and 834 millimeters on undisturbed lands (ORMVAT 1991).

Climatic factors have a tremendous impact on crop productivity throughout the study region, and this influence increases toward the south. In 1979–1980 (the agricultural year begins in the fall), a good year in the Tafilalet Plain, about 83 percent of the arable land was cultivated; the following year, 1980–1981, only about 43 percent of Tafilalet land was under crops. In the middle Ziz Valley, with its many reliable springs, farmers were able to irrigate about 81 percent of their arable land during both years (ORMVAT 1989, 24–25).

Soil formation in the Ziz Valley is retarded by arid conditions. Nevertheless, Ziz floodwaters have deposited thick, fertile sediments. As the Ziz River and other major streams flow out of the mountains and become less constricted, their floodplains become broader, and arable alluvial deposits become deeper. Ziz farmers employ a soil taxonomy that includes six classes. *Lhlu* (sweet) soils are a mixture of sand and deposits of silt. Relatively deep, rich in nutrients and fertile, and widely cultivated, they are easy to till and have good water storage potential, requiring irrigation once every four to six days. *L'aqad* (reddish-brown) soils are similar to lhlu but are compact and drought resistant. They are considered to be the most productive soils and are sought enthusiastically by farmers. They need less fertilizer than other soils and "are productive no matter how stingy one gets with the application of expensive fertilizer and manure and require less labor attention," a farmer conceded. L'aqad is irrigated once every fifteen to twenty days and is thus superior for agricultural uses. *Mramel* (sandy soils) dominate the Ziz banks but are less desirable because of their need for more frequent irrigation, at least once every four days. *Lharsh* (angular gravel) soils dominate the unworked foot of the mountains and areas of the Oued's banks and flood-plain. The lharsh fields are not as productive as l'aqad or lhlu. They are drought prone, and in order for them to be productive, large amounts of sand, silt, and green manure must be added. *Lmalh* (salty) soils are not desired by most farmers but are tolerated. They are sites of fields filled with pans of salt. To render them productive, farmers are obliged to practice preirrigation to flush out the salt deposits, and to turn the soil to bake in the sun every year before planting. Finally, *Lmsus* (unsalted) soils are the least desirable by farmers. They occupy waterlogged areas and are subject to too much shade (Ilahiane 1995).

Water in the valley is supplied by floodwaters, springs, wells, river resurgences, *khottarat* (the North African term for subterranean water conduit; they are called *qanats* in the Middle East), diversion dams, and the 380,000,000 cubic meter Hassan Addakhil storage reservoir. The river drainage basin supplies the reservoir with an annual average input of 164,000,000 cubic meters. Table 3.1 summarizes some quantitative data for these sources.

The Hassan Addakhil dam, completed in 1971, was a response to a November 1965 flood of 5,000 cubic meters that disabled most bridges below Rich and caused widespread field and crop losses. The valley's farmers also remember major destructive floods in 1949 and 1925. The dam demonstrated its value in 1989 and 1994 by capturing floods that knocked out roads and caused other damage above the reservoir, in the Kheng and Guers Tiallaline region. In addition to floods, droughts, sandstorms, salinization, sand dune

Table 3.1
Ziz Valley Water Supply

Source	Number	Output in million m³ per average year
Oued Ziz via		
Hassan Addakhil	n.a.	141.4
Meski Spring & Resurgences	n.a.	24.6
Artesian wells	n.a.	3.6
Private wells	5,000	n.a.
ORMVAT wells	7	9,964 milliliters
Cooperative pump stations	60	60 liters/second
Khottarat (qanats)	376	0.9
Floodwater	n.a.	24.0
Oued Ghris via Moulay		
Brahim Diversion	n.a.	95.0
TOTAL	n.a.	292.96

SOURCES: ANAFID (1990, 1991); ORMVAT (1989); Ilahiane, Mabry, and Welsh (1991).

encroachment, the date palm fungus known as *lbayoud*, locusts, and other pests are important limiting factors in the region's agriculture.

A primary canal from the Hassan Addakhil dam flows on the west bank of the Oued Ziz to irrigate the area extending from the foot of the dam to Targa and the New Perimeter villages. The east bank primary canal irrigates a perimeter extending to Meski. The Meski spring supplies 10 to 15 million cubic meters annually to lands controlled by the communities of Meski, Bousaid, Lkenz, Zaouit Amelkis, Jramna, and Zwiwia. In response to the severe drought (1979–1986), the regional office for agricultural development and water management (ORMVAT) established seventeen additional groundwater pumping stations to supplement the dwindling river flows and built and refurbished the Lahmida and Laghrissia canals to transfer flood waters from the Ghris Oued to the Ziz to irrigate the Tafilalet plain.

According to the 1994 census, the population of Errachidia province is 522,017, 42 percent urban and 58 percent rural. Population density is 10.8 to 22.4 per cultivated hectare, 5.1 per uncultivated hectare, and 2 per square kilometer for the rest of the province. Sixty percent of the province's population is engaged in full and part-time farming; the rest is involved in construction, government, commerce, national and international migration (Europe), and services (Ministère du Plan 1995).

Agricultural resources are concentrated mainly in cereal cultivation, arboriculture, and livestock. The area available for the practice of farming is 43,069 hectares, and the potential area covers 48,069 hectares, making up 45,000 farming household units. The average farmer's entire holdings total less than a hectare (.86 ha), with about 65 to 70 percent of his total holdings under cereal cultivation (.6 ha) and the rest under alfalfa and seasonal vegetables or occupied by perennials, such as olive, fruit, and date palm trees. On the provincial level, the farming system is partitioned as follows: cereals occupying 60 percent of the farming area, barley 14 percent, fava beans 4 percent, corn 9 percent, alfalfa 10 percent, vegetable gardens 2 percent, and henna and cumin 1 percent.

Arboriculture, mainly dates and olives, plays a crucial role in the economic development and ecological survival of the area accounting for 60 percent of household income. Livestock is the third important economic aspect of the valley's agriculture, with an average of five to six head of sheep per household (ORMVAT 1991).

In summary, the potential productivity of the region is restricted by climatic conditions affecting the resilience of the valley's irrigated farming. Water scarcity and its erratic variability over time and space, recurrent droughts, and frequent locust invasions have contributed to the impoverishment of the valley's environment. The lbayoud disease, which ravages the date palm trees, along with the annual alternating olive production, combine to reduce household welfare. All these factors have, in one way or another, impeded the optimization of the agricultural resources.

The Ziz Valley: A Society of Rank

For more than twelve centuries of recorded history the valley has been a the-ater of ethnic struggles, urbanization, and social change. Its medieval trade entrepôt, Sijilmassa, which flourished from the caravan trade, slavery, and the trading of African gold, shaped the valley's environment and its historical relations of production.

In the seventeenth and eighteenth centuries, the history of Tafilalet or the Ziz Valley was marked by resource scarcity, drought, famine, and diseases. This scarcity and competition over resources by various nomadic tribes opened the door to the *zawiyas* (religious orders) to act as peace brokers. The religious orders of the Shurfa and the Murabitin were rewarded by valuable gifts and economic favors by the surrounding tribes for resolving conflict among the nomads and sedentary communities. This period saw the rise of the Shurfa and Murabitin Arabs and other trading groups to the summit of the social and ethnic pyramid because of their involvement in the transaharan trade. The rise of the Ait Atta Berbers, natives of the Jbel Saghro due west of the Ziz Val-ley, was provoked when the Banu Ma'qil Arabs expanded to the west, depriv-ing the Ait Atta of their traditional Sijilmassa market and threatening their grazing lands. The Banu Ma'qil expansion would provoke a harsh reaction that changed the regional ethnopolitical balance of southeast Morocco. The Ait Khabbash, a clan of the Ait Atta tribe, took possession of many villages that they still occupy today, an area covering the best watered lands along the Ziz Valley. Ethnic and ecological factors combined to facilitate this expansion: drought periods of the seventeenth and eighteenth centuries, the Banu Ma'qil's encroachment on Ait Atta's escort of the transaharan trade routes, and the latter's control of the Ziz and other palm groves (a source of economic exchange with the sedentary Haratine), and France's incipient control of the Sahara Desert (Mezzine 1987).

The peoples of the Ziz Valley compose an ethnically-stratified society (of rank). The Shurfa Arabs are believed to be descendants of the Prophet Mohammed through the line of either Idriss al-Awal of Fez or Mulay Ali Sharif of Tafilalet. The former was the founder of the first Arab dynasty in Morocco in the eighth century; he founded the city of Fez in A.D. 892. The latter was the founder, in the seventeenth century, of the Alawite Dynasty, which still rules Morocco. They are entitled to a number of communal privileges and personal immunities.

The Murabitin are thought to be the descendants of holy men who were revered as saints. The living members of a saint's lineage are responsible for the maintenance of his shrine, and for the administration of gifts of money or sheep and goats donated by the followers of the saint. The difference between them and the rest of the population is their possession of *baraka*, the quality of divine grace. Because of their baraka, the Murabitin and the Shurfa serve as respected and credible men in deciding and mediating communal and personal conflicts (Gellner 1969).

Berber status derives from their social organization, historical military dominance, and persistent political power, factors prompting Berber self-perception as a dominant social class. Berber social organization is based on what structural-functionalist anthropologists call the segmentary lineage model. The notion of segmentation stresses the fact that order and peace are not maintained by specialized agencies or institutions of a state, but by the balanced opposition that unites forces and alliances in case of external menaces (Gellner 1969, 41–44). Such societies are divided into subgroups, which in turn further divide; all groups at the same level of segmentation are in balanced opposition. Households are inserted into this system of segments and subsegments in a defined manner, and social ties of any sort are insignificant. Gellner stresses the absence of ambiguity in a segmentary society. He argues that this type of society ensures that there will be groups in balanced opposition that can be mobilized in times of conflict. Most of these groups are not corporate, but rise to existence when in opposition to others (Gellner 1969, 116).

Another essential characteristic of Gellner's model of segmentation is the presence of the saints, who hold the segmentary partition of the Berber society in order. The Shurfa and the Murabitin, putative descendants of the prophet and holy saints, play the role of mediators among the Berber tribes of the High Atlas. The sacred cast of the holy mediators, according to Gellner (1969, 54–55), allowed the Berber tribes to have a democratic system in which no one group dominated economically and politically.

Berber social organization is essentially a product of a transhumant society based on force and power. Its elementary social unit of analysis is the household, or *takat*, and a number of households form what is called an *igezdu*. Households belong to *ighsan* (lineages). Villages may shelter different lineages, and often trace their genealogy to a common ancestor. Lineages belong to clans, and a number of clans make the *taqbilt* (tribe). Tribes, in turn, shape confederations.

During the nineteenth century the middle Ziz came under the control of the Ait Atta. According to the local reconstruction of history, the Ait Atta, specifically the Ait Khabbash clan, entered the middle stretches of the Ziz, at the time when France embarked on its colonization of Algeria in 1830. The Ait Khabbash, together with the Ait Umnasf in the Rtbat region, occupied sixteen villages by the end of the nineteenth century (Dunn 1972; 1977, 93; Mezzine 1987). In the Rtbat region, the Ait Khabbash expelled most of the inhabitants and confiscated most of their lands and property. They also extended their power through domination over trade routes escorting caravans between Touat in southwest Algeria and Tafilalet and also practiced the "piracy of the road" (Dunn 1972). The first language of the Ait Atta is Tamazight, a Berber dialect.

The Ait Atta expansion was directed toward the control of agricultural resources more than the occupation of pastures. The Ait Atta did not regard Blacks or Arabs as their social or political equals. By 1912 and the beginning of the French Protectorate, the Ait Khabbash were firmly established in the Rtbat region.

The Haratine are allocated inferior status and are typically responsible for menial labor. Because traditionally they did not own land, they worked as sharecroppers for Arabs and Berbers. As for the Haratine's history, there are many versions. Local ethnohistory differentiates between slaves and the Haratine. Slaves were integrated into Berber and Arab households, whereas the Haratine never assumed that position. They have always been characterized as "the workers of the soil." From a linguistic perspective, the etymology of the word "Haratine" is varied and has evolved through time. From the root of the Arabic verb *-haratha-*, to plant, one can say that they were referred to by the conquering tribes as *harathine*, or cultivators of land. This suggests that the Haratine might have been the ancient inhabitants of the Saharan frontier from the time of its desiccation. The other meaning is derived from breaking down the term "Hartani" into the two components *hor* and *thani*, two separate words meaning the "second free people" (as opposed to freeborn Arab commoners). In Berber, however, the Haratine are referred to as *iqbliyn*, meaning "the people of the east" or "the inhabitants of the southeastern oases," a term that could have been coined during the Berber takeover of the sedentary communities composed of Haratine and Arab commoners in the seventeenth and eighteenth centuries. Iqbliyn are, in turn, divided into *iqbliyn imalalan*, or white easterners, who own land, and *iqbliy ungaln*, or black easterners, who have no access to land and thus are subject to subordination, the Haratine. Iqbliyn imalalan, who are also called *qbala*, are of Arab descent—for example, the Beni Hcine, who populate a few villages around the Rich area. In other

Berber dialects such as the one spoken by the Ait Sgherushen tribe, the term *ahardan*, which is closer to the word "Haratine," refers to a person with a dark complexion. The term "Haratine" does not exist in Arabic. The Berber term apparently underwent an arabization process, transforming it from the original form of *ahardan* to the locally arabized version, "Hartani." This linguistic evolution testifies to the arabization drive of Islam since the eighth century. Outside the Ziz Valley, the Haratine are referred to as *drawa*, natives of the Dra'a Valley, an oasis to the west of the Ziz Valley (Ilahiane 1995).

In the valley's chain of ethnic stratification, the Arabs and the Berbers classify the racial and social status of the Haratine along at least five attributes: (1) their skin color, ahardan, implying "black, and not worthy of respect"; (2) a landless condition, people of no *al-asl*, denoting lack of ancestry and shamelessness; (3) an obtuseness attribute meaning "short of intelligence, like donkeys," and infantile; (4) a patronage attribute, *ait-tmurt*, or "our people," indicating protection pacts to which the Haratine were subject; and (5) a labor attribute, sharecropper, naming any Hartani working on the lands of the people of al-asl in exchange for one-fifth of the harvest. Before the advent of French colonialism, they were also deemed to be "like women" and not permitted to wear white turbans, the symbol of Ait Atta and holy Arab manhood. They were prohibited from participation in the village council of the Ait Atta, denied arms, and sometimes used as shooting targets for any Ait Atta member who wished to test his new gun (Hart 1980; Jacques-Meunié 1958).

The Irrigation System of the Zaouit Amelkis Village

The palm grove is the heart of the village of Zaouit Amelkis and its main source of subsistence. Concerns about the management of the palm grove and its irrigation system are the stuff of everyday life in the village. As a defensive strategy, the village and its council crafted a bundle of rules to govern the use of the palm grove. The stipulations of customary law reported in written documents, as in the *ta'qqit* of the Lgara village and oral history, testify to the determination of the Ait Atta Berbers to leave nothing to pure chance.

The palm grove has its chief, *amghar n'tamazirt*, to see to it that fields and produce are not subject to theft. The irrigation network has also its chief, *amghar n-tiruggin*, who supervises the cleaning and maintenance of the canals and the dam. The two chiefs are always Berber or Arab, and they are appointed by the council on the basis of their age, honesty, and religiosity, as these attributes are essential to the just management of the subsistence base. Communal institutions govern the agricultural calendar and land use, and fix the opening and closing of date and olive harvests. The legal organization of farming sanctions certain acts. Examples of these acts may include unauthorized weeding on the borders of irrigation canals and the river, unauthorized gleaning of dates, olives, and other fruit in the palm grove and around the gardens, bringing weeds or alfalfa into the village after sunset, and the picking of green wood.

Land use within the palm grove and around the village of Zaouit Amelkis follows a pattern of successive agricultural activities and zones. The first zone is the walled gardens located in front of the main gate and around the ramparts of the village. These gardens are used to grow vegetables and fruit trees; they are called *urtan* in Berber. The second zone is dedicated to the cultivation of alfalfa, and is characterized by the dominance of olive trees. The third zone is dominated by cereals, date palm trees, and other types of trees. The fourth zone is comprised of the fields that are rarely irrigated; these fields are almost devoid of trees. Here barley is planted in rainy years. These fields are known as communal or village lands. In the fifth zone are stretches of infertile land, *al 'asi* in Moroccan Arabic, used for grazing. This land is found outside the palm grove in the nearby hills and along the surrounding mountains and plateaus.

Ethnographies of water rights in rural Morocco have been traditionally confined to a simple interpretation and description of rules, whether these rules were based on the *Shari'a*, introduced by the French and Spanish Hydraulique network colonial administrators, or were a product of tribal customary law. Research on the relationship between the rules of water and social stratification has been ignored or only mentioned briefly in passing. Some anthropologists and other social scientists have tried to find the relationship between the social order and the way irrigation functions, and have correlated water distribution with segmentary models of various tribes (see, e.g., Abdellaoui 1987; Aït-Hamza 1993; Bencherifa and Popp 1992; Berque 1978, 143–145 and 153–155; Bouderbala et al. 1984; Chiapuris 1977, 211–213; Geertz 1972, 32–35; Gellner 1969; Glick 1970, 172–174; Hammoudi 1985; Hart 1976, 107–116; 1980, 1984; Miller 1984, 77–86; Nadir 1980, 126–136; Ouhajou 1993; Pascon 1978, 1979; Welch, Mabry, and Ilahiane 1996).

Hammoudi, writing on water rights and water distribution in the Dra'a Valley of southern Morocco, maps out the historical and ethnic dynamics that influenced the land and water tenure system. He discusses the impact of the religious status of the Arab Shurfa and Murabitin, the power of the Berber nomads, and the low social status of the Haratine on water distribution in the valley. Describing a situation similar to that in the Ziz Valley, where water and land rights are joined, resulting in what is called *mulk* (private ownership),

Hammoudi discusses two systems of water distribution in the Dra'a Valley: the *allam* system, in which water is a common property and resembles the Ziz Valley's system; and the mulk, in which water is a commodity subject to market demands. According to Hammoudi, the difference between the two systems is that under the allam system people are entitled to a water share to irrigate their fields; in mulk, water becomes a commodity sold and bought (Hammoudi 1985, 39–41).

In the Ziz Valley, the irrigation community is usually made up of one or several villages along the river sharing communal main canals that irrigate the palm grove. Each village has a local council (*taqbilt* in Berber) that administers the economic, political, and social organization of the village. The border limits are known and recognized by neighboring villages. The management of water and land fall under the responsibility of the council. Typically, the main canal (*targa* in Berber) draws water from a diversion dam built out of dirt, sticks, and stones. The canal is considered the property of the village or the villages that use it and maintain its operation. The neighboring villages recognize each other's rights of ownership, construction, and maintenance duties.

The irrigation network of the village of Amelkis, for instance, could be best described as a local folk model. The Amelkis palm grove stretches on both sides of the Ziz River. Thus, its system of irrigation is fed by two diversion dams, the Jarmonia dam on the west bank and the Salhiya on the east bank of the Ziz River. Each dam feeds a main canal: The Salhiya dam feeds the Salhiya canal on the east bank, and the Jarmonia dam feeds the Jarmonia canal on the west bank of the river. These two diversion dams are situated at about 7 kilometers north of the village. The location of dams requires pacts with neighboring villages whose territories the canals traverse, as well as permitting topography and slope. For these reasons, and for the main canal's right of passage through the neighbors' lands, a tradition of weekly division of water regulates water use among the villages. The Salhiya canal on the east bank runs through the Lkenz, Amelkis, and Zwiwia villages and water distribution is performed on a weekly basis. Lkenz, to the north of Amelkis, uses its water share from sunset Saturday to sunset Sunday, Amelkis from sunset Sunday to sunset Friday, and Zwiwia to the south of Amelkis from sunset Friday to sunset Saturday. On the west bank of the river the Jarmonia canal traverses the villages of Bousaid, Amelkis, and Jramna. Bousaid, to the north of Amelkis, is entitled to use its water share from sunset Saturday to sunset Sunday, Amelkis from sunset Sunday to sunset Thursday, and Jramna, south of Amelkis, from sunset Friday to sunset Saturday. Water channeled through the main canals is the property of all members of the community and is everyone's concern.

Breaking dams or diverting water illegally from the main canals has led to bloody disputes and water wars among the villages.

As the Jarmonia canal reaches Amelkis's fields, it channels water into the village's upper and lower targa, which in turn divide into secondary canals, and then into tertiary canals called *lmsarf*, leading water straight to fields. Although the main canal is the responsibility of several villages, once within the boundaries of a village it becomes the business of all members of that village. The lower and upper targas are of concern to the whole village as well, whereas the secondary and tertiary canals are the responsibility of owners who get their water from them and, therefore, are in charge of their maintenance and repair. In some places, however, the main canal feeds directly into the tertiary canals.

The same rules apply on the east side as on the west side. The system of water distribution in Amelkis is based upon the principle of mulk. Thus, the water that a person gets is as much each person's property as is land property. The owners of the upper canal fields can take as much water as they wish without taking into account the interests of the lower canal field owners. This distribution of water is reinforced through the customary rule of the priority of the upper canal lands over the lower canal lands. Water rights are not alienable from land rights; nevertheless, water is still considered to be the outcome of collective obligations.

Land is divided into units of measurement called *taggurt* (plural *tiggurin*). After the settlement of the Ait Atta Berbers in the riverine villages of the Ziz Valley in the nineteenth century, the set of tiggurin was the homestead share to which each conquering lineage within each lineage was entitled. A taggurt owner, theoretically, would have three or more *igran* (singular *igr*) or fields and, depending on the abundance of land, a piece in every zone. Each field usually runs from the bank of the river, perpendicular to its axis, to the marginal and uncultivated lands of the valley, being shouldered by other tiggurin owners to the right and left. Fields incorporate upstream lands irrigated by the main canal, then other lands irrigated by tertiary and secondary canals, and finally lands extending over the slopes above the valley and outside the irrigation network, an area called *amardul*. Fields thus extend from the river to the mountains; this diversified set of land property gave rise to the too often quoted Berber expression about establishing the rights of a taggurt owner: *sag islman ar udadn*, "from the fish to the mountain goats."

R. De Monts de Savasse pointed out in 1951 that the concept of "taggurt" is one part land and one part water. It is of variable size, and its dimensions are subject to a host of ecological variables such as location, annual precipitation, and the amount of labor needed to extend and develop the land. In the Ziz

Valley, in particular in the Ait Atta Berber villages, water rights are linked to rights of land. When land changes hands, water rights follow the land. Distribution of irrigation water is based on the concept of *mulliy*, or "turns." A turn of irrigation belongs to each household and can be applied to any field, and is not tied to individual fields because, in the villages of the middle Ziz Valley, there is thought to be enough water. Whereas the maintenance and clearing of the secondary and tertiary ditches is the responsibility of the beneficiaries, labor required for the upgrading and maintenance of the diversion dam and the main canals, the lifeline of the village, is provided on a pro rata basis by each taggura owner. The meticulous division of property into tiggurin measurement units along the three ecological zones of the valley is ingenious in maximizing each household's chances of benefitting from the scarce and variable supply of water.

Taggurt is a sum of land and water in the upper, middle, and lower reaches of the river estimated to provide the annual subsistence requirements for each takat. Despite changes in the original taggurt system that prohibited land fragmentation, taggurt has survived to our day and still remains the preferred local unit of water repartition and defines the expenses and duties of each owner in the operation and maintenance of the irrigation network of the ksar. In the Zaouit Amelkis village, "taggurt" not only refers to a standard unit of measuring land, but also evaluates olive and date production. The number of muds planted per taggurt has increased over the decades. Farmers and elders talk about the twelve-mud taggurt system prior to 1968 that evaluated only land production, a system we call the classic taggurt system. In 1968, the number of muds constituting a single taggurt doubled and has been increasing by an eighth of the original twenty-four at regular intervals since.

During this period, the classic taggurt system evolved into a composite one, taking into account not only agricultural production of sown area but olive and palm date production as well. In 1968, it was 24 muds per taggurt, 27 in 1976, 30 in 1984, and 33 in 1992. When asked about the changes in the assessment of the taggurt system, farmers contend that it is linked to the necessity imposed by recurrent floods and the damage they cause the palm grove. The land area of the village, however, has remained more or less the same despite the impact of floods. What is intriguing is that these changes coincide with the period when the Haratine started to become affluent by converting their migration remittances into land and tree acquisitions (Ilahiane 1998).

The reason the system continues in this only slightly modified form despite the considerable changes in land tenure and population may reside somewhere in the village's lukewarm reaction to Haratine upward mobility and access to land. The composite system acknowledged the increased emphasis by Arabs and Berbers on tree production perhaps due to low prices for grains linked to U.S. and European grain exports. Increasing the amount of production needed to qualify as a taggurt may reflect increased intensification in the oasis due to the impact of the Hassan al-Dakhali dam not far upstream. The Berbers and the Arabs would still want to mobilize Haratine labor for most of the upkeep of the irrigation infrastructure at traditional levels. Their claims on Haratine labor are increasingly resisted, and if their increased output were to be interpreted as a legal right to demand correspondingly increased levels of labor, it might cause insuperable social problems.

Today, a taggurt is equivalent to an area taking 33 muds or 16.5 'abras of seeds, given that one 'abra equals 2 muds, or 16.5 muds of seeds, and the other 16.5 represent olives and palm dates. The measurement of tree production differs from that of seeds. Tree production is measured in what is called *l-watad*. One l-watad of palm dates or olives equals 8 'awinat or 1 mud, and one ta'wint is equivalent to 1 kilogram of seeds or fruit produce. It follows from this that for canals and diversion dam maintenance, each taggurt has its necessary labor evaluated over twelve *shhar* (months) and each month in the past corresponded to one-twelfth of the total (24 muds); in other words, two muds of seeds or a combination of one l-watad and one mud of seeds. Local tradition in the Ziz stressed that every taggurt owner must provide an able-bodied man, and not a teenager, and a beast of burden with a container, preferably a mule, for work on the main canals and the diversion dams as need be. To prevent the obligation from increasing in tandem with increases in production, the taggurt had to be redefined.

The conceptualization of dividing taggurt obligations into twelve months makes provision for the mobilization of labor on a monthly basis to deal with the mishaps and the emergencies of the irrigation system. A small landowner who has less land than that making up a taggurt is supposed to cooperate and trade labor days with another owner within his lineage for the completion of monthly labor requirements. In times of emergencies, however, such as floods that damage the diversion dams and the main irrigation canals, the able-bodied of the whole village or all those people capable of fasting through Ramadan *(had Sa'im)*, whether they were taggurt owners or not, had to participate in fixing the system. Every household also had to bake an extra loaf of bread, and provide a bowl of olive oil to feed the irrigation laborers (Ilahiane 1998).

The Social Organization of the Irrigation System

Social organization presupposes cooperation and resolution of conflict among members of the community as issues of private and communal property have to be regulated. The perpetuation of the Amelkis folk model has relied heavily on the use of force and symbolic power rather than rules and norms of behavior agreed upon by the community. The maintenance and perpetuation of the water system is the objective of the well-positioned segment of society.

Historically, for the Ait Khabbash Berbers, land tenure was the founding pillar of law and tradition, *azerf*. Land and tree tenure was virtually the decisive vehicle through which the Ait Atta's social organization expressed itself. Exclusion of outsiders was the chief operational element of the Ait Atta's construct of property, and the perpetuation of *tamazirt*, the patrimony of the community, was jealously guarded by the keepers of customary law and tradition. Those who were not members of the Ait Atta and the holy Arab lineages, particularly the Haratine, could never acquire any of the Ait Atta land. Property was the primary cementing block of the "conservative closed corporate community," and was embedded in complex contexts of violence, ecology, power, and cultural concepts to keep outsiders and the conquered from accessing it (De Monts de Savasse 1951; Dunn 1977; Gellner 1969; Hammoudi 1974; Hart 1980, 1984; Mezzine 1987).

The concept of *shafa'a*, or preemption, for instance, was and still is mobilized to block land transfers from Berber lineages to non–Ait Atta groups. In the Berber villages, any land transactions or selling of trees had to be made public so that the right of shafa'a could be applied by distant clan and lineage members who might be away from the village during the sale. Before the sale was concluded, a three-week-long auction was held in order that an absentee could have enough time to make his shafa'a claim. Practically any stranger, to the exclusion of the Haratine, wishing to buy a piece of land belonging to a certain lineage or any of its members, could offer a price. Any lineage or clan member could make a counteroffer of half that price, and would acquire the land. The shafa'a claim ensured that land remained in the hands of the clan or lineages because a lineage member's price and blood negated those of a stranger or a Haratine. Land tenure for the Ait Khabbash is referred to as *al-asl*, or origin and ancestry; in other words, origin, social structure, and identity were and are still writ large in property (Ilahiane 1998, 139).

As soon as the Berbers settled their accounts with the sedentary population of the village, they started dividing the lands among themselves. Mezzine describes the Ziz Valley's situation in the eighteenth and nineteenth centuries as follows:

Among the Ait Atta for whom the sedentarization process is relatively recent (XVII–XIXth centuries), oral tradition states that when
a group decided to settle, whether on virgin lands or not. . . . As was
the case in Rteb, conquered land was divided into as many shares as
there were families to settle. These shares of land were generally made
up of several fields perpendicular to the valley. . . . Each share
contained one field in the upstream, another in the middle stream,
and a third in the downstream so as to guarantee an equal distribution
of water and good quality land among the members of the group.
(Mezzine 1987, 202)

In the Amelkis village, another oral tradition reports that once the Ait
Khabbash nomads conquered a village, the first thing that any member of the
group did was to drive a claim stake on the property that happened to be
before him or her. This is known as *wat tagut*: to hammer a stake on a piece of
land, giving the member the automatic right of ownership regardless of who
the past owner was. While oral tradition and customary rules still dominate
the mode of resource management, the political life and social organization of
resources of some villages are documented in local legal treatises or constitu-
tions called *ta'qqit* in Berber and *shurut* (conditions) in Arabic. While the
term "shurut" implies the conditions imposed on the conquering groups by
the sedentary population, the ta'qqit is the result of the conquerors' determination to impose their legal norms and values. These documents provide
information on power relations within villages, and spell out the social organization of the palm grove, the irrigation system, sharecropping practices, and
intervillage relations (Ilahiane 1998).

The management of the irrigation system falls under the village council.
The system is fixed, and everyone knows the rules. The priority and access
that Berbers and Arabs enjoy reflect their higher status in the community.
For instance, in the constitution of 1883 of Lgara, a Berber-dominated village in the middle of the Ziz Valley where the Haratine were institutionally
blocked from owning or having access to the means of production, it was
stipulated that, "If anyone sells a house to a Hartani the seller as well as the
buyer will be fined one hundred *mithqals* each. Purchase of any sort of land by
the Haratine is equally fined by the same amount" (Mezzine 1987, 193, section [21]).

For the maintenance of the dam, there is a yearly campaign on the village
level to mobilize the work force to repair and fix the dam, the canal, and the
major branches. Communal help is called upon when the dam is destroyed by
floods. For the maintenance of the irrigation system, all males past the age of
puberty have the obligation to take part in the upkeep of the dam regardless of

whether they own land or not. The constitution of Lgara makes it obligatory that "when the *shaykh* demands the mobilization of youth labor for an irrigation maintenance task all the Haratine must be present. He who is absent is fined 5 *uqiyas*" (Mezzine 1987, 234, section [21]). Despite the landlessness of the Haratine, their participation in the maintenance of the irrigation system was mandatory and justified on the basis of their low and subservient status in the village community.

In normal times, the workforce provided by each holder is a function of his or her holdings. The Shurfa and Murabitin are usually exempt from this kind of work; "their Haratine volunteer" does their share. It is believed that by sparing the Shurfa and Murabitin from this menial work, the Haratine gain some *hassanat* (afterlife rewards) and a blessing that counts as a good point in paving the road to Heaven. The element of divine grace that the Shurfa possess or believe themselves to own induces the Haratine to perform labor for them. This divine power is also employed to contain the Haratine's compliance, and at the same time, to disengage, if not to arrest, any forms of social change and disobedience. The monopoly of divine power by the Shurfa and the Murabitin succeeds in extracting menial and agricultural labor from the Haratine that the Shurfa and Murabitin are exempt or pretend to be exempt from on the basis of their religious genealogy. The Berbers usually hire the Haratine to fulfill their share in the upkeep of the irrigation network.

Nevertheless, water-stealing and produce theft from the palm grove and gardens are the two major sources of labor for the maintenance of the irrigation infrastructure in normal times. The rate of theft tends to be high because almost all the Haratine are landless, and they are barred from the right to cut and collect grass on the banks of the river and the canals as well as on field boundaries. While the landless Haratine are required to participate in the operation and maintenance of the irrigation infrastructure of the village, they are denied the right of use of wild grass and forbs patches found on the banks of the river and canals as well as on field boundaries. These grassy areas, particularly those on the banks of the river, are used by Berbers and Arabs to graze their mules and bovines. Blocking the Haratine from using what is supposedly communal property of the village, even though the Haratine must provide labor for the upkeep of the community's communal irrigation system, is justified by the high-status groups on the principle that a villager who does not own or sharecrop property has no business going to the palm grove and the gardens. The offender is subject to a public denunciation from the minaret and later given the choice between feeding a party of ten or twelve people for a lavish dinner (usually involving six members of the council, the *fqih* of the mosque [the imam, who leads prayers], the prayer caller, the water and palm grove guards, and another member or two of the community), or one or two days' community service clearing and cleaning the main canals so that water runs smoothly.

The dinner expenses are usually too stiff for the poor and landless to bear, and to save face he is compelled to negotiate his way through credit, which in turn, makes him indebted and dependent on his patrons. This practice of "feasting" is locally called *n'zul*, from the Arabic verb *nazala*, meaning "to fall on someone." The n'zul has a practical function, which is to impose sanctions upon the offenders and to teach others a lesson in communal administration and morality. The underlying motive, however, is to bankrupt an offender, and at the same time to reinforce the religious ideology and power of Arabs and Berbers, and to perpetuate the vulnerability and dependence of the landless Haratine. The water guard and the palm grove guard are paid in kind for their community service, besides their prestigious position in the council's circle, and they are entitled to the tithe of the harvest (cereals, dates, and olive oil) delivered to them on the day of *'id al-fitr* (the day of breaking the fast).

Recently, however, access to land by the low-status Haratine has been facilitated by revenue streams linked to migration to Europe. Certainly, the Haratine have accumulated more land over the last two decades (22 percent of the village's private land) and have harvested more economic and political representation at the local and regional levels. They have slowly repudiated the patron-client society and have hailed the opportunity to migrate. In fact, it seems that the Haratine's drive to amass land could be understood only in connection with the policies of the colonial and postcolonial state and remittances from Europe. Though a few Berbers and Arabs have migrated, they have adopted Western consumption patterns, thereby taxing their participation in land investment. What is interesting, however, about present-day social changes sweeping the Ziz Valley is that the Haratine are using their new wealth to short-circuit the traditional barriers of access to resources and appropriate what is inherently a Berber cultural concept, al-asl, to construct a multiplicity of cultural and power bases to challenge the traditional cultural hegemony of the Berbers and the Arabs (I am in the process of publishing a thorough analysis of these interethnic changes and their impact on resource management elsewhere).

Despite the Haratine's success in acquiring some land, they still run into difficulty at a number of levels. The Haratine's rapid trend of social mobility, driven by remittances, is being silently resisted by the declining traditional nobility of Berbers and Arabs. This nobility is being forced to sell or "eat its fields" and al-asl, one by one, to meet its subsistence and ceremonial fund obligations and to face up to the new demands of the community's cultural economy of jealousy and monetization. These dynamics of social mobility, though interesting, are beyond the scope of this chapter.

In the mulk system of Amelkis, it seems that the maintenance of the irrigation system not only is governed by social relationships, but also is subject to intracommunity relationships and institutions designed to disguise the extortion of collective labor, especially when the level of technology and resource management techniques are simple, yet demand communal participation (Bourdieu 1972, 178, 237–39). The combination of the Berber use of force and the Arabs' mobilization of holy genealogy and saintly ideology legitimized through ethnic stratification succeeded, over time, in naturalizing and reproducing the process of exploitation of the Haratine's labor, while also forming "la forme la plus précieuse d'accumulation" (Bourdieu 1972) for the high-status Berbers and Arabs in the ethnically segregated and fragmented communities of the Moroccan Saharan frontier.

Acknowledgments

I would like to thank the National Science Foundation and the Wenner-Gren Foundation for Anthropological Research for support of my dissertation fieldwork in Morocco and France (1994–1995). I would like also to thank the inhabitants and the members of the *taqbilt*, the council of the village of Zaouit Amelkis, for their cooperation and for helping one of their own, and the Office Régional de Mise en Valeur Agricole du Tafilalet (ORMVAT) for its support and institutional affiliation. Many thanks go to Tad Park, Tom McGuire, Charles Stockton, Moh Rejdali, and Nabil Chbouki (IAV Hassan II), Abrou Hro (ORMVAT), and the late Bob Netting for their valuable input and encouragement. Special thanks also go to the anonymous reviewers for their superb guidance.

Bibliography

Abdellaoui, R. M. 1987. "Small-Scale Irrigation Systems in Morocco." In *Public Intervention in Farmer-Managed Irrigation Systems*, ed. IIMI, 165–74. Digana Village, Sri Lanka: IIMI.

Aït-Hamza, M. 1993. "Irrigation et stratification socio-spatiale dans une oasis sans palmier: le cas du Dades." In *Aspects de l'agriculture irriguée au Maroc*, ed. M. A. Alaoui and P. Carrière, 71–85. Rabat, Morocco: Publications de la Faculté des Lettres et des Sciences Humaines.

ANAFID. 1990. *Gestion des grands périmetres irrigués au Maroc*. Volume 1. Distribution de l'eau d'irrigation. Rabat: Association Nationale des Oeuverages d'Irrigation.

———. 1991. *L'irrigation au Maroc*. Rabat: ANAFID.

Arnould, E. 1990. "Barriers to Sustained Development: Embedded Institutions and Arid Resources Management." *Office of Arid Lands Newsletter* 21:7–13.

Bencherifa, A., and H. Popp. 1992. *L'oasis de Figuig: persistence et changement*. Passau, Germany: University of Passau, Department of Geography.

Berque, J. 1978. *Structures sociales du Haut-Atlas*. Paris: Presses Universitaires de France.

Bouderbala, N., J. Chiche, A. Herzinni, and P. Pascon. 1984. *La question hydraulique*. Rabat, Morocco: Institut Agronomique et Vétérinaire Hassan II.

Bourdieu, P. 1972. *Esquisse d'une théorie de la pratique: précédé de trois études d'ethnologie Kabyle*. Geneva: Librairie Droz.

Chambers, R. 1989. "Editorial Introduction: Vulnerability, Coping, and Policy." *IDS Bulletin* 20(2):1–10.

Chiapuris, J. P. 1977. *The Ait Ayash of the Central Atlas: A Study of Social Organization in Morocco*. Ph.D. Dissertation, Department of Anthropology, University of Michigan. Ann Arbor: University Microfilms.

De Monts de Savasse, R. 1951. *Le régime foncier chez les Ait Atta du Sahara*. Paris: Centre des Hautes Etudes sur l'Afrique et l'Asie Moderne (CHEAM).

Dunn, R. 1972. "Berber Imperialism: The Ait Atta Expansion in Southeast Morocco." In *Arabs and Berbers: From Tribe to Nation in North Africa*, ed. E. Gellner and C. Micaud, 85–107. Lexington, Mass.: D. C. Heath.

———. 1977. *Resistance in the Desert*. Madison: University of Wisconsin Press.

Geertz, C. 1972. "The Wet and the Dry: Traditional Irrigation in Bali and Morocco." *Human Ecology* 1(1):23–29.

Gellner, E. 1969. *The Saints of the Atlas*. Chicago: Chicago University Press.

Glick, T. 1970. *Irrigation and Society in Medieval Valencia*. Cambridge, Mass.: Cambridge University Press.

Hammoudi, A. 1974. "Segmentarité, stratification sociale, pouvoir politique et sainteté: réflexions sur les thèses de Gellner." *Hespéris* 15:147–180.

———. 1985. "Substance and Relation: Water Rights and Water Distribution in the Dra'a Valley." In *Property, Social Structure and Law in the Modern Middle East*, ed. A. Mayer, 27–57. Albany: State University of New York Press.

Hart, D. M. 1976. *The Ait Waryaghar of the Moroccan Rif: An Ethnography and History*. Tucson: University of Arizona Press.

———. 1980. *Dadda Atta and His Forty Grandsons: The Socio-Political Organization of the Ait Atta of Southern Morocco*. Cambridge, U.K.: Menas Press Ltd.

———. 1984. *The Ait Atta of Southern Morocco*. Cambridge, U.K.: Menas Press Ltd.

Ilahiane, H. 1995. *Fieldwork notes* on file with the author.

———. 1998. *The Power of the Dagger, The Seeds of the Koran, and the Sweat of the Ploughman: Ethnic Stratification and Agricultural Intensification in the Ziz Valley, Southeast Morocco*. Ph.D. dissertation, Department of Anthropology, University of Arizona, Tucson.

———. 1999. "The Berber Agdal Insitution: Indigenous Range Management in the Atlas Mountains." *Ethnology* 38(1):21–45.

Ilahiane, H., J. Mabry, and J. Welsh. 1991. *Rapid Rural Appraisal of Moroccan Irrigation Systems: Methodological Lessons from the Pre-Sahara*. Report submitted to USAID/Rabat, Morocco.

Jacques-Meunié, D. 1958. "Hiérarchie sociale au Maroc Présaharien." *Hespéris* 45:239–270.

Mezzine, L. 1987. *Le Tafilalet: contribution à l'histoire du Maroc aux XVII et XVIII siècles*. Rabat, Morocco: Publications de la Faculté des Lettres et des Sciences Humaines.

Miller, J. 1984. *Imlil: A Moroccan Mountain Community in Change*. Boulder and London: Westview Press.

Ministère du Plan. 1995. *Preliminary Results of the 1994 Population and Housing, South-Central Morocco*. Meknes, Morocco.

Nadir, M. 1980. *Lecture de l'espace oasien*. Paris: Sindbad.

ORMVAT. 1989. *Office Regional de Mise en Valeur Agricole du Tafilalet*. Public Information brochure distributed in Errachidia, Morocco.

———. 1991. Dossier synoptique portant sur l'évolution des principales productions et actions agricoles, 1972–73 à 1989–1990. Document on file with the author and ORMVAT Office of Agricultural Production.

Ouhajou, L. 1993. "Les rapports sociaux liés aux droits d'eau: le cas de la Vallée de Dra." In *Aspects de l'agriculture irriguée au Maroc*, ed. M. A. Alaoui and P. Carrière, 87–98. Rabat, Morocco: Publications de la Faculté des Lettres et des Sciences Humaines.

Pascon, P. 1978. "De l'eau du ciel à l'eau d'état: psychologie de l'irrigation." *Hommes, Terre et Eaux* 8(28):3–10.

———. 1979. "Théorie générale de la distribution des eaux et de l'occupation des terres dans le Haouz de Marrakech." *Revue de Géographie du Maroc* 18:3–19.

Welch, J., J. Mabry, and H. Ilahiane. 1996. "Rapid Rural Appraisal of Arid Land Irrigation: A Moroccan Example." In *Canals and Communities: Small-Scale Irrigation Systems*, ed. J. Mabry, 119–138. Tucson: University of Arizona Press.

Chapter 4

Reidentifying Ground Rules

BETTINA NG'WENO

Community Inheritance Disputes among the Digo of Kenya

T HE RAINS WERE PARTICULARLY GOOD in 1993, leaving the grass lush and tall and the forest deep green. We walk down the hundreds of paths and roads in the countryside that cut across compounds and turn by the sides of houses. I am stunned by the view of grass patches and gardens, twisted cashews and gigantic baobabs, and houses and compounds softened by the light of coconut plantations. Distributed throughout this landscape are patches of dense forest, abundant with life both natural and spiritual. The elders of Kinondo say that ever since the forests have been protected they have once again been able to see the mist rise above the sea in the early morning.

In 1992 the government of Kenya, under the Antiquities and Monuments Act, gazetted (designated by law) as national monuments twenty coastal forest patches known as *kaya*, including Kaya Tiwi, Kaya Waa, and Kaya Kinondo in Kwale district. To the Mijikenda of the past the kaya were fortified forest hilltop villages established by various Mijikenda peoples along the low plateau running north-south some twelve miles inland from the Kenya coastline. Today, the kaya are considered to be sacred forests and the seats of the highest Mijikenda courts and ceremonies. Gazettement was the result of the combined efforts of the Coastal Forest Conservation Unit (CFCU) of the National Museums of Kenya and local Mijikenda communities to preserve and protect the quickly vanishing forests.

More than half of Kenya's rare plants are found in the coast region, many within these forests on the coastal strip. The conservationists were originally interested in the unique endemic biodiversity of the forests. They quickly came to realize that they would not be able to protect or justify protection of these forests on the basis of biodiversity alone in an area where land pressures, land prices, and limited forest resources provided competing interests in the land the forests occupy. They thus decided to work with local Mijikenda communities for whom for centuries these kaya forests have been sacred and home.

Kaya forests are attached to and protected by specific communities and clans. The very existence of the kaya lies not so much in efforts to control the cutting of trees or the sale of the land, as it lies in the continuation of the social existence of the communities and the forest's cultural significance within these communities. Nevertheless, as the CFCU also found out, these communities were neither homogeneous nor united in their conceptualization of the forests. For instance, for the Muslim Digo, a subgroup of the Mijikenda, the kaya do not hold as much religious significance as they do to other non-Muslim Mijikenda. In trying to get the participation of the communities in conservation efforts, the CFCU had to recognize the divisions of the community by age, wealth, gender, and religious belief. At the same time some groups like the Digo are engaged in long-term disputes over common property and the very meaning of "community" itself. At the center of these disputes is inheritance, which acts as a site for the definition and negotiation of community. The prevalence of multilayered land disputes indicates an insecurity in land tenure in Kwale district. However, the perception of insecurity differs between community members and the state. If conservation efforts are dependent on "community," then what can these inheritance and land disputes tell us about the relationship between common property, the construction of community, and insecurity of landholdings among the Digo?

This chapter focuses on why common property and inheritance disputes remain important to the matrilineal and Muslim Digo people of the southern coast of Kenya. I consider landholdings "common property" when use, allocation, and access are determined by a particular kind of membership in a group rather than being bound to specific persons. In this chapter I use concepts of social continuity (the continuation of practices and societies through time), and categorical identity (the categories by which people are recognized as groups) to understand how "community" is constructed in the negotiation of inheritance practices and the intergenerational transfer of land.

As such, I am using Williams's (1989) argument to investigate relations of power in the way people group themselves and are grouped within the context of states. Williams argues that this identity formation should be understood as the societal production of enduring categorical distinctions. These distinctions are produced through the control over the criteria for property distribution within the context of nation-states. My discussion of Digo inheritance and property is framed by Berry's (1993) concern for the meanings and use of land in social relations, extending the definition of politics to include actions beyond those of the state. Key to this understanding is Bowen's (1988) notion of social continuity as a principal image of society. I use Bowen along with Berry and Williams to argue that although communities may be constructed, community invention takes place in the context of the sociocultural priorities of local societies and is not just a matter of ideological convergence. The political meanings of categorical identity allow for the investigation of how these sociocultural priorities take on significance and are developed through time to define what is, and who belongs to, a community.

To do this I look at how divisions of the community by kinship, religion, and gender are expressed in inheritance disputes. The overlapping nature of these divisions demonstrates the difficulty of making clear categorical distinctions between subsections of the heterogeneous community. I do not focus directly on kaya land, but rather I look at other kinds of land relations and disputes to put the kaya in the wider context of Digo community formation and to understand this wider context's implications for the management of the kaya.

In the first section I address different understandings of relatedness and clan membership. Legal structures frame these understandings within specific religious and civic categories. I focus on Digo efforts to control the definition of the meaning of these categories to open spaces for community membership unrecognized by the state. In the second section I look more closely at government efforts to fix categories of community membership and therefore inheritance practices, through titling of property. This section also addresses the legal and social aspects of Islamic belief in Digo society. In the final section I return to kinship to explore the gendered effects of land transfer dependent on group membership. This section concentrates on Digo efforts to retain land as common property and to convert private property into collective property. It looks at the moral significance of different types of property holdings and types of property transfer. The conclusion focuses on the importance of fluidity and ambiguity in community for the retention of common property, raising questions about how kaya conservation needs to accommodate these notions of community.

The Digo have two forms of common property, one that is defined by residence as well as kinship, the kaya or sacred forest; and one that is defined by

descent alone, *fuko* or clan land.[1] Individual landholdings also exist, and property disputes often involve the individualization of common land. In other
words, disputes arise when people try to transform commonly held land into
individual property. Nevertheless it is not uncommon for family members to
hold property jointly. Common property is central to disputes of membership
and property. These conflicts reflect a situation of insecurity of landholdings
in Kwale. Insecurity can be a result of lack of understanding or compliance
with the law, or it can be felt by a complex number of people who claim land
but who lack the institutions with sufficient authority to guarantee one set of
claims over others. Insecurity can be not knowing which set of laws and procedures can protect sacred forests from real estate development, the tourist
industry, or local forest resource use.

Conservation and development projects, government policies, and the
multiple legal systems have not successfully addressed such situations of insecurity. While these efforts have focused on identifying or mandating a single
system of property ownership to increase land tenure security, or gazettement
to protect forests, they have not paid attention to the effect of relations
between community membership and access to resources. I suggest that these
relations have a critical effect on security of landholdings. Specifically, this
chapter argues that although being a member of a group is of fundamental
importance to land allocation among the Digo, an unstable and ambiguous
relation between community membership and access to resources increases
the insecurity of landholdings, including those of the sacred forests.

Three systems of law—customary, Islamic, and statutory—are drawn into
debates to support definitions of, and ascriptions to, various communities. The
manner in which property relations are understood through the competing
ascriptions of what is characterized as Islamic, Western, and Digo personhood
is especially important to the Digo in conceptualizing kinship and constituting community identity. These competing and often contradictory systems of
classification are negotiated and mobilized to retain certain practices regarding landholdings and certain conceptualizations of community. Related to
political authority and forms of power, these inheritance conflicts shed light
on the important but fraught position of community constitution in development, production, and conservation.

The Digo of Southern Kenya

The Digo are one of nine peoples who make up the Mijikenda, the name itself
meaning "the nine kaya." In the late 1940s, when they were forming the

cooperative political organization, the Mijikenda Union, these nine peoples chose to be called Mijikenda.[2] In Tiwi sublocation, six kaya forests were set aside to the Kwale county council in the 1974–1975 land adjudication and registration process. Most are less than one hectare in size, but the largest, Kaya Tiwi, is over nineteen hectares. Among the Digo the word "kaya" is synonymous with "home," so that when people say they are going home they say "*akavia kaya.*"

The Digo live predominantly in the coastal hinterland of Kwale District bordering Tanzania in the south. The cool tops of the Shimba hills around Kwale town look out over the narrow eight-mile coastal strip for a good thirty kilometers south of Mombasa toward Tiwi. From these cloud-forested hills where the air is cool and heavy with mist, you can see all the way to the ocean, over Shimba hills settlements, the coconut and cashew plantations of the flatland, and the whitewashed beach hotels. On a clear day you can see both Mombasa in the north and Chale Island jutting out at the end of the Diani peninsula, with the whole bay of Galu-Kinondo stretching out behind it to the south.

Between the base of the hills and the sea are dispersed settlements typical of coastal Kenya. Coconuts, mangoes, and cashew trees dot this flat landscape of sandy soils. No fences divide the compounds with houses made of either coral and mud with thatched roofs (cool in this hot, humid environment), or concrete and stone houses with corrugated iron roofs (that last much longer but burn under the sweltering sun). Vegetable gardens and clumps of indigenous coastal forest or patches of grassland fields stand between the planted trees.

Tiwi is situated in this area, a few meters from the main road and reaching toward the sea. Although Kwale district is 8,260 square kilometers with a population density of 46 people per square kilometer, Tiwi is one of the more densely populated areas with a density of 274 people per square kilometer: with only 52 square kilometers, Tiwi has a population of 14,267 people in 2,659 households.[3] It is divided into 2,352 plots of land registered to 3,668 people (almost totally Digo), with an additional 77 plots set aside for the Kwale County Council for schools, mosques, or kaya.

As is typical of Kwale district, few people in Tiwi are dependent solely on agriculture for a livelihood. They "rely basically on non-farm income," be it the tourist industry, government employment, fishing, or quarrying.[4] Many people work in Mombasa, only forty-five minutes away by public transportation, or in other centers like Ukunda or Kwale town. In this semiurban/semirural society, families rely upon land for agriculture, accommodation, various forms of energy and nutrition, and employment.

Belonging and Distribution of Property: Digo Kinship

The CFCU quickly realized that one of the major problems in preserving the forests was the decline of what they term "traditional values." Particularly troublesome was the decreasing significance of the forests to the surrounding communities. Unlike other Mijikenda peoples, the Digo are Muslim and express social continuity through concepts of matrilineal kinship and the continuation over time of matrilineal clans. With Islam the religious meaning of the kaya has been weakened. The significance of kaya forests for the Digo relies on the relationship to matrilineal clans, and the cultural traditions and history of the Digo in general. These clans and traditional practices constitute the Digo as Digo and connect them to the many kaya of Kwale district.

The Digo have a single set of named matrilineal clans known as *fuko* (Spear 1978; Wamahiu 1988).[5] Oendo argues that the fuko "plays an important role in giving individuals their identity and supplying the idiom by which membership in Digo society is claimed or demonstrated" (1987, 47). Although maternal clan ties are the most important kinship ties, Digo people consider paternal lineage ties to be important as well. The Digo differentiate between the mother's clan, the fuko, and the father's lineage, the *mbari*. A couple in Mombasa described fuko and mbari to me as follows: "*Mbari* [father's lineage] is whose family one belongs to and goes back probably no further than grandfathers. It is a shorter unit than *fuko* [matrilineal clan] which ranges all the way back to all ancestors and the founder of the *fuko*. However, *mbari* is also mainly patrilineal and your grandfather's family, while *fuko* is all your mother's mothers back to the beginning."[6]

Fuko and mbari provide two different ways of belonging to a community that set out rights, duties, and obligations to members. These may include the obligation of your father's sister, who is part of your mbari, to replace objects that you damaged, or the obligation of fathers to provide land to divorced daughters, or the rights to products from fuko or mbari farms, or the rights to inheritance of fuko land. Fuko belonging is considered to be a relationship that ranges back to the founder of the fuko, while mbari is a relation to a specific person of the not very distant past.

The relationship between fuko and mbari determines in what manner land should be distributed. Kinship relations are defined by membership in a clan that differs by gender. Although sons belong to the fuko of their mother, their children do not, and have no rights to *mashamba ya mafuko* (clan land). Common land connected to social kin relations such as fuko land materially reproduces these social ties when the land remains in the hands of women or passes maternally from mother's brother to sister's children or from mother to child.

Lineage land apparently changes the gendered nature of land relations, for a terminal duration. At times in the past, fuko land could be inherited by sons and became known as *mashamba ya mbari* (lineage land). However, this form of inheritance was not a continuous inheritance but rather lasted about three generations. The grandfather would have gotten the land from the fuko originally. The great-grandchild is said to be very far from the fuko of the grandfather, as s/he has no immediate relatives who belong to that fuko. The grandchild's connection to the fuko is the father, but the great-grandchild belongs to a still further removed fuko. When the intersection of two different idioms of relatedness, mbari and fuko, cease to function or hold meaning, a tension is created between the person with whom the land is associated, and the one who might be holding it at the time. In other words, a tension is created between the rightful inheritors by clan, and the rightful inheritors by lineage. Mashamba ya mbari then returns to the fuko instead of going on to the great-grandchildren. On returning to the fuko it goes to the nearest relative of the grandfather's sister.[7]

Inheritance is important to the Digo for a number of reasons. Over 70 percent of Kenya's people are rural and rely on agricultural production for their livelihood. Due to restrictions on settlement, the economic marginality of Kwale district, the poverty of the rural areas, and the resulting lack of substantial monetary income, intergenerational transfer remains the only way of obtaining land for the majority of the population. Compared to wages in Kwale district, land prices are exorbitant; but compared to rural incomes they are particularly prohibitive. Even though a fivefold population increase occurred between 1939 and 1989, inheritance was the crux of Digo land disputes even before 1939.[8] I would argue that it is not the spatial competition for land, or demographic increase, but an economic inability to compete for land in marginal areas that produces a reliance on inheritance. For those who rely on land for their survival, yet cannot fully participate in a capitalist land market, inheritance remains fundamentally important.

Heeding Sally Falk Moore's (1991, 109) caution against projecting into another time the current centrality of land, how has inheritance become so central to arguments over land? Discussing three Muslim societies in Sumatra, Bowen states that "the central ideas of social continuity in each of these societies—village community, alliance relation, material continuity—have shaped their reactions to socioeconomic change and to judicial reinterpretations of property transmission" (1988, 287). The central ideas of social continuity in Digo society are expressed through concepts of matrilineal kinship and the continuation over time of the fuko. Thus, I contend that aside from its material importance, inheritance of property becomes the chosen expression of this social continuity when nonmembers of the fuko contest ownership of fuko land. In other words, fuko members express social continuity (their kinship and the continuation of the clan) through inheritance practices. This becomes particularly important when nonmembers try to dispute their ownership of fuko land, because in doing so they present competing claims of belonging that could legitimate their claims to the land.

The Digo understand ownership as relations between persons in regard to things. This concept of ownership, declared in relation to other persons rather than things, creates a shared rather than unique identity. Although the land is common property in that its "ownership" resides with the fuko, the fuko is not a corporate entity that acts as an individual, neatly and concretely bounded. Fuko land is land in which various clan interests inhere and rights and duties of clan members exist. These rights are not the same as individual claims, or something owned by a proprietor of rights; rather they are a guarantee of relational existence. As Gluckman noted for the Barotse, if the "right" is removed, the relationship that brought it into being has to change (1965, 145). Fuko and fuko lands are social networks that enable people to access a whole series of material and nonmaterial resources.

A kaya is not productive land in the sense that mashamba ya mbari or mashamba ya mafuko are; rather it is a sacred forest that serves a religious purpose, although a declining one since most people are Muslim. Its ownership can be thought of in territorial/locational terms as the kaya are described as belonging to everybody of the area.[9] For instance, Kaya Tiwi, the largest of six kaya in the area, is considered to be for everyone in Tiwi to use for prayer. However, a kaya elder has to come from the founder's clan.[10] Ownership is more general than clan ownership but specific people and clans are important for ceremonies and activities. Neither of the two common landholdings, neither kaya land nor clan/family land, is officially recognized by Kenyan laws, as there is no legal provision for common property. Rather, common property is negotiated in practice within the confines of the laws of land registration. I deal with these complexities of the Kenyan legal system later in the chapter. Kaya forests are emerging as an axle around which issues of ethnic identity, Mijikenda unity, tradition, and religion turn.[11]

Claims from the Past: Memory

The watershed case of *Ganyuma vs. Mohamed* concluded in 1927 in the Court of Appeal for Eastern Africa. It can be seen as a sign of the tensions between different concepts of community and landholdings. The case disputed "whether the estate of a deceased member of the Wa-Digo tribe, who was a

Mahommedan, descends in accordance with Mahommedan law or in accordance with the customary law of the Wa-Digo tribe" (Colony and Protectorate of Kenya 1931, 30). The Native tribunal had decided that the estate descended by Wa-Digo custom, that is, matrilineally. In the first appeal at the Second Class District Court at Kwale, the appellant attempted to prove that "in the clan of the Wa-Digo tribe to which the deceased belonged the customary law of inheritance was patrilineal" (30). This possibility was not recognized by the courts who "held that the inheritance was governed by tribal custom, that the estate descended matrilineally and accordingly upheld the decision of the native tribunal" (30). However, the decision was appealed to the Supreme Court, where the appellant argued for patrilineal inheritance in accordance with Islamic law, as the deceased was Muslim.

In the Supreme Court of Kenya the presiding judge decided that Islamic law applied and the estate should descend patrilineally. In these various court cases the appellant had first made his plea under Digo customary law. Yet he was contesting what was perceived to be customary law and what it constituted to be Digo by claiming that his particular clan inherited patrilineally. When the plea was unsuccessful, the appellant claimed legitimization by Islamic law in the higher court to establish patrilineal descent. In both cases these were claims of identity and community belonging, as well as claims on the meaning of this belonging or identity itself. His claims of identity were first as a member of a Digo clan and later as a member of a "society of Muslims transcending the claims of village communities or traditional sources of authority" (Bowen 1988, 279). The appellant was contesting and defining what it meant to be Digo and what it meant to be Muslim, and especially what it meant to be both. In spite of what his intentions might have been, having debated the meaning of, and the right to define these categories publicly, he engaged in the process of transformation for which he is remembered today.

A son born to the appellant during the time of the *Ganyuma vs. Mohamed* case is today known as Mzee Keisi (pronounced KAY-see, stemming from the word "case").[12] This case is now seen, sixty-eight years later, as the turning point in land disputes regarding Islamic law in matters of Digo inheritance. Mzee Keisi is named Keisi after the circumstances of his birth. His name a constant reminder; the community recalls the case as a marked point of change. An elderly man in Tiwi explains that: "Mohamed Bin Hadji was the first person out of Digo land to disagree and openly challenge the inheritance of *mjomba* (inheriting from a maternal uncle). He is the father of Mzee Keisi. He took his father and uncles to the Liwali [Islamic judge] and complained that he should inherit from his father and not his cousins, because his father was Muslim. The Liwali agreed that the son should inherit and it went to the court in 1917–1918. It was finally decided that he should inherit in accordance with Islamic law. This is the case Mzee Keisi is named after."[13]

One elderly woman remembers the circumstances that allowed Mzee Keisi's father to make such claims, as well as the consequences of the claims: "Mzee Keisi's grandfather was the village elder. This position at that time was hereditary by *fuko*. The fight for Mzee Keisi's grandfather's land was between Mzee Keisi's father and his father's maternal cousins. Mzee Keisi's father was challenging not only the nephews' right to inheritance but also the nieces'."[14]

The son of an important man with considerable power and a history of land accumulation in the family, Mzee Keisi's father was in a good position to challenge his cousins, and he was able to take the case all the way to the court of Appeal (Ng'weno 1997). His grandfather's authority and status as village elder had been inherited from his mother's family, the very family that the son was to challenge over inheritance.

However, the *Ganyuma vs. Mohamed* case did not diminish disputes, nor did it establish clear guidelines for the colonial administration's regulation of access to land, as was hoped in 1927. Rather, it produced increased acrimony in the arguments over what it meant to be Digo and Muslim in relation to the distribution of resources. This acrimony reflected the importance of inheritance and belonging to the communities and the lack of power of the legal institutions over these matters. It showed how Digo identity is built on ambiguity and fluidity that contrasts with what the colonial government imagined were the confines on limits of being either Digo or Muslim. The increased disputes also reflect the importance of the relations between affiliation in a community and the distribution of resources in the security of landholdings.

Registration and Adjudication

European imperialism and colonialism in Africa and Asia in the nineteenth century coincided with debates in Europe over the relation between property, proprietors, and the state. Collier, Maurer, and Navaz argue that Western legal practices identify "the primary creator and beneficiary of law as an individual who 'owns' property, even if only in 'his' person" (1995, 2). Property took on a moral character that defined persons as individuals and as subjects of the emerging European nation-states. This moral character included viewing private property as having positive values and common property as having negative values. Grossi (1981, 3) argues that the state was viewed as the guarantor of wealth of whoever held it legitimately, and the proprietor was seen as the ideal citizen.

These property considerations contributed to the form property law took in countries such as Kenya. In 1895 the coastal strip became part of the Kenya Protectorate of Britain. As in other parts of the world, British land policies regarding tenure in Kenya were implemented in the interest of improved agricultural production. As a result, between 1910 and 1920 the colonial government "set out to establish the *legal* structure for capitalist development" (Cooper 1992, 217) creating "Native" reserves, including the Digo reserve that was set up in 1914. The Digo were considered to be noncapitalist within a broader idea of development, a policy that continues with the independent government today, as I show later in this chapter. Native reserves were set up to demarcate and contain land held by specific ethnic groups; thus no Digo person could officially hold land outside the Digo Reserve. The British made a distinction between "Native" and "Muslim" regarding the ownership of land, making Digo and Muslims subject to different property laws. This legal structure made community (or ethnic) belonging central to rights to land for anyone with a Digo identity.

While the colonial state was instrumental in enforcing changes in social relations through demands on labor and court decisions over land, the independent state takes on that role today.[15] The independent state inherited a colonial agrarian policy along with European property law. This included an extension of the logic of the Swynnerton Plan that argued "that the issue of accessibility of land was essentially one of tenure and the technology of production" (Okoth-Ogendo 1991, 69). That is, transforming tenure and technologies of production could solve problems of land accessibility and productivity. The Swynnerton Plan was put into effect during colonialism through first, the Native Land Tenure Rules of 1956, which set up the machinery for the adjudication and consolidation of land conferring legal title on individual holders; and later, the Native Lands Registration Ordinance of 1959, which allowed every owner freehold title. In this chapter, "registration" and "adjudication" refer to this process that turned Native reserves into private or trust lands just before and after independence in 1963. For the Digo this process took place primarily in 1974–1975.

Inheriting the concern for the transformation of agricultural production, the postcolonial government in Kenya has based its development policy on a specific type of landholding (private property) and land-subject relations (citizen). In this way the Kenya government essentially continued colonial policy toward agrarian change by considering private registration of title to land essential to improving agricultural output. Okoth-Ogendo (1991, 164) points out that "the continuity of agrarian law was simply an aspect of the wider process of the continuity of the political economy of colonialism as a whole."

The Registered Land Act of 1963, which provided a single code of property law for the whole country, reinforced by the Succession Act of 1981, removed government sanctions on claims to customary law in nationalist attempts to secure tenure and regularize succession. As others have argued about other parts of Kenya (Haugerud 1989; MacKenzie 1993; Shipton 1992), these attempts were largely unsuccessful.

The Kenya government offers three explanations for continuing privatization. The first reason is that adjudication provides a secure tenure by establishing title, thus bringing an end to land disputes and enabling "progressive" use of the land. The second is that it enables capital accumulation and development because the title can act as a mortgage in raising credit. Last, it will regularize inheritance. According to the 1994–1996 Development Plan: "The Government's strategies towards this need are to ensure that all land is planned, surveyed, adjudicated (where applicable) and registered with a view to issuing title deeds. This in turn provides security of tenure and encourages the people to invest in and develop their land. This leads to higher incomes, increased productivity, general rise in economic growth and improved standards of living" (Government of Kenya 1994, 187).

The government argues that the land adjudication concept parallels a farmer's own "urges." Thus, this farmer has become a possessive individual defined through having. As expressed by the Central Bank of Kenya: "The rationale behind the concept of land adjudication is the natural urge and wish of all farmers to own their land. Such ownership has proved a vital spur to development. Once an individual or group of individuals owns land, a title deed is issued to the holder who can then use the document as a means of securing funds for development" (Central Bank of Kenya 1991, 119).

Through a system of property with naturally possessive individuals qua citizens, the government is trying to create the citizen as a subject who will aid development and increase productivity. However, Digo claims to land, patterns of inheritance, personhood, and community definition question and disrupt the connection made between increased productivity and individual ownership.

Present Claims with the Past and Future in Mind

In spite of efforts to register property and regularize inheritance, disputes over inheritance continue today, and people continue to mobilize diverse community belonging and legal systems in efforts to secure particular modes of inheritance. The fuko, mbari, and kaya lands are forms of common land that are dependent on Digo notions of belonging and clan membership. Metaphors of stealing are used to refer to the process under which these properties turn individual, which are linked to the overlaying of Islamic and Western forms of law, legal systems, and conceptualizations of persons, community, and belonging. Women from Kinondo lamented that "there is no longer a sense of community. Now people live very separate from each other; one family here, another there, with no sharing."[16] They were particularly concerned that brothers were able to register land under their own names, without their sisters' names. Because the sisters' names did not appear on the title, the brothers were able to sell land or the produce from land without consulting or paying the sisters. They considered the registration of land in a brother's name to be stealing land and produce sisters "have a right to."[17]

Brothers are able to steal land through a combined appeal to two competing systems of classification of belonging. Because of large-scale Digo conversions to Islam in the 1920s, today it is taken for granted that a Digo person is Muslim, although not all are.[18] Through claims to Islamic laws of inheritance and understandings of family, as sons brothers have a greater right than daughters to control and ownership of land.[19] Sisters, in fact, have no claim over their brother's property. The brothers then register land using statutory legal provisions for private property based on claims, as Muslims, to Islamic law.

A large number of land disputes that deal with administration of estates for those who have died intestate end up in the Attorney General's Office in Mombasa. Only the most fraught cases make it to this office or the courts since most are settled within the community. The majority of the disputes that do arrive at the Attorney General's Office are between Digo people, 20 percent of which are presented under the rubric of customary law.[20] These formal settings join informal ones in the resolution of disputes and the construction of identity.

In this manner customary law is not a static, ahistorical product of a self-contained particularity, as legal structures often perceive it to be. It is mobilized and produced within traditional spaces such as local moots and official spaces such as the Attorney General's Office. Customary law is not simply a colonial construct as Chanock's (1991) analysis of the construction of customary law and Ranger's (1983) of the invention of tradition would suggest. Rather, as a fluid element in a system of legal pluralism, customary law becomes "one of the legal spheres to which disputants have recourse" (MacKenzie 1993, 201). It becomes another formal option in a complicated and multilayered system of law. Digo claims to customary law mainly take the form of bothers and sisters or nieces and nephews claiming a deceased person's land.[21]

Rather than reducing conflicts over land, land registration, which is tied to notions of citizenship, exacerbates an already conflictual situation. Since the 1991 amendment to the Succession Act, the Attorney General's Office has applied Islamic law (as recognized in the Kadhi's courts) to inheritance cases where the deceased was Muslim.[22] Claims to inheritance by brothers and sisters highlight the discrepancy between claims and rights in law. They are making claims to a legal system that officially does not recognize their rights to inheritance as brothers and sisters of a deceased Muslim. This discrepancy reflects the discord of belonging produced by a single civic identity (a Muslim citizen) that is separate from clan or ethnic identity. The person who is a Muslim citizen is considered a different kind of legal actor than the person who is Digo from a particular clan, each one with a different set of rights. One would assume that these changes in law would be followed by changes in inheritance practices. However, actual practice can often be contradictory, as the following case shows.

Ali's case is a dispute about the division of land in accordance with general aspects of Islamic and customary law.[23] The struggle is about what it means to be simultaneously Muslim and Digo, especially within an official framework in which only specific kinds of claims can be made. Although the final decision does not hold such historic relevance as the case *Ganyuma vs. Mohamed*, this case underscores the critical role played by the understanding of belonging in the distribution of resources, even after independence. It traces out how, whether in the arguments of claimants, or the decision of the judge, the understanding of the ways people were related to each other took precedence even over the legal stipulation of a registered land title.

The case started in 1983 when Ali's father tried to plant trees on a portion of his deceased father's land, on which he had previously planted other crops. Ali's grandfather, the original landowner, had died prior to land adjudication and registration of title in 1974–1975. He left behind three wives; one with nine children, one with two children, and one with one child—Ali's father. At the time of land adjudication, the land was registered in five names, which is the maximum number of names permitted on one piece of land registration in Kenya. These names were those of three of the nine siblings, one of the pair of siblings, and Ali's father.

Ali's father tried to plant trees on his land, but the nine siblings refused to allow him to do so. He ignored them and began to plant. The siblings complained to the subchief. The subchief sided with the nine siblings and ordered Ali's father to uproot his trees. Again he refused, and he went to the chief to ask assistance. The chief sided with Ali's father in favor of a division of the land by "house," that is, land divided among the families of each wife, rather than among all the children. Thus, he was advocating a three-way division of the property rather than a twelve-way division. At this point, the nine siblings invoked Islamic law by arguing that the land should be divided by children, although they did not want the specific divisions of fractions of land that Islamic law prescribes. Ali's father was invoking Digo customary law by arguing for division by house.[24] The dispute was not settled there and went first to the District Officer and then to the courts.

At the court level the dispute left the hands and discussion of the elders, and was instead argued by lawyers. As the court at that time had no mandate to enforce or uphold either Islamic law or customary law, the lawyers argued for the division of land by the five registered names.[25] The court, however, ruled for a three-way division by house. A surveyor then divided the land into four and the father had to take it to court again, where the surveyor was threatened with contempt of court if he did not divide it by three. The land dispute caused terrible family strife. The families involved stopped talking to each other and even threatened each other with weapons. This final court case was concluded in 1985.[26] This case highlights the consequences of group membership as well as the changing recognition of the authority of Islamic or customary law at different levels of the dispute.

Claims on Meaning and Authority: Islam

Ali's case demonstrates the many ambiguities of legal structure and the contradictions of government administration. These contradictions and ambiguities show the importance of forms of authority tied to group membership. First, not all people with interests in the land could register the land in their names. There were thirteen siblings, but only five could legally register their names. Membership in the family could not be recognized equally in the title deed for all the children. Second, various parts of the local administration supported differing sides in the argument. The level of government authority being engaged influenced the terms of debate. Thus, the recognition of a person's membership in a specific community carried more authority at various levels of government.

Last, the court did not necessarily follow its mandate regarding customary law. After the Law of Succession Act (1981), customary law was not supposed to apply to succession cases. In its actions the court contradicted the state's claims on persons as citizens free from customary and religious constraints. Discussing paternity cases in American society, Janet Dolgin argues that "each court aimed to preserve a certain kind of family by protecting the rights of a certain kind of parent" (1995, 62). In Ali's father's case, and in the case of

Ganyuma vs. Mohamed, the courts aimed to preserve a certain kind of family by protecting the rights of certain kinds of offspring, although the two courts had very different families in mind, and thus, different communities. As a result, they were protecting different kinds of legitimate forms of socially organized identities in relation to a broader political context. Specific moments of political governance render certain kinds of social organization more legitimate. The gazettement of the kaya as national monuments renders what is considered Digo customary social organization more legitimate than social organization based on Islam or citizenship. The CFCU recognizes the authority of elders within this customary social organization by funding registered kaya committees of elders as part of their support of local communities in the protection of sacred sites.

The Digo desire and ability to retain both a Mijikenda and an Islamic identity is unique among the Mijikenda, arising most probably from patterns of residence, which integrated Islam in most aspects of Digo life. Willis points to the importance of this combined identity, stating that "only among the Digo did a non-Swahili Muslim identity really develop, which may explain why some Mijikenda Muslims on the coast north of Mombasa, anxious to assert both their identity as Mijikenda and their religion as Islam, have adopted Digo identities" (Willis 1993, 197). For the Digo, being Muslim and Digo overlap and are interconnected.

Being Muslim means confronting how differing notions of relations and kin belonging lead to differing distribution of resources. Digo "customary" classification of belonging comes into conflict with alternative classifications of sameness and difference such as "Muslim" or "citizen." This is done through administrative and legal processes that support concepts of Islamic and statutory law above customary practices of inheritance or common ownership. Digo common ownership differs from Islamic inheritance as stipulated in Kadhi's courts, which designate the specific division of property in specified amounts to a number of heirs. Some people expressed concern to me that too many people have rights to property under Islamic law. As inheritance provides primary access to land, this is particularly problematic. Regarding a case disputed between sisters and brothers, I was told: "Islamic law greatly increases the number of people who then have a right to the land. For instance, if my aunt dies her land could go to her husband and the children."[27]

The concern is expressed mainly in regard to nonclan members' gaining access to clan land and thereby removing it from circulation (e.g., the aunt's husband). Individual holdings are considered divisive both of land and of the clan. However, this is not a uniquely Digo concern, for there is a long tradition in Islamic law of circumventing the divisive effect of laws of inheritance through *waqf* (public or family endowments). These *inter vivos* distributions of property often take the form of collective holdings and can inhere in individuals, collectivities, and institutions. As Dominguez points out in her discussion of indirect inheritance and legal categories of kinship in Louisiana, it becomes common practice to circumvent legal rules for the transfer of property, through disguised sales, donation, and adoptions, in cases in which rules prohibit making certain persons kin (1986, 79). She draws crucial attention to patterns of avoiding legal rules where they contradict understandings of kin and belonging similar to those patterns adopted by Digo people with reference to religious, customary, and legal rulings. Arguments about who is kin are also arguments about how someone is a member of a community.

The Contradiction of Kinships

Some Digo people opt to distribute their land while they are still alive. Omar's grandfather had land from which he gave plots to all his children, male and female, and to his two wives, while he was alive. He retained a plot as his own, which he declared would go to all his family/descendants to use communally after his death.[28] *Inter vivos* land distribution is customary under both Digo and Islamic law, and the Digo use either system to justify intergenerational distribution of land. However, the high incidence of inheritance disputes among the Digo would indicate that *inter vivos* land distribution is not standard practice, and inheritance remains the major mode of intergenerational land transfer.

Beyond transforming ideas of family belonging, the more individual conceptualization of land and person under Islamic moral and legal structures is at odds with Digo notions of clan land. As a result many Digo make provisions for a separate pattern of inheritance involving self-acquired land and clan land. Self-acquired property (acquired by clearing the bush or by purchase, but not inheritance) began to take on the more individual form of Islamic property holdings that included the possibility of patrilineal inheritance. Nevertheless, Islam did not remain static but was incorporated in Digo practice changing both the categories of "Digo" and "Muslim."

Property held in common can be retained within an Islamic tradition of inheritance, not only through waqf or the registration of common title (up to five names only), but also through equal distribution of land to sons and daughters. The Digo argue that brothers and sisters should (and most often do) inherit equally from their parents as opposed to the lesser percentage (half) stipulated for women under Islamic law. Digo men and women emphasized to me that in the past, land went matrilineally to the nieces and nephews (remaining in the same fuko), but today it goes to the children of the deceased equally.[29]

Oendo (1987, 61) argues that brothers accept inheriting land equally with their sisters because this distribution allows some property to go to their sisters' children, as it would by Digo tradition. The land inherited by sisters under Islamic law belongs to them personally and does not become their husbands' property. That is, part of what the brothers would have inherited by Islamic law goes to their sisters, and through the sisters to the sisters' children (the brothers' nieces and nephews). Thus, some of the land that would have gone to nieces and nephews by customary law still does go to them. In this way, the land remains in the fuko. However, some of this land is transferred to another fuko by being passed on to the brothers' children. Oendo argues that "while formally meeting the demands of Islam for female inheritance, brothers use it to circumvent Islamic injunctions which permit only parent-child inheritance" (Oendo 1987, 61). This practice partially returns fuko land to the fuko, although now the criteria for distribution are a mixture of membership inclusion of women and individual rights held by women. This transforms the person-land relation and the very construct of community in the reproduction of community.

The resistance to private ownership of land in Kwale is also part of a continued contestation of land registration that has taken place since the beginning of adjudication in 1974. Registration involved a series of community meetings and a referendum to decide on the type of landholding into which the reserves would be divided. Individual tenure of land was strongly encouraged by the adjudication administrators. However, Digo women and men did not vote the same way on this issue. Adjudication records indicate that women were against the titling to private property and men were for it. Unlike their neighbors to the west, the Duruma, who voted to hold land as group ranches (whereby land held in trust is now being privatized), the Digo voted for private property and individual tenure (Gray 1972). This remains a contested area where registration makes possible a certain kind of "stealing" that is both gendered and individualizing.

In a way that was similar to what MacKenzie (1993) and Haugerud (1989) argue for highland Kenya, contrary to the goals of adjudication, the number of land disputes in Kwale did not decrease after adjudication. In fact, registration provided another area for land disputes within the community. Security of tenure, recognized in the decrease in disputes, was not improved after adjudication either. The insecurity of tenure exemplified by the circumstances of Ali's father's case indicates the tenuous relation of title deeds to increased productivity. Ali's father's land became less secure and less productive with registration as registration provided a third method of distribution and contestation.

Adjudication and registration policy was conceptualized around a notion of a radically individualized farmer that the fuko and mbari barely fit. When land is registered it ceases to be clan land in the view of the government, as registration is meant to remove all customary law claims. Thus, registered land should be private property transferred in accordance with the Succession Act of 1981, or since 1991, by Islamic law. Currently the claims to land by clan are less easy to uphold, especially in court. Privatization of clan land causes conflict because it questions and challenges Digo kinship structures and the basis of social relations.

Making the Individual Common

Although land adjudication in Tiwi in 1974–1975 resulted in the registration of land to private title, 34 percent (825 plots out of the 2,426 plots registered) were registered by common equal undivided share. In Kenya, "common title" legally means that up to five people can register land in equal, undivided shares. Offspring, rather than the other shareholders, can then inherit this land. The land registration records indicate that the proportion of land registered to common title has not decreased in recent years. Rather, most plots where the proprietor has passed away since adjudication (1974–1975) have been registered in common to the heirs, or are undergoing arbitration. The majority of the land held in common share is held by siblings or, in the case of inheritance since adjudication, by the children (and often wives) of the deceased. This is especially evident for women in Tiwi, where 80 percent of the 1,032 women who have registered title to land hold it in common.[30]

Common registration can be thought of as an effort to introduce dynamism to a system that is concerned with fixity. As is argued for Romania by Katherine Verdery, such practices can be seen as a "struggle of certain groups and persons to tie property down against others who keep its edges flexible, uncertain, amorphous" (1994, 1073). Various people benefit from the fixity or dynamism of categories and possibilities at certain specific moments. In Ali's case, rather than securing landholdings, registration further caused dissension in society and fueled disputes. In his critique of Zionist land policies in Israel, Atran analyzes problems that became evident when "peasants were suddenly forced to live with the results of their last redistribution as if caught in an arbitrary moment of 'musical chairs' " (1989, 727). Registration of fuko land had a similar effect of making permanent the last redistribution of land within the clan, thus stopping the dynamism. The high percentage of women with title in Tiwi reflects the customary relation of women to land. However, registration radically changes their relation to the land and the process through which land is transferred from or to women. Kaya elders and fishermen at the Port of Chale felt that this registration was robbery. To express the ultimate in stealing through registration, the registration of kaya land was compared to the registration of a mother's or grandmother's land. The comparison of the mother's or grandmother's land to the most sacred land of the kaya stresses that land "stealing" is not gender neutral but is always perceived as containing a gendered moral component.

Gendered Relations and Female Kin

Gender becomes implicated in debates between individuals and collectivities, as women are located and relocated in a negotiation of kin relations. In short, social relations of land are gender specific. Land associated with women plays an important part in Digo inheritance disputes. In Tiwi sublocation of Kwale district, 28 percent of the people to whom land was registered in 1974–1975 were women.[31] This percentage (on record) has not changed significantly today in spite of some sale and subdivision of land in Tiwi. However, in most of Kenya, women are subordinate rights holders in land. As Shipton (1992, 370) points out, well over 90 percent of land titles in Western Kenya are issued to men at registration of title. Kwale district has the highest percentage of land registered to women in the country: approximately 30 percent.[32]

Women owned and gained access to resources because, as women, they were the central units through which clan properties and property were transferred. They claimed land as clan members, although the land was considered common property as clan land. A woman may inherit in this way along with her brothers, who later would transfer the land to her children, or as in Omar's grandmother's case, in spite of her brothers. Omar explained to me that his grandmother had inherited land from her mother's brother (mjomba), although he had had five sons. She then left her land to her daughter's daughters, although she herself had two sons as well as one daughter. Omar's grandmother's land first passed maternally from mother's brother to sister's child, and then remained in the hands of the women of the fuko. Thus, the land passed through the women of the family only.[33] Both adjudication records and interviews indicate that most land inherited matrilineally had at one time belonged to a woman.[34] Ownership through matrilineal inheritance no longer constitutes a large proportion of the plots in Tiwi, as patrilineal inheritance is more often practiced today. The conceptualization of family under Islam changes the manner in which women gain access to resources. Women are able to own land and have access to land as daughters, as spouses, and as individuals. The land they then hold is their personal property.

What is at stake in the loss of common property for women? As Muslims and as Digo clan members, women have access to land through relationships. However, the type of access and the form of the person and community who holds land are radically different. As Oendo argues, Digo insistence that sons and daughters inherit equally, both verbally and in practice, is a way of joining matrilineal and patrilineal inheritance by providing for the sisters' children. Thus, it is also a way of keeping part of the property within the clan from which it originates. If we consider this practice in relation to the registration of clan land that is seen as stealing, it is less free from dispute than it first implies. The involvement of registration in negotiating Digo/Muslim categorizations indicates that none of these systems are working in isolation from one another, but rather are imbricated in a complex manner, thus making the definition and content of community ambiguous. Digo land practices challenge individual title to private property as envisioned by the state and development communities. To a lesser extent, they challenge and appropriate Islamic inheritance stipulations within Digo cultural practices while reinforcing family, whether matrilineal or patrilineal.

Conclusion: Out of Chaos, Order?

In 1992 the CFCU embarked on an innovative program to preserve both the biological and cultural heritage of the kaya in conjunction with local communities. This chapter has described the context in which this program takes place. It is a situation in which land is highly contested, people come to property through different and often competing criteria, the categorization of people is at stake, the state is unable to enforce a specific method of transfer of property, and security of tenure is a major problem. One cannot just wish away such a complex community setting. Rather one should ask: What can this complex understanding of Digo society and Digo land relations contribute to conservation efforts that work with and through communities?

The insecurity and ambiguity of land tenure in the area surrounding the kaya affect the composition of the community, the retention of common property, and the use of resources associated with the kaya. In the development policy of Kenya, and as a principle of neoliberal economics, common property is seen as less secure and less productive than private property. The argument is that individual people with private property have a stake in that property; thus they will look after it more and invest in it. The stake in property is produced because of the absolute individual nature of the property holding—no one else has claims over the property. Rather, multiple claims on property do not necessarily reduce the stakes people have in property, so long as the manner in which various claimants relate to the property and each other is clearly defined. In other words, people have a stake in property when they can define the relationship between belonging and the criteria for the distribution of resources. Thus, although being a member of a group is of fundamental importance to land allocation among the Digo, an unstable and ambiguous relation between community membership and access to resources increases the insecurity of landholdings, be it private property, clan land, or kaya forests.

Since 1992 a total of thirty-six out of the possible forty-seven kaya sites have been gazetted as national monuments, twenty-nine in Kwale district. The forests are protected for their high cultural value as sacred sites. The most recent gazettements were based on forests that have direct cultural significance and are still used by elders. Gazettement offered an innovative way to preserve the forests regardless of the official ownership of the land, as the Antiquities and Monuments Act prohibits the destruction of national monuments even if they are located on private property. However, at the same time it is yet another way to categorize communities and to set the criteria for the distribution and use of property under legal strictures.

Ironically the CFCU has had to promote the kaya among the Mijikenda themselves. The kaya have been promoted as a unique symbol of Mijikenda identity in an effort to increase the significance of and interest in the forests, especially among the youth. This interest in the kaya as a cultural heritage is promoted through the education system with the sponsorship of workshops and competitions in schools. This identity formation is not at the same level as being Digo but rather in the broader grouping Mijikenda, and it is constructed in opposition to other ethnic groups in Kenya that do not have kaya. Nevertheless, it recognizes the importance of group membership for conservation, while recognizing the divisions, mainly by age, in the community in regard to the significance of the forests.

Fiona MacKenzie (1993, 200) argues that in a system of legal pluralism such as Kenya, insecurity arises from the contest of rights over land by individuals drawing on various sets of legal rights, which interact with each other. Taking into account the ideology and power behind differing legal processes, I contend that the insecurity arises from the contest over the social ordering of productive units for the continuation of groups. That is to say, insecurity is produced as people struggle over the manner in which how land is ordered into clan land, lineage land, individual land, kaya land, and/or land held by

Muslims or Digo people affects the continuation of communities as Digo communities, or as Muslim communities, or as a fuko.

Rather than an unambiguous desire for belonging leading to property claims, in Kwale there are competing grounds for unity, so that sameness can be understood in multiple ways. It is this particular state of conflict between categorization of persons (Digo, Muslim, Kenyan) and criteria for distribution of property (clan membership, religious brotherhood, citizen) rather than a mode of ownership (common or private) that produces the insecurity of tenure resulting in decreased productivity. As Beidelman argues, disorder and ambiguity may characterize central moral concerns rather than deviancy and subversion. Thus, "what represents disorder and conflict at one level may represent inclusive and instrumentally powerful and valued categories at another" (Beidelman 1980, 35). The kaya are not immune to the surrounding land conflicts. If we take Beidelman's suggestion seriously, conflicts provide windows into inclusive and instrumentally powerful and valued categories within societies. These are categories that cannot be swept under the rug when conservation efforts are constructed in conjunction with the community. Rather, they must be addressed as having an impact on and, often, being crucial to the relationship between communities and conservation.

Production is related to the degree of security of the categorization of personhood, of sameness and difference, in a society. Thus, there is no "natural" stability or increased production with private property. With registration as private property in Kwale, reduction in production has been increased by the institutions that were meant to free it. Beidelman points out that rules emphasize maintenance of boundaries and order, yet social action often involves bridging categories such that there is a moral ambiguity or a choice in conduct and ends (1980, 32). The Digo property relations can be seen as the constant tension between fluidity and fixity. Fluidity in belonging, and the imprecise and multiple ways of categorizing persons, dispersed power, and authority, provide for a movement between categorical systems that allows access to resources. Individuals and collectivities try to fix specific categories that benefit them to secure access to resources. Instead of looking at the apparent land as private or common property, we need to look at the classificatory order (the grounds for and limits to unity) that sets criteria for the distribution of property.

The ever-changing nature of community belonging necessitates a fluid concept of the community rather than a concept that tries to tie communities down to specific forms. Conservation efforts cannot afford to work with categorical identities that stand as fixed opposition to each other, for instance,

Digo versus Muslim. Rather they need to make space for communities that are both Digo and Muslim in their management of the forests, while building on the promotion of property relations that support the continuation of these groupings through time. It is only through the understanding of the grounds for and limits to belonging that this space can be opened up. These categories of meaning and social relations are at stake in restructuring and defining community through common property. Thus, rather than just negotiating various land laws that exist simultaneously in Kenya—statutory, Islamic, and customary law—conflicts in inheritance and practice must be read as fights over defining community and belonging along with access to wealth, power, and resources.

Notes

1. Another kind of land is communal grazing land, called *vuwe*.
2. The other eight Mijikenda peoples are the Giriama, Kauma, Ribe, Kambe, Jibana, Rabai, Chonyi, and Duruma. The Duruma also mainly live in Kwale District, while most others live north of Mombasa. Brantley notes that "the Giriama's own term, *Makayachenda*, the nine *makaya*, was changed by them to *Midzichenda* but the Swahili term Mijikenda is best known and has now been accepted by the Mijikenda themselves" (1981, 6). *Miji* in Swahili means "town," "city," or "village," while *chenda* is the old Bantu word for "nine," replaced in Swahili by the Arabic tisa'a.
3. 1989 Kenya Population Census.
4. Government of Kenya, Ministry of Planning and National Development and UNICEF, *Socio-Economic Profiles*, 1990.
5. For a more in-depth discussion of the matrilineal and patrilineal relationship, see Bettina Ng'weno, "Inheriting Disputes: The Digo Negotiation of Meaning and Power through Land," *African Economic History* 25(1997): 59–77.
6. BK and HK, December 1993, Tiwi. All names of people interviewed have been replaced by initials to retain confidentiality.
7. HM, December 1993, Tiwi.
8. The combined Digo and Duruma population in 1939 and 1947 were 63,822 and 103,992 respectively (Native Affairs Reports, quoted in Wamahiu 1988, 57). In 1989 this population of 316,240 people made up 80 percent of the 380,000 people of Kwale district (Kenya Population Census 1989, 1–35).
9. CWG women's group, October 1993.
10. HB, December 1993, Tiwi.
11. The Coastal Forests Conservation Unit plays a role in reestablishing kaya as a symbol of Mijikenda identity and unity in their efforts to conserve the biodiversity in the forests.
12. People are often named after important occurrences at the time of their birth such as famines, independence, or the Gulf War.
13. HM, November 1993, Tiwi.
14. The Swahili terms *shangazi* and *mjomba* mean "paternal aunt" and "maternal uncle," respectively. However colloquially they are used to refer to nieces and nephews as well. MM and SM, October 1993, Tiwi.
15. For more information about these changes see Ng'weno, "Inheriting Disputes," 59–77.

16. CWG women's group, October 1993.
17. Ibid.
18. Later in the chapter I go into further detail describing how Islam came to hold this dominant position in definition and classification of persons as Digo, and Digo people as Muslim.
19. I refer to Islamic law as an entity only insofar as it exists as part of the national legal system through the Kadhi's courts, recognizing that in calling it law, I am doing an injustice to a system that has moral and legal features to it, but is not limited to law. "Family" refers to networks of extending relations that cannot necessarily be thought of as an entity that is bounded and can act.
20. MS, November 1993, Attorney General's Office, Mombasa.
21. Ibid.
22. The Kadhi's or Islamic courts are a branch of the Kenyan Judiciary that deals with family law involving Muslims, and are administrated and monitored by the Kenyan government. Appeals are decided by the secular High Court rather than at the Kadhi's courts. In 1991 the Succession Act was amended so that Islamic law regarding family matters applied to Muslims.
23. These names have been changed to protect the identity of the informants.
24. No distinction is made between order of wives or children, as an elder child does not inherit more than another child. Throughout the area property seemed to be evenly distributed among those who qualified to inherit.
25. This was true after the 1981 Succession Act and before the 1991 amendment to the Act.
26. AH, December 1993, Tiwi.
27. AV, November 1993, Mombasa.
28. KR, December 1993, Mombasa.
29. Kaya Elders, October 1993, Waa.
30. These titles were given during the land adjudication of 1974–1975.
31. This is not the same as the percentage of plots of land registered to women, since 35 percent of the plots of land in Tiwi sublocation of Kwale district are held in common. The statistics were compiled from land adjudication records for Tiwi sublocation, 1974–1975.
32. Personal communications with Okoth-Ogendo.
33. KR, December 1993, Mombasa.
34. Lands Office, Kwale District, 1993.

Bibliography

Atran, Scott. 1989. "The Surrogate Colonization of Palestine, 1917–1939." *American Ethnologist* 16(4):719–744.

Beidelman, T. O. 1980. "The Moral Imagination of the Kaguru: Some Thoughts on Tricksters, Translations, and Comparative Analysis." *American Ethnologist* 7:27–42.

Berry, Sara. 1993. *No Condition Is Permanent: The Social Dynamics of Agrarian Change in Sub-Saharan Africa*. Madison: University of Wisconsin Press.

Bowen, John R. 1988. "The Transformation of an Indonesian Property System: *Adat*, Islam and Social Change in the Gayo Highlands." *American Ethnologist* 15(2):274–293.

Brantley, Cynthia. 1981. *The Giriama and Colonial Resistance in Kenya 1800–1920*. Berkeley: University of California Press.

Central Bank of Kenya. 1991. *Kenya Land of Opportunity*. Nairobi: Central Bank of Kenya.

Central Bureau of Statistics. 1994. *Kenya Populations Census 1989*. Vol. 1. Nairobi: Government Printers.

Chanock, Martin. 1991. "Paradigms, Policies and Property: A Review of Customary Law of Land Tenure." In *Law in Colonial Africa*, ed. K. Mann and R. Roberts. Portsmouth, N.H.: Heinemann.

Collier, J., B. Maurer, and L. S. Navaz. 1995. "Sanctioned Identities: Legal Constructions of Modern Personhood." *Identities: Global Studies in Culture and Power* (2)1–2:1–28.

Colony and Protectorate of Kenya. 1931. *Law Reports of Kenya*: Volume XI, 1927–1928. Nairobi: Colony and Protectorate of Kenya.

Cooper, Frederick. 1992. "Colonizing Time: Work Rhythms and Labor Conflict in Colonial Mombasa." In *Colonialism and Culture*, ed. N. B. Dirks. Ann Arbor: University of Michigan Press.

Dolgin, Janet L. 1995. "Family Law and the Facts of Family." In *Naturalizing Power: Essays in Feminist Cultural Analysis*, ed. Sylvia Yanagisako and Carol Delaney. London: Routledge.

Dominguez, Virginia. 1986. *White by Definition: Social Classification in Creole Louisiana*. New Brunswick, N.J.: Rutgers University Press.

Gluckman, Max. 1965. *The Ideas in Barotse Jurisprudence*. New Haven, Conn.: Yale University Press.

Government of Kenya. 1994. *Development Plan 1994–96*. Nairobi: Government of Kenya.

Government of Kenya and UNICEF. 1990. "Socio-Economic Profiles." Nairobi: Government of Kenya, Ministry of Planning and National Development and UNICEF.

Gray, Nancy. 1972. "Acceptance of Land Adjudication Among the Digo." Nairobi: Institute of African Studies, University of Nairobi.

Grossi, Paolo. 1981. *An Alternative to Private Property: Collective Property in the Juridical Consciousness of the Nineteenth Century*. Chicago: University of Chicago Press.

Haugerud, Angelique. 1989. "Land Tenure and Agrarian Change in Kenya." *Africa* 59(1):61–90.

MacKenzie, Fiona. 1993. "'A Piece of Land Never Shrinks': Reconceptualizing Land Tenure in a Smallholding District, Kenya." In *Land in African Agrarian Systems*, ed. Thomas J. Bassett and Donald E. Crummy. Madison: University of Wisconsin Press.

Moore, Sally Falk. 1991. "From Giving and Lending to Selling: Property Transactions Reflecting Historical Changes on Kilimanjaro." In *Law in Colonial Africa*, ed. K. Mann and R. Roberts. Portsmouth, N.H.: Heinemann.

Ng'weno, Bettina. 1997. "Inheriting Disputes: The Digo Negotiation of Meaning and Power through Land." *African Economic History* 25:59–77.

Oendo, Ayuko. 1987. "Marriage Instability and Domestic Continuity in Digo Society." *Cambridge Anthropology* 12(2):47.

Okoth-Ogendo, H.W.O. 1991. *Tenants of the Crown*. Nairobi: ACTS Press.

Ranger, Terence. 1983. "The Invention of Tradition in Colonial Africa." In *The Invention of Tradition*, ed. Eric Hobsbawn and Terence Ranger, 211–262. Cambridge, U.K.: Cambridge University Press.

Shipton, Parker. 1992. "Debts and Trespasses: Land, Mortgages, and the Ancestors in Western Kenya." *Africa* 62(3):357–386.

Spear, Thomas T. 1978. *A History of the Mijikenda Peoples of the Kenya Coast to 1900*. Nairobi: Kenya Literature Bureau.

Verdery, Katherine. 1994. "The Elasticity of Land: Problems of Property Restitution in Transylvania." *Slavic Review* 53(4):1072–1109.

Wamahiu, Sheila Parvyn. 1988. "Continuity and Change in Adigo Women's Roles,

Status and Education: An Exploratory Anthropological Study." Ph.D. dissertation, Kenyatta University, Nairobi.

Williams, Brackette F. 1989. "A Class Act: Anthropology and the Race to Nation Across Ethnic Terrain." *Annual Review of Anthropology* 18:401–444.

Willis, Justin. 1993. *Mombasa, the Swahili and the Making of the Mijikenda.* Oxford, U.K.: Clarendon Press.

Communities, States, and the Governance of Pacific Northwest Salmon Fisheries

Chapter 5

SARA SINGLETON

AFTER DECADES OF BEING IGNORED, "community" now occupies a central role in discussions about what it is that allows people to govern themselves effectively. This is particularly true with respect to natural resource management and environmental policymaking. In both so-called developing countries and industrialized, wealthy countries such as the United States, governments at all levels are being urged to "reinvent" themselves as facilitators of community capacity and empowerment, and communities themselves are now seen as reservoirs of social capital. Yet no serious student of natural resource management or community governance would suggest that communities are infallible or that local governance is a panacea for all that is wrong with the way natural resources are managed. An open-minded approach is needed with respect to what both communities and states can contribute to conservation, and how their particular strengths and weaknesses might be productively combined to encourage sustainable, equitable management of natural resource systems. This is especially true where large-scale or transboundary resource systems necessitate the involvement of multiple groups of users or where public goods such as biodiversity are part and parcel of a resource system that supplies private goods (lumber, fodder, fish, game, etc.) to a particular population. The universe of cases falling within one or the other of these categories is obviously very large.

In this chapter, I begin with a discussion of what seems to me to be some confusion in the literature regarding what communities can do and how their collective capacities relate to the conservation of natural resource systems. The bulk of the chapter then explores the evolution of a complicated and highly sophisticated regime for comanagement of salmon fisheries in the Pacific Northwest region of the United States. The case involves twenty American Indian tribes that, as the result of a 1974 federal court decision, have the legal right to take half the area's harvestable salmon and share equally in salmon management with various state, federal, and international regulatory authorities. Pacific Northwest salmon are a migratory or trans-boundary resource involving multiple actors, both tribal and nontribal, and disparate and widely separated user groups. There are both shared and com-peting interests between government agencies and the tribes and both between and within different tribal communities. How the tribes, collectively, grapple with intertribal conflicts while simultaneously presenting a unified front when they bargain with external, nontribal regulatory entities demon-strates a complex, nuanced process in which different sorts of situations are framed in terms of diverse interests and various sorts of social identities. The case study also describes the conflictual, difficult, and time-consuming process by which tribal and state managers have been able to create a set of workable institutions that allow them to manage this important resource system coop-eratively. The depiction of a third level of institutions at the level of internal governance shows how tribal communities have attempted to deal with the distributional issues that accompany management of a scarce resource in the context of varying degrees of heterogeneity among user groups.

The Concept of Community

Like many important ideas, the concepts of community and community gov-ernance attract the attention of people with very different political ideologies, disciplinary backgrounds, and theoretical perspectives. It is not surprising that some degree of conceptual ambiguity results. Specifically, there are at least three areas where unexamined assumptions or poorly worked out causal rela-tionships between variables may create unfounded expectations about the role of community in the conservation of natural resources or in the service of other goals such as equitable distribution. They are: (1) a failure to distinguish between a group's collective capacities and its goals—that is, the assumption that if a group has certain capacities, it will necessarily adopt certain goals such as conservation or the protection of public goods; (2) the idea that strong communities are necessarily socially homogeneous or harmonious com-munities, or that such homogeneity or harmony is a requirement for them to be reasonably effective in realizing shared goals or acting collectively; and (3) a failure to distinguish between different kinds of problems and to recognize that both communities and state agencies have positive roles to play in the management of many sorts of natural resource systems and other sorts of commons. I will develop each of these points in more detail before going on to the case study, which I hope will illuminate these issues with concrete examples.

COLLECTIVE CAPACITIES AND COLLECTIVE GOALS

It is not necessary to hold a romanticized vision of communities in order to believe that the collective capacities of a group of individuals—their ability to accomplish shared goals—are greater when membership is relatively stable, when relations between members are direct and multifaceted, and when members expect to go on interacting with roughly the same group of people for the foreseeable future (Taylor 1982). There is considerable empirical evidence to support this finding (Acheson 1987; Baland and Platteau 1996; Ellickson 1989, 1991; Feeny et al. 1990; McKean 1982, 1986; Netting 1981; Taylor 1982). And, as at least some theorists have taken pains to point out, social relations within communities in the sense defined above are not necessarily particularly harmonious or even amicable. What is necessary is that members are mutually interdependent or connected (Bowles 1999; Taylor 1982). Such communities are not always spatially delineated, although spatial proximity increases the likelihood that relations between people will be direct and multifaceted and also may lower the costs of gathering various sorts of relevant information and of monitoring compliance with rules, and so on.

It is at least plausible, then, to argue that close-knit communities possess certain collective capacities or, alternatively, a greater stock of social capital, that will, *ceteris paribus,* allow them to act collectively more effectively than groups of people who lack such capacities. Yet even if we grant that communities meeting these conditions have such capacities, this says nothing about their goals with respect to natural resource systems.[1] While there is evidence to suggest that local communities can indeed be successful at managing local CPRs (common pool resources) more or less endogenously, in order to do so they must meet at least four necessary conditions: First, they must have a preference for sustainable management relative to, for example, liquidating the resource and investing the proceeds elsewhere. In other words, they must consider sustainable management to be a worthwhile goal.[2] Second, they must have the material resources necessary to solve a variety of collective action problems associated with creating and maintaining resource management institutions. Third, they must understand or have appropriate beliefs about what actions need to be taken and how human actions affect the viability of the physical or biological systems they are interested in.[3] Fourth, they must have sufficient information available to them to allow for the creation of effective management institutions (Singleton 2000). The extent to which this information is readily available at the local level will depend partly on characteristics of the resource system such as its geographical scale, the extent to which its functions and health or deterioration are discernible to local observers, and the extent to which other users of the system are able to affect its productivity without the consent or perhaps even the awareness of the community in question. Large-scale, transboundary resource systems are very difficult for (sets of) local users to manage well because the conditions noted above must be met and because there also must be sufficient social capital between the (possibly numerous) user groups to allow them to create and maintain a set of management institutions to coordinate their joint use. And as Elinor Ostrom has argued in the case of small-scale CPRs, the governance mechanisms themselves must also satisfy certain conditions (Ostrom 1990).

The fact that a community has the capacity to solve collective action problems does not mean that it will choose to manage resources sustainably, that it will solve internal distributional problems in an equitable manner, or that it will manage resources in such a way as to provide public goods such as biodiversity to larger collectivities. What the literature on local-level natural resource management does seem to indicate is that communities meeting these conditions are generally able to utilize certain comparative advantages in managing local resources effectively and efficiently. For example, local users have access to detailed and timely information about local resource conditions, which allow them to devise regulations to diverse and changing environmental conditions. Close-knit communities are able to use preexisting systems of social control to create and maintain institutions designed to sustain resource systems; consequently, it is often easier and less costly for local communities to monitor and enforce regulations themselves, or hire and supervise an agent to do so, rather than relying on poorly funded state enforcement.[4]

SOCIAL HETEROGENEITY AND ECONOMIC INEQUALITY

Returning to the issue of social homogeneity, we find that many of the communities cited above exhibit some level of social heterogeneity or economic inequality, but this does not seem to cripple their effectiveness. Yet while neither homogeneity nor social harmony appear to be prerequisites for effective collective capacities, obviously if there are very large income or wealth differences between those political actors or subgroups who have the power to significantly affect outcomes, various bargaining problems are likely to ensue, with the result that either problems remain unsolved or they are solved less efficiently or less equitably than they could be. If there are significant divisions between relatively powerful and relatively powerless groups, the substantive content of the emerging institutions is likely to favor the powerful (Knight 1992), while shirking, foot-dragging, and other "weapons of the weak" will be deployed by the less powerful in an effort to shape the process by which formal rules are interpreted in local practice (Scott 1987). Yet despite internal conflicts, even divided communities may be able to coalesce very effectively in defense of common interests in the face of an external threat.

The effects of inequality on environmental outcomes are mixed. Bargaining problems resulting from economic inequalities may present insurmountable barriers to the resolution to various sorts of "commons" problems including overexploitation and overcapitalization (Johnson and Libecap 1982). Or, as is apparent in the Pacific Northwest case, otherwise attractive solutions to management problems may simply be ruled out by virtue of the fact that they would make one or more parties worse off and that compensatory mechanisms, where they exist, lack credibility. On the other hand, the presence of at least some relatively wealthy users who are better equipped to bear the short-term costs of conservation efforts may make it more likely that a common pool resource will be managed sustainably. As Jean-Marie Baland and Jean-Philippe Platteau have argued, inequality of access rights to commons has two divergent effects on the incentives of users of common pool resources. Drawing on Mancur Olson (1965), they note that, because they expect to derive greater benefits from a sustainably managed commons, large users are more likely to contribute (conserve). Yet while increasing inequality enhances the incentives of big users to contribute, it simultaneously encourages small users to have a free ride. If the cooperation of all or nearly all users is necessary to sustain the commons, then inequality will decrease the likelihood of a successful outcome. Thus the effects of inequality on environmental outcomes are ambiguous, turning in large part on the political or social "technology" of collective action (Baland and Platteau 1999, 781).

Comanagement: State/Tribal, Intertribal, and Intratribal Institutions

Prior to contact with Western Europeans, the Salish people of the Pacific Northwest Coast of North America had created a complex system of property rights, contracts, and division rules that was extremely effective in allowing them to organize their use of natural resources, especially the large and plentiful salmon that provided the most important element of their spiritual and material culture. Whether or not such institutions were also directed toward conservation, as some authors have claimed, would be difficult to establish conclusively, but they were unquestionably highly efficient in terms of organizing labor and allowing people to migrate along resource-harvesting routes that coincided with periodic superabundance of fish, berries, bulbs, and other resources.[5] It is difficult to escape the conclusion that the emergence of these highly efficient institutions was facilitated by the stable, multidimensional, direct relations that are characteristic of what is defined as strong community (Singleton 1999).

A very different regime subsequently came to regulate use of the salmon resource, and still another set of institutions governs the fishery today. As native people were pushed aside by settlers during the nineteenth century, the salmon fishery came to be dominated by immigrant fishermen who competed with one another for an opportunity to supply what had become a global market for canned salmon. Early fishing methods imitated native practices, but as time went on, the basis of competition became the ability to intercept the returning salmon before they reached the nets or weirs of others. Fishing began taking place farther and farther from the mouths of rivers and tributaries where the tribes had traditionally fished. Not only was the fishery becoming less efficient—it required bigger boats and more expensive gear to catch the same fish—competition through interception had the effect of driving Native Americans out of the fishery, since they were unable to raise enough capital to compete. By the 1960s, the fishery was seriously overcapitalized, the salmon were under severe strain, and the tribes were collectively taking only about two percent of the catch. The State of Washington, which had been singularly ineffective in protecting the resource against an ever-expanding, highly capitalized fleet and an extensive system of dams that today block more than a thousand miles of salmon spawning streams, persisted in enforcing "conservation" regulations prohibiting Indians from using traditional methods of fishing in the rivers. In an atmosphere of festering conflict and escalating civil disobedience, the U.S. government, acting in its role as trustee for the tribes, sued the State of Washington in order to recover the fishing rights tribes claimed had been guaranteed to them when they signed treaties in 1854–1855. The federal district court's decision in 1974 to divide the harvestable salmon equally between the treaty tribes and the State of Washington set off howls of protest from non-Indian fishermen, newspaper editors, state resource management agencies, and political leaders.

The reallocation of fishing rights was a shock to state managers, but even more cataclysmic from their perspective was the fact that the court granted tribes the right to manage their own fisheries. The effect of this was to require that the state and the tribes reach agreement on nearly every decision governing when, where, and how many fish would be caught. For the first seven or eight years following the legal decision, the amount of conflict, both on the fishing grounds and in the courtroom, was extraordinary. The state initially refused to implement the decision, and eventually the federal district court was obliged to take over the day-to-day management of the fishery. Formal disputes numbered in the hundreds, and nearly every fisheries management decision made by the tribes was challenged in court by the state (Cohen 1986). Throughout the later 1970s and early 1980s, the Washington salmon fisheries were a textbook example of how little a regulatory system can accomplish if it must rely solely on formal, coercive authority. Despite this inauspicious beginning, in the subsequent decade the two sides were able to create a relationship based on at least a measure of mutual respect and to design a set of institutions that worked far more effectively than either those that existed under traditional state regulation prior to 1974 or those instituted by the court in the early stages of comanagement (Pinkerton 1989; Singleton 1998).

STATE/TRIBAL INSTITUTIONS

Even before the introduction of twenty sovereign Indian tribes into the decision-making process, the management of Pacific salmon had become, by the mid-twentieth century, a very complicated process involving numerous state, federal, and international regulatory agencies. Salmon travel thousands of miles on their return to natal streams and pass through a gantlet of fishermen as well as a series of natural and man-made obstacles on either side of the international border. Each of the six species of Pacific salmon and steelhead is actually composed of a number of stocks, which are defined as separate populations adapted to a particular river or tributary. If genetic diversity is to be maintained, as many as possible of these individual stocks must be sustained. Stocks begin to separate as they get closer to the terminal areas, but prior to that time, it is difficult to conduct a fishery on strong stocks without catching weak stocks. The large number of widely separated fisheries, the need to protect weak, wild stocks while allowing fishermen the opportunity to catch strong stocks, the complexity of salmon ecology, and the number of poorly understood factors affecting their survival combine to make salmon management extremely difficult.

Like the salmon themselves, the regulatory process follows a cyclical pattern. Early each February, representatives of the Pacific Northwest states, the federal government, the treaty tribes, and Canada attempt to work out fishing regulations that allow them to share common stocks. Between 1985–1992, the guidelines established by the Pacific Salmon Treaty guided this process, but in recent years, negotiations have continued into the fishing season, with enormous expenditures of time and energy. In March and April, the Pacific Fisheries Management Council (PFMC)—one of the regional councils established by the 1976 Fishery Conservation and Management Act—develops a management plan for the fisheries conducted from three to two hundred miles off the U.S. coast. In so doing, they unavoidably set the parameters of the subsequent fisheries inside Puget Sound and within three miles of the coast. Next, the state and the tribes must work out a plan to coordinate their joint utilization of the resource. Finally, individual tribes develop regulations for their own fishermen, and the state develops regulations for the non-Indian fishery. Beneath the surface of the negotiations taking place at each step of the process are patterns of shared and divergent interests that continually strain internal relations between members of state, tribal, and national coalitions.

Competition between treaty and nontreaty fishermen involves both spatial and temporal dimensions. As the fish return to spawn, they pass through a succession of fisheries, each of which must be limited in order to allow enough fish for escapement and for subsequent upstream fisheries. The recreational and commercial offshore fleets are the first to intercept the fish, and they are almost entirely non-Indian. Next are the commercial net fisheries in the marine waters inside Puget Sound, which are somewhat more mixed between treaty and nontreaty, but in which nontreaty fishermen predominate. The majority of tribal fishermen fish in the bays, river mouths, and rivers adjacent to their reservations.[6] Thus the composition of the commercial fishing fleet changes from predominantly nontribal to predominantly tribal as the fish move from the ocean through the Strait of Juan de Fuca and into the rivers that drain western Washington. One environmentally beneficial consequence of this is that the tribes can be counted upon to raise conservation concerns early in the season, when most of the fishing is taking place in the ocean, and the state plays a similar role later in the season, when the fisheries at issue are primarily Native American.

To further complicate matters, both the tribes and the state have heterogeneous interests within their own coalitions. The state must balance the needs of recreational fishermen, both in the ocean and in the rivers, with those of commercial fishermen, both ocean trollers and net fishermen inside the bays. Rivalry between these groups has been intense in recent years. There are few Native American recreational fishermen, but each tribe is limited to fishing within particular geographical areas, called "usual and accustomed places" (UAPs), which have been established by the court according to the locations where specific tribes fished at the time of the treaties. As a result, each tribe has claims only to particular stocks, which makes it particularly important to them that management decisions are made on a stock-by-stock basis, rather than by looking at aggregate yields.[7] Decisions regarding conservation and when and where the treaty and nontreaty shares will be taken have distributional consequences not only for the two sides in relation to each other, but also for different interests within each coalition. Thus a variety of issues having to do with fisheries biology and stock management get played out against a morass of distributional conflicts.

One legacy of the nearly continuous litigation that followed the initial court decision is that there is an extensive system of formal rules that stipulate what each party must do in particular management situations. Given the history of conflict and the clear distributional consequences of most of these decisions, it would be expected that one side or the other would insist that the formal rules be rigorously adhered to. Yet this is not the case. The system in the mid-1990s reflected a surprising amount of mutual accommodation and willingness to depart from formal rules.

For example, the nontribal ocean recreational fishery takes place early in the season in an area where stocks are mixed. It invariably has negative impacts on one or more weak, wild stocks. Since each tribe essentially exercises veto power over fishing that could compromise either its own harvest of, or the escapement goals for, wild stocks passing through its "usual and accustomed places," it has the legal authority to shut down a fishery that is of critical importance to a very influential constituency of the Washington State Department of Fish and Wildlife. The fact that such a fishery generally does take place is indicative of the degree of cooperation between the state and the tribes. In addition, although formal rules require it, neither side does annual accounting of allocation shares in anything but the most cursory fashion. Finally, the number of disputes requiring formal adjudication has declined from a high of more than a hundred a year to fewer than five.

INSTITUTIONS GOVERNING INTERTRIBAL
CONFLICT AND COOPERATION

The 1974 federal court decision that reallocated the salmon resource also altered the environment of intertribal relations, creating new areas of potential stress and fracture and the need to create new intertribal institutions. The tribes had a prior history of shared sacrifice and civil disobedience during the struggle to regain fishing rights, and many tribal members are related to members of other tribes either through intermarriage or as a result of the somewhat arbitrary process with which the territorial government created "tribes" and reservations out of the much more complex system of kinship relationships that existed at the time of the 1854–1855 treaties. Tribes also continue to hold a variety of shared interests specifically related to fishing. These include the need to present a united front to external groups in state, federal, and international bargaining forums; various economies of scale for certain management tasks; the desire to reduce confusion and limit potential conflict by agreeing on a set of consistent regulations for the many areas where they share fishing rights; and the need to create a sense of security among individual tribes that investments in hatcheries, effective management, and enforcement regimes will be matched by other tribes and that all tribes will share in the results. Nonetheless, tribes are distinct political entities that must compete for what is an increasingly scarce resource. And since the court decision limits individual tribes to fishing where their ancestors fished, some tribes are able to intercept fish headed for other tribes' areas, in much the same way that they themselves were intercepted by nontreaty fishermen in the past. As state/tribal conflicts began to recede in the mid-1980s, wrangling—both in and out of court—over allocational shares became a prominent feature in intertribal relations. Yet contrary to what might be expected, dissension between tribes had little effect on their ability to act collectively in pursuit of shared interests vis-à-vis nontribal regulatory agencies.

Over the years, tribal representatives have discussed a number of principles under which tribal shares might be allocated. These have been seen by some tribes as a way of redressing what is perceived as the current inequitable distribution, or by others simply as a method of increasing predictability and decreasing potential conflict. Some of the principles proposed by tribes could be interpreted as reflecting aspects of efficiency—that is, with expanding overall quantities of fish that can be harvested or reducing overcapitalization of the collective fishing fleet—or in increasing the degree of predictability in fishing regulations. Other principles focus on equity, defined in various ways. Several principles are conspicuous by their absence. For example, none of the tribes has suggested that the open access rule that governs the nontreaty fishery and most fisheries in the United States and elsewhere be replicated in the tribal fisheries. Nor has any tribe endorsed the method of allocating fishing opportunity that is currently much in favor with economists, which creates a de facto property right in fisheries by establishing individual transferable quotas (ITQs) that, after their initial distribution, can be exchanged in a market. Given the sophistication of tribal managers in the area of fisheries management, it is clear that this is not simply an oversight, but that tribes have rejected such principles.

The efficiency-enhancing principles include several proposals that appear to be designed to reward investment of one sort or another. For example, one principle would base allocation shares on investment in hatcheries and habitat protection. Another would bias shares toward those who have been the most active in pressing litigation to enlarge the collective tribal share or to extend the scope of the legal decision to other species of fish. Either of these principles is efficiency-enhancing relative to a set of institutional arrangements that have the effect of rewarding interception. Large tribes, poor tribes, and tribes without access to good hatchery sites have objected to these principles.

Another set of principles reflects various conceptions of equity. These include: shares proportionate to the size of the tribe; shares proportionate to the number of fishermen in each tribe; and shares based on the extent to which a tribe is dependent on fishing. None can be said to be efficiency-enhancing, and all would generally tend to work against efficiency. The problem of too many fishermen with too much equipment chasing fewer and fewer fish is endemic in fisheries, and rewarding large tribes or tribes with a large number of fishermen or fishermen with a large investment in gear is obviously not conducive to controlling it.

Although several of these principles would likely result in an increase in allocative efficiency, none has, in fact, been adopted for the simple reason that none are Pareto superior to the status quo—none can be achieved without making at least one tribe worse off. This is true even though some of these principles satisfy a standard often used by economists to judge efficiency—the Kaldor Hicks definition of Pareto optimality, whereby through the adoption of one of these principles it would be possible for those who gained under the new institutional arrangement to compensate those who lost and still be better off. Without a network of social institutions that gives the participants some assurance that they will, in fact, be compensated, it would be irrational for them to agree. Thus, distributional conflicts between the tribes have prevented them from reaching agreement on any of the nine principles that have been discussed over the years.

Nonetheless, after considerable effort and a great deal of time and expense, the tribes have been able to achieve some progress toward solving many of the problems of uncertainty and unpredictability that triggered discussion of the disputed principles in the first place. Rather than reaching agreement at the level of general principles and then constructing institutions based on those foundations, the tribes have, over the years, constructed a dense network of interrelated agreements that functions as a workable framework for managing day-to-day conflicts and organizing the fishing season. Some of these have been entered as court orders after being signed by the parties; others exist only as written minutes of meetings or oral agreements. This incremental process has produced two sorts of institutions that guide the process of managing fisheries: property rights and allocation share agreements.

The tribes recognize three types of property rights in addition to the spatially defined UAPs established by the court. Primary rights are those areas where a tribe is recognized to have a special claim or interest in an area within a larger area where several tribes share a UAP, for example, areas within or immediately adjacent to a reservation. Here, a tribe is said to have primary rights and can exclude others from fishing. Secondary rights convey the authority to set regulations, but they do not include the right to exclude other tribes with UAPs from fishing. A third category is in-common rights, which cover areas where all tribes with UAPs are entitled to fish and where each tribe may set its own fishing regulations. One of the strongest conventions, and one that emerged very early, is that tribes who share in-common fishing areas must agree to common fishing regulations.

The second type of institution is comprised of a series of allocation share agreements between so-called terminal tribes—those whose fishing rights extend only to the areas where particular stocks spawn—and the intercepting tribes, who fish those stocks as they pass through the marine waters. Most such agreements are based on a three-tiered sharing formula, in which different levels of harvestable salmon trigger different proportional shares between groups of tribes. At the lowest level, 85 percent of the fish originating in a particular watershed are allocated to those tribes who have fishing rights in those areas and the intercepting tribes' share is capped at 15 percent. The guiding principle here seems to be a sort of basic-needs version of equity. At the next level of abundance, the additional fish are divided equally between the intercepting tribes and the terminal tribe(s). At the highest level of abundance, the tribes at the terminal areas are again given the lion's share of the additional fish (85 percent), which serves to create incentives for restoring fish habitat (or convincing local governments and landowners to do so) and investing in fish hatcheries.[8]

The tribes recognized very early that they shared an interest in creating and maintaining a supratribal organization that could provide various public goods. The Northwest Indian Fisheries Commission (NWIFC) was created in part to address problems related to the initial asymmetry of information between the tribes and the state. The outcome of bargaining over shares and the timing and duration of fishing regulations often turn on data collection and the ability to justify fish run-size predictions and escapement goals (goals for the number of fish that must be allowed to escape in order to perpetuate the species) based on competing scientific models. While state managers were supposed to provide such information to the tribes, they often did not, and even when they did, the tribes generally felt the data were unreliable. One important function of the NWIFC in the early years of its existence was to enable the tribes to generate their own fish run-size predictions, with which they could challenge state-initiated closures of tribal fisheries. The NWIFC continues to provide information and technical training wherever there are economies of scale, as well as facilitating coordination between different tribes in the areas of data collection, hatchery production, and habitat rehabilitation. This provides the tribes with a source of information for comprehensive, systemwide planning. The NWIFC also monitors and disseminates information about political and economic developments throughout the state that are relevant to fisheries. Perhaps most important in the context of intertribal disputes, NWIFC provides a forum in which tribes can settle differences and arrive at a unified bargaining position prior to entering the yearly cycle of negotiations with the state and other external regulatory agencies. In addition to the NWIFC, several smaller organizations have been created to perform more specialized services for particular subsets of tribes (Pinkerton and Keitlah 1990). Despite the fact that relations between tribes, particularly with respect to the issue of allocating shares of the collective tribal share of the fisheries, are far from harmonious, the tribes have been very successful at solving a variety of collective action problems related to the creation and maintenance of intertribal organizations.

INTERNAL GOVERNANCE

Winning the right to comanage the area's salmon was a great victory for the tribes, but it also presented enormous political challenges. The court granted each tribe the authority to regulate its own fisheries, but this right was conditional on a tribe's being able to demonstrate that it had the necessary technical skills and regulatory and enforcement capability to manage its fisheries in accordance with conservation requirements. Although a few tribes already had fisheries departments, for most this meant the creation of a whole new set of management institutions and supporting infrastructure for the enforcement of tribal fishing regulations. In this, tribal leaders faced formidable challenges. They needed to create a system of regulation and enforcement in a social context in which illegal fishing had been tolerated and even applauded; they had to confront the potentially divisive issue of how tribal membership was to be defined for purposes of fishing rights; and, given the paucity of professionally trained tribal biologists and statisticians, they had to hire predominantly non-Indian professional staffs, while still maintaining democratic accountability and participation. The fishing rights decision, then, was a catalyst for institutional development and change. Just as relations between the tribes and the state were to be significantly altered by joint participation in comanagement, the institutional structures of governance within tribes have also been profoundly changed in this evolutionary process.

Tribal fisheries are unusually diverse, covering the spectrum from traditional river fishermen to those with large gill net or purse seine boats who appear indistinguishable from their nontreaty counterparts. While a few tribes fish only in the rivers, using methods not too dissimilar from those used by their ancestors, most tribes must balance the needs or their set-net and small-boat fishermen with those of the highly efficient, mobile large-boat fleet. The potential for distributional conflict between fishermen using different types of gear is always present, which means that any and all management decisions regarding when or how people can fish are inherently political. Different tribes have experimented with a variety of methods to manage such potential conflicts, including lotteries for some types of in-shore fishing, staggered openings between upriver and downriver sites, and adjustments to the duration of fishing openings to maintain a rough balance between different gear types in the marine waters. The underlying principle that is articulated by fisheries managers is that each group should receive a "fair" opportunity to fish, which in this context appears to mean that no qualified group of fishermen should be excluded from participation in the fishery and that the pattern of intergroup distribution should remain relatively constant from one year to the next.

While the twenty tribes vary widely in terms of the size of their fisheries, the number of tribal members, and the degree of nontribal ownership within reservation boundaries, the institutional structures they have created to manage fisheries share certain key features. The management institutions of most tribes involve three decision-making bodies. The fisheries management staffs, who carry out day-to-day management, are composed of one or more biologists as well as a fisheries director and perhaps several hatchery workers, administrative staff, and enforcement officers. The biologists tend to be non-Indian, while tribal members often hold other positions. There is a convention that tribal members give up fishing while holding jobs in the fisheries department in order to reduce potential conflicts of interest while also spreading economic opportunities through the tribe.

Directing the fisheries staff are two overlapping decision-making bodies. The first is a committee of fishermen, either elected by the fishermen themselves or appointed by the tribal council, who draft regulations regarding when fisheries should be opened or closed, what sort of gear limitations should apply, and how fishing opportunities should be allocated between various types of fishermen. Overseeing both of these is the tribal council, which must approve all fishing regulations, capital projects, or fisheries-related litigation. Practices regarding how decision-making is divided among these three entities vary from tribe to tribe. Some councils work closely with the fisheries staff and fish committees, while others rarely become actively involved. All fish committees rely on the staff to generate various regulatory options, but the extent to which fish committees seek to actively shape fisheries, as opposed to simply choosing between preset alternatives, varies.

The institutional structure achieves a reasonable balance between participatory management and professional expertise. The consensus rule used by the fish committees obviously makes decision-making more time-consuming, but it also ensures that decisions are invested with an added measure of legitimacy. In addition, it gives each member a certain amount of political protection when decisions are expected to be controversial. The fact that the tribal council oversees decision-making by the fisheries department helps to ensure that conservation goals are maintained in the face of pressure by fishermen. And the fact that the fisheries staff is, to some extent, insulated from the socioeconomic concerns that enter into policy decisions helps to maintain the scientific integrity of the information presented to the Fish Commissions and the Tribal Councils. Although there is no tribe in which the system works perfectly, in most cases it works fairly well, and, considering the initial obstacles, the current system is something of a minor miracle.

Conclusion

As the case of the Pacific Northwest salmon fisheries demonstrates, both conflict and cooperation are perennial features of the process through which groups attempt to construct and maintain institutions to manage common pool resources. This is not surprising, given the underlying structure of shared and conflicting interests that exists both within and between communities. Even if we make the unrealistic assumption that individuals are interested solely in material interests, it is obvious that differences that loom large at one level of social relations could be submerged at another. While there is a contingent aspect to the way groups alternately unify and divide, a view of this as primarily opportunistic would be a distortion. Rather, the process seems to reflect the crosscutting nature of social identity and the dynamic process through which social identities are formed and reconstituted. The extent to which groups are able to maintain this sort of balance obviously varies. The skill of political leadership certainly affects the outcome, but outcomes are also affected by historical circumstances—the extent to which cleavages between groups are an integral part of local political culture or, conversely, the extent to which relations within or between groups are open to reinterpretation.

Turning to the issue of conservation, it is clear that large, transboundary ecosystems present especially difficult problems to managers. State agencies and local communities have different interests, and a certain amount of conflict between them is perhaps not undesirable as long as the institutions in place keep it from becoming debilitating. For example, until recently, when the State of Washington Department of Fish and Wildlife began to listen more closely to the warnings of many biologists, the Department had focused on producing the greatest number of fish without too much regard for the individual stocks or breeding populations that make up the genetic building blocks of the system. Individual tribes, on the other hand, were primarily interested in protecting particular stocks because their fisheries are place-bound—they can claim fishing rights only on particular stocks. The result was that because of the legal requirements of the comanagment regime, the state was forced to take account of a set of concerns that it had previously been able to ignore. Eventually the tribal view—that wild stocks, not aggregate numbers of fish—ought to form the focus of management objectives, has come to dominate both tribal and state management.

It is clear that states and local communities can bring different resources to bear on the commons problems such systems engender. For many resource systems, centralized monitoring and enforcement are difficult, costly, and apt to be ineffective, because resource harvesting takes place across a wide area or is hard to monitor for other reasons. There is also often a considerable degree of scientific uncertainty associated with the management of renewable resource systems, and fishermen or other users frequently perceive this as justification for failing to comply with regulations. Eliciting the cooperation of users is probably essential for the successful management of any such system. In the regulatory regime just described, while the parameters of the fishing season are set during prior negotiations between the state and the tribes, the actual fishing regulations are implemented locally. The direct involvement of fishermen means that rules and regulations are accorded greater legitimacy and allows the group's collective capacities to govern itself to be used effectively. Scientific information and scientific methods are disseminated through the day-to-day activities of biologists employed by the tribes and are thus more credible to fishermen. In addition to the formal monitoring system, monitoring is carried out by fishermen themselves who use a number of effective, relatively inexpensive methods to enforce regulations that they find acceptable and to force rule-makers themselves to adhere to norms of fairness. These include name-calling via the short-wave radio as well as other forms of gossip. Given the importance of reputation and mutual aid in what are generally small, fairly close-knit communities, these measures seem fairly effective.

At the same time, Pacific salmon are a transboundary resource, and the conservation of one group can easily be undone by the overexploitation of another. Conservation is not a straightforwardly rational strategy for any particular group or community, since incentives to conserve are continually being undermined by the high degree of uncertainty about the actions of competing users. There are also public good dimensions to the Pacific salmon resource system that extend beyond the immediate region or group of participants. In general, state managers are probably in a better position to uphold conservation standards, since they might be expected to have greater leverage over competing users and greater accountability to broader constituencies.

Tribal-state relations can scarcely be described as being characterized by community, as defined earlier. Nonetheless, tribal and state managers share some beliefs and have certain common, as well as competing, interests, and both sides now have the expectation that they will continue to interact over an extended period of time. This is largely responsible for the profound transformation of state/tribal relations in the period between 1974 and the mid-1990s. Whereas in the early period virtually no management decisions were made without recourse to either a formal dispute mediation or a court hearing, disputes are now normally resolved directly between the parties. While both the timing and duration of fisheries openings was once extremely chaotic and unpredictable, it is now fairly orderly. And where the high costs and potential for conflict once precluded negotiation of any but the narrowest issues, the state and the tribes now engage in mutually beneficial projects in a number of areas—habitat protection, stream assessment and rehabilitation, and so on.

Transboundary resources present very difficult problems to environmental policymakers, and there simply may not be a set of institutional arrangements that will consistently function in an entirely satisfactory way. In the comanagement regime, the differing capacities of centralized state agencies and local community managers are given the freedom to operate. Management objectives are established through a system in which the state and the tribes check and balance each other. In the Byzantine world of piscatorial politics, this is no small accomplishment.

Notes

This chapter is a substantially revised version of an article that appeared originally in the *Journal of Theoretical Politics* (1999) under the title "Commons Problems, Collective Action and Efficiency: Past and Present Institutions of Governance in Pacific Northwest Salmon Fisheries." It is reprinted with the permission of Sage Publications, which is gratefully acknowledged.

1. Successful collective action is, of course, not necessarily good for society as a whole. When firms form cartels and defraud consumers, or white residents band together to resist integration in South Africa (Jung 1998), they obviously possess certain collective capacities, but these capacities are being deployed in ways that fail to meet other important standards.
2. If the state within which a particular community exists is unwilling or unable to

pay the costs of defending a community's property rights, the community will have to defend those rights themselves. Resources with which to do so are, of course, scarce, and community leaders' decisions as to how to allocate such collective resources will be in part determined by the importance placed on the continued availability of the resource system by various constituencies within the community. Thus both internal power distributions and relations with external authorities contribute to how community leaders define goals.

3. The belief that hunting, fishing, etc., have little influence on the subsequent abundance of fish or game, and that to believe otherwise is a somewhat presumptuous misinterpretation of the relationship between humans and wildlife, is not uncommon among traditional people around the world. With similar effect, farmers, fishermen, and other resource users in both rich and poor countries often deny or substantially understate the contribution their own actions make to the deterioration of resource systems.

4. While I am primarily thinking of local users in the sense of people who live in close proximity to a particular resource system or systems, the same facility may be present among people who use a resource system regularly, but not continuously, over an extended period of time such as shifting cultivators, migrant shepherds, or native people of the Northwest Coast of North America, who moved regularly from winter villages to various summer fishing and gathering locations.

5. Many writers have assumed that Coastal Salish customs such as the potlatch or the ceremony that accompanied the arrival of the first salmon in local waters were developed as part of a conscious strategy to manage and conserve salmon (Johnsen 1986). Since I am not convinced that native fishers approached the carrying capacity of salmon stocks except perhaps in a few places along the Columbia River, I find this explanation for such practices unconvincing.

6. It is also true that the minority of fishermen with large gill net or purse seine boats take the largest share of the treaty catch. This pattern of a small number of fishermen harvesting the majority of available fish appears in nearly all commercial fisheries.

7. The principle of balancing the treaty/nontreaty catch on a river-by-river basis, rather than in the aggregate, was established in a case brought by a coastal tribe with limited UAPs after a year in which the PFMC regulatory process had resulted in its receiving no fishing opportunities at all. Under the present regime, the regulatory agencies must negotiate with each tribe, rather than lumping all tribal shares together and negotiating with the tribes collectively.

8. At the time, increasing the production of hatchery fish was thought to be a good thing for everyone, since once a fish is released into the wild, it increases the number of fish available to all. Fish hatcheries have subsequently fallen into disfavor because hatcheries stocks are now known to displace wild stocks, either through predation, disease, or competition for food or habitat.

Bibliography

Acheson, James M. 1987. "The Lobster Fiefs, Revisited: Economic and Ecological Effects of Territoriality in the Maine Lobster Industry." In *The Question of the Commons*, ed. Bonnie J. McCay and James M. Acheson, 37–65. Tucson: University of Arizona Press.

Baland, Jean-Marie, and Jean-Philippe Platteau. 1996. *Halting Land Degradation of Natural Resources: Is There a Role for Rural Communities?* Oxford, U.K.: Clarendon Press.

————. 1999. "The Ambiguous Impact of Inequality on Local Resource Management." *World Development* 27(5):773–788.

Bowles, Samuel. 1999. "Social Capital' and Community Governance." Unpublished paper. Amherst: University of Massachusetts Press.

Cohen, Fay G. 1986. *Treaties on Trial: The Continuing Controversy over Northwest Indian Fishing Rights.* Seattle: University of Washington Press.

Ellickson, Robert C. 1989. "A Hypothesis of Wealth-Maximizing Norms: Evidence from the Whaling Industry." *Journal of Law, Economics and Organization* 5:83–97.

————. 1991. *Order Without Law: How Neighbors Settle Disputes.* Cambridge, Mass.: Harvard University Press.

Feeny, David, Fikret Berkes, Bonnie J. McCay, and James M. Acheson. 1990. "The Tragedy of the Commons: Twenty-two Years Later." *Human Ecology* 18:1–19.

Johnsen, D. Bruce. 1986. "The Formation and Protection of Property Rights among the Southern Kwakiutl Indians." *Journal of Legal Studies* 15:41–67.

Johnson, Ronald N., and Gary D. Libecap. 1982. "Contracting Problems and Regulation: The Case of the Fishery." *American Economic Review* 72:1005–1022.

Jung, Courtney. 1998. "Community Is the Foundation of Democracy: But What If Your Community Looks Like This?" Paper presented at American Political Science Association meeting, 1998, Washington, D.C.

Knight, Jack. 1992. *Institutions and Social Conflict.* New York: Cambridge University Press.

McKean, Margaret A. 1982. "The Japanese Experience with Scarcity: Management of Traditional Common Lands." *Environmental Review* 6(2):63–88.

————. 1986. "Management of Traditional Common Lands (*Iriaichi*) in Japan." In *Proceedings of the Conference on Common Property Resource Management,* 533–589. Washington, D.C.: National Academy Press.

Netting, Robert McC. 1981. *Balancing on an Alp.* New York: Cambridge University Press.

Olson, Mancur. 1965. *The Logic of Collective Action.* Cambridge, Mass.: Harvard University Press.

Ostrom, Elinor. 1990. *Governing the Commons: The Evolution of Institutions for Collective Action.* New York: Cambridge University Press.

Pinkerton, Evelyn, ed. 1989. *Cooperative Management of Local Fisheries: New Directions for Improved Management and Community Development.* Vancouver: University of British Columbia Press.

Pinkerton, Evelyn, and Nelson Keitlah. 1990. "The Point No Point Treaty Council Innovation by an Inter-tribal Fisheries Management Cooperative." University of British Columbia Planning Papers Series No. 26, School of Community and Regional Planning, University of British Columbia, Vancouver, B.C.

Scott, James C. 1987. *Weapons of the Weak.* New Haven, Conn.: Yale University Press.

Singleton, Sara. 1998. *The Construction of Cooperation: The Evolution of Institutions of Comanagement.* Ann Arbor: University of Michigan Press.

————. 1999. "Commons Problems, Collective Action and Efficiency: Past and Present Institutions of Governance in Pacific Northwest Salmon Fisheries." *Journal of Theoretical Politics* 11(3):367–391.

————. 2000. "Cooperation or Capture? The Paradox of Co-management and Community Participation in Natural Resource Management and Environment Policymaking." *Environmental Politics* 9(2):1–21.

Taylor, Michael. 1982. *Community, Anarchy and Liberty.* New York: Cambridge University Press.

Chapter 6	Boundary Work
TANIA MURRAY LI	*Community, Market,* *and State Reconsidered*

MY CONTRIBUTION TO THIS VOLUME is an exercise in critical "boundary work" that challenges the assumed separation between communities and what lies beyond them. By positing a boundary, advocates of community-based conservation constitute community as a unit of analysis and action. This conceptual move is not, in my view, a simplification made in error or oversight; it is crucial to the ways in which communities figure in conservation agendas. It therefore requires serious scrutiny. Here I focus attention upon the ways in which boundaries are constructed, the purposes they serve, the processes they obscure, and the consequences that ensue. Community is not an easy concept to analyze in this way, because as Raymond Williams (1976, 66) points out, there is no positive, opposing term on the other side of the boundary. Most often, community is counterposed to market and state, and these are therefore the relevant relational categories that situate, and that must be examined together with, community.[1]

In the first part of this chapter, I undertake such boundary work at a conceptual level, drawing upon a range of theoretical literature and ethnographic illustrations from several contexts. In the second part, I focus upon an area of Central Sulawesi, Indonesia, in which indigenous farmers in a rather densely populated, deforested mountain area relatively remote from centers of state power might be expected to be ideal or even natural subjects for community-based resource management. As it turns out, neither community nor conservation are especially self-evident. Whatever the idiosyncrasies of this particular locale, it serves the important purpose of disrupting associations that are too easily taken for granted, thereby exposing processes and relationships too often overlooked.

Key Words

The idea of community as a bounded entity both separate and distinct from that which lies outside is deeply embedded in our language, imagery, and practices. Even when it is recognized that the "local" and the "community" are constituted in intimate interactions with the "global," the "state," and the "market," the notion that there is a boundary separating internal from external is reinscribed. This may be unavoidable, since distinctions between state and community are embedded in the language and concepts we have available to us, as well as the images associated with these terms.[2] While scare quotes can be used to indicate that the key words are recognized as problematic, they also indicate that these words cannot be readily abandoned. One central reason for retaining the concept of community is the political potency of the notion. It is a key term invoked in struggles over resources that are also, simultaneously, struggles over meaning and identity, and that occur at a range of levels and sites, from the local to the global.[3] Moreover, the imagined community of the nation or ethnic group that is experienced as "a sense of belonging together," a "feeling of solidarity," or "understanding of shared identity" is produced, in part at least, through the naturalization of arbitrary boundaries (Brow 1990). When boundaries are simultaneously constructed and occluded, this is politics at work, not coincidence.

A useful starting point for boundary work is Doreen Massey's (1993, 66) attempt to conceptualize community or place in terms that emphasize connection rather than separation: "What gives a place its specificity is not some long internalized history but the fact that it is constructed out of a particular constellation of relations, articulated together at a particular locus."[4] At the level of theory, this formulation is very persuasive, and it accords with the current emphasis in anthropology upon the connectedness of people, places, and ideas (e.g., Comaroff and Comaroff 1992; Gupta and Ferguson 1992; Roseberry 1989; Wolf 1982). It seems likely that it also accords with many rural people's experience of living in the world, where prices, wages, remittances, the comings and goings of kin, school exam results, national election campaigns, taxes, policemen, and identity cards figure at least as large as earth and plants.[5] But it is not the notion of community that underlies the classical literature examined by Agrawal and Gibson in their introduction to this volume, nor is it the one behind current attempts to promote community-based resource management. The communities literature, old and new, shares a vision in which state and market processes impinge upon communities from the outside. It does not envision a countryside characterized by processes of state formation and market involvement that are articulated into unique but provisional constellations at particular places. Despite disclaimers to the contrary, the community as a domain separate from, and counterposed to, market and state continually reasserts itself. How does this happen, and what are the consequences for understanding and addressing the predicaments of rural people in relation to resources?

SUBSISTENCE

"Subsistence" is one key term that makes, marks, and maintains a boundary. It is used in discussions of rural development to suggest that the social and economic life of (some) rural folk is both different from that of the encompassing system, and isolated from it. Like the term "community," "subsistence" is seriously underspecified in the literature on resource use and conservation. Often a simplified market/subsistence dichotomy is deployed but not discussed, even when de facto crossings are observed: markets intruding into communities, subsistence producers selling goods and labor. A label is used as a substitute for empirical analysis (Carrier 1992). The term has several referents: livelihoods that barely meet the minimum requirements for survival; livelihoods that are acquired (with greater or lesser adequacy) primarily outside market relationships; also, when framed as subsistence orientation, it refers to a cultural style or way of life characterized by limited material needs and desires, in which increased production and prosperity are apparently of low priority. Critical scrutiny of each of these meanings provides a window on the ways in which community is both differentiated and separated from what lies beyond.

If poverty is the main feature of communities labeled subsistence, then subsistence can be denaturalized by tracing the historical trajectory through which such poverty has been generated. Poor people, rather than being without history, may have had all too much exposure to world economic processes. The experiences of Kalahari San are a case in point. A generation of researchers read them as original hunter-gatherers, and explained their social organization and livelihood practices in terms of adaptation to the desert environment (Lee and DeVore 1976). But recent historical studies have shown that their ancestors were herders and laborers, and some were also miners, craftsmen, and traders, active participants in a mixed regional economy (Gordon 1992; Wilmsen 1989). They were relegated to their "subsistence" niche in the course of a vicious colonial program of genocide, enslavement, and land appropriation, and kept there in the postcolonial period by both

Tswana and donor racism, paternalism, and neglect (Hitchcock and Holm 1993). Similarly in Amazonia, the image of natural natives living in a state of nature (and poverty) arose only after precolonial trade and production had been eliminated, and people once forced to labor in the rubber sector were ejected back into the forest to which, it was conveniently assumed, they properly belonged (Fisher 1996). In Indonesia, too, the poverty and isolation that resulted from the economic and political dislocations of colonial rule have been interpreted, incorrectly, as prior natural states. In several highland areas lively and diverse regional economic systems were eliminated by the Dutch in the course of their efforts to impose coffee production. Later, after coffee's demise, during a period of world market depression, highland regions began to take on the characteristics usually assumed to be typical of subsistence farming systems: household-based enterprises working tiny plots of marginal land, growing food for home consumption and producing for the market only sporadically (Hefner 1990; Kahn 1993). Only when such regional histories are ignored can so-called subsistence farming, together with isolation and poverty, be interpreted as the natural or normal condition of rural economic life.

The second feature associated with subsistence economies, relative isolation from markets, even in the contemporary period, is also problematic. Many discussions of rural livelihoods from a conservation perspective underestimate the extent and nature of market involvements, or assume them to be recent accretions to a more fundamental subsistence base. Perhaps this occurs because conservationists, who are primarily interested in the condition of natural resources, focus their attention upon activities relating directly to those resources, such as fodder and fuel collection, or farming. Components of the local economy that are not directly resource dependent, or that take place in a broader arena, may therefore be overlooked. Local wage work and short- or long-term labor migration are important examples. The use of a "green lens" (Zerner 1994) not only leads to the interpretation of ritual activities in a functional, conservationist light, it also highlights those economic activities that fit assumptions about communities in harmony with their environment while obscuring others that are environmentally harmful and/or market based. For example, Borneo Dayaks are best known in the environmentalist literature for their swidden rice system, and not for the forest-products trade, migrant labor, or smallholder rubber production that have been crucial to their livelihoods over the centuries (Healey 1985; Sellato 1994). Similarly, in the Garhwal Himalayas, international fascination with Chipko and forest conservation has obscured the significance of market-oriented activities, including the sale of timber, in local livelihoods (Rangan 1993).

Ironically, the recognition that communities have been in contact with outsiders and engaged in trade and exchange since ancient times may also support conservationist imaginings, since it seems to confirm that market engagement (past or present) does not necessarily undermine sustainable resource management. This outcome is explained by drawing upon another meaning of subsistence, framed in this case as "subsistence orientation." This phrase is usually used to describe a cultural milieu or way of life less driven by economic ambition and the search for increasing productivity and profit. The implication is that people in communities must be satisfied with the (often marginal) economic niches to which they have been assigned. This idea is implicit in conservationist agendas that propose that minor forest products be promoted to meet the (limited) income needs of forest-dwelling people (Dove 1993a). Critiquing this logic, which he dubs "rainforest crunch," Michael Dove points out that those who lack power are excluded from enjoyment of the most profitable forest product (timber), and punished for converting land to export-oriented tree crop production (Dove 1993b). If and when the land or some minor forest product become especially profitable, these too are usually taken away from categories of people whose poverty renders them ineligible as beneficiaries. Therefore, according to Dove, the "search for 'new' sources of income for 'poor forest dwellers' is often, in reality, a search for opportunities that have no other claimants—a search for unsuccessful development alternatives" (1993a, 18). Poverty, powerlessness, and exclusion from valuable resources are integrally related. Such economic and political linkages are obscured when forest communities are viewed through a lens that stresses subsistence and implies that marginality is an elected way of life.

The cultural definition of needs and wants is, in part, a reflection of what is possible under existing constraints. It is also a reflection of desire mediated by the imagined community to which an individual belongs. This point is made very clearly in Robert Hefner's (1990) study of mountain Java. Villagers growing vegetables on steep slopes witnessed erosion on a scale that would make any type of farming difficult or impossible for the next generation, yet they persisted. Tengger highlanders show few signs of being naturally ecological peasants, but they cannot be dismissed as simply greedy or foolish. Their actions make sense when considered in relation to an arena of want formation that is not limited to the immediate locale. Tengger highlanders imagine a future in which they participate, together with lowlanders and city folk, in an increasingly generic, nationwide, middle-class consumption style. Many Tengger highlanders do not anticipate a future in the hills. They are counting on intensive (and destructive) vegetable production to pay for their children's education and to launch them on nonagrarian careers, preferably in the bureaucracy. Conservationist agendas that assume that mountain farmers have (or should have) subsistence goals can neither explain nor alter this scenario.

Questioning subsistence and examining the nature of rural people's engagement with the market has important implications for practical agendas concerned with conservation. Rural lives and livelihoods are not constituted in opposition to or isolation from market processes. It cannot be assumed that the direct use of resources (including labor) has priority over their exchange or sale, or that resource management decisions will reflect a long-term view. For rural people as for urbanites, cost-benefit analysis is an everyday matter to which conservation agendas must respond. Unexamined assumptions about the subsistence-and-conservation priorities of farmers, and the overwhelming conservation preoccupations of outsiders, have resulted in the promotion of agroforestry programs whose economic potential is unproven (Enters 1994). In Thailand, for example, those who adopted alley cropping did not experience the increases in production that were promised, and found their fields invaded by grasses or ravaged by wild animals seeking easy forage. Resistors therefore limited their participation to a "token line" designed to please outsiders and/or avoid sanctions (Enters 1995). In the similar case of the Philippines, Elaine Brown (1994, 56) describes the vigor with which non-government and government agencies have promoted "sloping land agricultural technology" (SALT) and the reluctance of upland people to adopt it, presumably because it does not benefit them. Even agroforestry programs that are successful in economic terms can fail to meet the conservation objectives of their proponents. A major agroforestry program in Indonesia was designed on the assumption that increased profitability of tree-crops (through improved seed stock and marketing) would relieve pressure on neighboring forests. However, instead of sitting back when their (supposedly limited) needs were met, farmers responded to the new opportunities by expanding their production into the forests, and migrants (not necessarily poor ones) were also attracted into the area (Angelsen 1995; Tomich and Noordwijk 1995). These are not exceptional situations, and it is not clear that they can be rectified by better technologies and program incentives. They are the predictable outcomes of changing patterns of production and the dynamics of culture and class in many, if not most, rural areas.

Only when communities are imagined as distinctive kinds of places, characterized by subsistence (poverty, limited market involvement, and limited wants), can they be charged with responsibility for conserving resources that other, more powerful players (states, corporations, large landowners) located outside communities are free to exploit. The logic of biodiversity conservation suggests that they may also be made responsible for species that they do not regard as *resources* at all (Leach et al., 1997), because they figure only marginally in their repertoire of livelihood sources, or are irrelevant to the long-term futures that they imagine and toward which they strive. In some instances, the environmental threat that appears to demand a conservation response may itself be exaggerated, misperceived, or even fabricated (Enters 1994; Leach and Fairhead 1994). Unless outsider-driven efforts to design better resource management institutions are clearly rooted in local priorities, they will fail to find the active, concerned local constituency that the notion of community seems to guarantee.

Conservationists have turned to communities not only because of their location, close to particular resources, but because there is a hope and/or an assumption that they are (to varying degrees) different in their practices, motivations, or aspirations from the world beyond. The idea of difference depends upon a boundary separating inside from outside. The discourse that relates communities to subsistence (or even "livelihoods," a term that can carry some of the same baggage) permits and accomplishes the necessary separation. Conservationists can acknowledge that coercive measures will fail where they threaten subsistence and everyday livelihood, but they are more reluctant to acknowledge that rural people may also resist conservation measures for reasons that are very much like those of urbanites (including ourselves): convenience, greed, or the desire to catch up with, or get ahead of, others near and far.

THE STATE

Many advocates for communities in conservation are aware that conservation seldom comes naturally and does not inhere in any particular identifiable group, hence their insistence upon the need for regulatory institutions, rules, and enforcement At this point, it is necessary to turn to questions of power, and to the marking of the boundary between community and state. Like the market, the state is a shadowy, underspecified, and apparently external factor for the communities that are the subject of conservation initiatives. Even when there is a recognition of the myriad ways in which states and communities are not only mutually implicated, but in some respects (and for some purposes), inseparable, the use of hybrid terms such as "semiautonomous" reinstates boundaries even as it problematizes them.

What is the work accomplished by positing a boundary between community and state? In much of the literature cited in the introduction to this volume, the marking of a boundary between state and community is more than a convenience: it is intrinsic to the narrative that links community to conservation. The central proposition of this literature is that, since states have failed to manage or conserve resources, then communities—outside or at least operating differently from states—offer an alternative. If it is states that spoiled previously existing local resource management regimes, then the withdrawal of states, their devolution of control and authority to communities (or local institutions), is the solution. This particular development narrative or "cultural script for action" (Hoben 1995, 1008; Leach et al. 1997) is more plausible than one based on the conundrum of market involvement: states can (perhaps) be persuaded to back away from or move out of communities, leaving people happier as well as more effective in conservation. In contrast, policies directed at restricting the market involvement of rural people are, by and large, ineffective and intensely unpopular (cf. Dove 1993b). Perhaps it is for this reason that "the state,"[6] more often than the market, stands as the proxy for whatever is outside the boundary of community.[7]

Yet this narrative begs important questions about the relationship between state-systems and rural populations. Many of the small-scale population units that are viewed as communities do not exist (structurally at least) outside or counterposed to an external state: They are units of local government. Therefore, the development of new institutions that allocate more control over resources and management authority to local units cannot really be seen as the transfer of power from state to community, envisaged as separate entities. It is more useful to regard such measures as rearrangements of the ways in which rule is accomplished (Corrigan 1994).[8] If local administrative units are set up so that, singly or in federations, they have the (apparent) autonomy to bargain or cooperate with "the state," or even to struggle against it, this has to be seen (paradoxically perhaps) as an arrangement internal to the structure of the state-system. To appreciate this point it is necessary to abandon the idea of an urban or extravillage location of the state, and explore the ways in which state power is generated and actualized in rural settings (Hirsch 1989, 35).

Territorialization is one mechanism through which state institutions attempt to assert control over rural citizens and natural resources. According to Vandergeest and Peluso (1995, 387), "all modern states divide their territories into complex and overlapping political and economic zones, rearrange people and resources within these units, and create regulations delineating how and by whom these areas can be used." Territorialization has been a project of both colonial and postcolonial regimes. Particular territorializing initiatives may stem from a search for profit by favored elites, for tax revenues to support administrative systems, or from the need to assert state authority in areas that, although they may lie clearly within national boundaries, are not fully enmeshed in state-defined institutions and processes. Always ongoing and incomplete, territorializing initiatives are commonly contested by the populace. Moreover, they involve many government departments, each with different and possibly conflicting approaches. Strategies for increased control may include privatizing natural resources (within state-defined frameworks) or direct state management; encouraging settlement in unpopulated areas or forbidding settlement and enforcing exclusion; centralizing administrative authority or devolving authority to lower levels. The making of maps, the conduct of censuses, the drawing up of village boundaries and lists, classification and staking of forests can all be seen as measures to define, regulate, and assert control over the relationship between population and resources.

In view of the long history of territorializing projects in most parts of the world, the status of communities that appear to be autonomous from the state formations in which they are located requires careful scrutiny. For example in Indonesia, contrary to the assumption that orderly, homogeneous villages are a natural feature of the Javanese landscape, Jan Breman argues that Dutch colonial policy itself created the peasant village. This was accomplished by pinning hitherto rather mobile people down into households and villages, surveying land, fixing and enforcing local administrative boundaries, and representing the result in maps, lists, and censuses (Breman 1980, 9–14, 1988; Kemp 1991). The colonial regime also took measures to cut off the personalized chains of command, extraction, and cooperation that previously linked rural people to patrons located elsewhere, thereby increasing the density of localized interactions and concentrating relations of face-to-face dependency within the village. As a result, the village, constituted by the state, came to take on an appearance of completeness or autonomy, while the colonial regime, its power instantiated, consolidated, and occluded through these very arrangements, appeared to be ever more separate, more abstract (Abrams 1988; Mitchell 1991). Similarly, in Indonesia's uplands and interiors, there is mounting evidence (e.g., Kahn 1993; Tsing 1993) that both colonial and postcolonial regimes have been deeply implicated in the formation of communities (sometimes envisaged as tribes) that advocates (Lynch and Talbott 1995; Moniaga 1993) present as sites for preservation or restoration of autonomous, community-based institutions.

It is important to recall Vandergeest and Peluso's caveats about the unfinished and contested nature of territorializing processes. Sometimes, attempts to intensify rule produce unintended effects: vigorous communities constituting themselves in opposition to state projects deemed contrary to local interests. Produced by the state (in part at least), such communities can hardly be seen as external to it, yet they can be actively engaged in obstructing, subverting, or otherwise undermining particular state agendas. They may use the powers vested in one state institution against another. Rural people comfortable with the official framework of rural administration may also organize themselves into groups (of a partial and contingent kind) in order to advance particular projects and oppose others (Leach et al. 1997, 7) and they routinely present their claims in a rhetoric of community, invoking as appropriate the local, national, and global resonances of that term (Li 1996a; Nugent and Alonso 1994). They may seek access to state resources or oppose state projects, including those framed as community-based conservation. Such processes cannot be grasped when community and state are viewed as separate and opposed entities.

The effects of the decentralization measures proposed by community advocates as a mechanism to roll back state power and strengthen communities need to be carefully considered. These measures have the capacity to further state territorialization projects and provide various other opportunities (e.g., through bureaucratic expansion, donor funding, international legitimation) for the intensification of rule. One possibility for intensified rule arises directly from the nexus of knowledge and power (Davies 1994; Escobar 1984–85; Foucault 1981). A state agency charged with responsibility for designing, supporting, and monitoring formal institutions for local resource management must become engaged in the collection, codification, and cataloguing of ever more finely grained information. Some advocates suggest that every aspect of society, including class, gender, ethnic differences, local histories, conflicts, and, of course, patterns of resource use and access, is relevant to the design of appropriate institutions. Such information must then be represented in standard formats, if institutionalization is to occur. When complexity is reduced to standardized bits of information, resources and resource users are rendered amenable to management and planning (Escobar 1984–85, 1992). Information "gathering," planning, and the design of institutions are simultaneously instances of, and vehicles for, the exercise of power. Moreover, critics of development suggest that the power-laden effects of information-and-planning operations are the same whether they are undertaken by state institutions directly, or by other "external agents" working for, with, or around state authorities (Ferguson 1994; Rahnema 1992). Planning itself *is* political. So too is surveillance, which increases in intensity the more local the watchdogs.

Note that new institutional arrangements that enmesh the countryside more deeply in state systems of information and control are not necessarily a bad thing for the rural people involved. In many cases, these are engagements that they seek. Just as state power is not absolute, it must be stressed that it is not necessarily malevolent: Territorialization, for example, is a normal activity of modern state systems, not one peculiar to oppressive regimes. Environmentalists and supporters of peasant struggles who assume that "traditional communities" are inclined to oppose "the state" in order to preserve "their own" institutions and practices may overlook the extent to which rural people seek the benefits of a fuller citizenship. As others have also noted, the oppositional characterization of "virtuous peasants" and "vicious states" (Bernstein 1990, 71) fails to do justice to the complexities of state-formation and associated class structuring processes (Hart 1989; Nugent 1994). It neglects also the claims upon the state-system for access to modernity that characterize many peasant and indigenous people's movements (Schuurman 1993, 27), just as others reject and resist state imperatives.

New institutional arrangements, of the kinds proposed by Agrawal and Gibson in the introduction to this volume, could open up opportunities for the advancement of local agendas. Democratic spaces and procedures may be designed into the institutions themselves. Alternatively, or in addition, unplanned opportunities for popular mobilization or strategic action by particular social groups or individuals may arise around the edges and in the gaps and fissures between levels and branches of government, especially in the course of adjustment to new roles and modes of operation. In these ways, institutional innovations may bring about a shift in power in the sense of rechanneling, diverting, or reconfiguring power and tying it up in new knots. The overall result, however, is unlikely to amount to the kind of transfer envisaged by advocates who would like to see power moving across a boundary from state to community. By problematizing the boundary that appears to separate communities from states, it is possible to assess both the promise and the limitation of efforts to engage with power through the development and reform of institutions.

Constellations of Relations at a Particular Place

The critical boundary work I am attempting in this chapter can be deepened by a sustained illustration. The problem of boundaries looms large in the hills of Sulawesi where I have been carrying out research since 1990. It is a place in which it is not obvious who or what should count as a community, nor is it easy to imagine what community-based resource management is, or could become, in that context. By describing this place, which may perhaps be an unusual one, I hope to problematize some of the features that seem to be natural (and therefore invisible, taken for granted) in other places where the existence of community is more apparent. There is space for only a summary outline here, and I refer the reader to other work in which I have explored some of these issues in more detail.

COMMUNITIES AS NATURAL UNITS?

How communities are formed is a question routinely asked about migrant populations, but less often posed in relation to indigenous farmers, especially those
occupying forested or hilly terrain relatively remote from centers of state
power. For such people, it is often assumed that the coincidence of kinship,
geography, language, culture, and modes of livelihood yields communities
"naturally" in place. But the Lauje people, currently numbering about thirty
thousand, who occupy the hilly interior and the narrow coastal strip to the
north of the Tomini Bay, do not appear to view themselves, or to be organized
or treated, as a community in the two most familiar senses: as a bounded ethnic
group with a shared culture, or as villages or neighborhoods. They are concentrated in the present-day districts of Tomini and Tinombo, but their numbers
shade off gradually along the coast in both directions. Their language shades
into Tiaolo and Tajio, the languages of their neighbors. No strongly ethnicizing
or demarcating signs have been articulated to mark the borders of the Lauje
domain. Nor has there been an influx of neighboring groups or more distant
outsiders into the hills to provoke the articulation and defense of ethnic
boundaries associated with claims to a specific territory (Li 1997, 2000). The
bilateral kinship system produces overlapping kindreds rather than bounded
descent groups, and people are active in tracing kinship links wherever they
travel in the hills. Flexible arrangements for access to land encourage people to
move on to better terrain when their current swiddens are worn out, although
few people alive today have ever cleared primary forest. Finally, the preference
of people to live at some remove from kin and neighbors leads to a pattern of
residence in which single family households are scattered across the hillsides,
sometimes clustered in groups of three or four, but seldom collected into a unit
that resembles, or is regarded as a hamlet, still less a village.

In many contexts, the articulation of an ethnic or community identity is
facilitated by the local elite, eager to assert group pride vis-à-vis others. This
has not occurred in the Lauje case. According to Nourse's (1999) account of
local history, in precolonial times, most Lauje kept to the hills for fear of slave
raiders and pirates, although they traded jungle produce, and those occupying
the drier lower slopes produced tobacco for regional markets. Lauje who
moved down to the coast during the nineteenth century constituted themselves as a class of aristocrats, and intermarried with traders originating from
other coastal regions of Sulawesi (Kaili, Bugis, Mandar, and Gorontalo).
There is no evidence that this coastal elite exercised direct control over the
hinterland, deriving their wealth instead through the familiar practice of
trade monopoly. Those with Lauje ancestry allied themselves with the more

powerful outsiders and, increasingly, defined their identity in terms of Islam. Although literate, especially in this century, few have shown any interest in articulating a specifically Lauje identity, and most regard their shared ancestry with the heathen and backward interior as a source of embarrassment (Nourse, 1994, 1999). The geopolitics are such that coastal Lauje share the economic fate of the hill people only indirectly (through trade), and do not identify with their everyday lives or concerns. Most coastal Lauje have never hiked into the hills, and have only vague (and usually quite inaccurate) ideas about how people live there. Coastal elites tend to be preoccupied with securing linkages to other powerful coastal places and cities, and are not engaged in projects intended to consolidate a distinctive Lauje identity or sense of community at home.

STATE INTERACTIONS AND COMMUNITY FORMATION

There are few, if any places on earth that are autonomous from the state systems of the nations in which they are located, although the intensity of state efforts to enmesh rural populations has varied according to the geopolitical significance of the area and the resources involved. State intervention in rural areas, rather than destroying or undermining communities, has been a significant factor in community formation. It follows that where state attention is weak or absent, communities are not strongly formed.

The Lauje area was of only peripheral interest to the Dutch. It contained little natural wealth, and the coastal elites were quiescent and easily coopted, posing no threat to Dutch authority. A halfhearted attempt was made early this century to move the interior population to the coast, but it was clear that they could not survive on the resources of the narrow coastal strip, and they were soon allowed to return to their scattered hillside homes. Some served occasional corvee duty, working on the construction of the coastal road and bridges, while others moved farther inland to evade such obligations. Dutch revenues from the area, such as they were, came from taxing the owners of coconut groves planted along the coast at Dutch insistence.

Rule over the interior was indirect, via coastal chiefs, and it was relatively light. The minimal obligation of the coastal chiefs toward their Dutch overlords was to keep peace in the interior, and prevent feuding and bloodshed. The standard model for governing the interior, both in the colonial period and still today, has been to select highlanders of renown, people who appear to command respect, and make them responsible for maintaining order over "their" people. This is a task such so-called leaders have found onerous, since they had few routinized forms of authority over their mountain peers, merely personal charisma and the powers of persuasion. While in some areas of Indonesia the Dutch were active in discovering, constituting, or recording traditional law as a vehicle for rule, they did not bother with the Lauje. As a result, Lauje identity and traditions remained ad hoc and dynamic, with their "customary" law generated anew upon each encounter, much in the way that Tsing (1993) has described as happening in the Meratus hills of Kalimantan. Individuals are appointed by coastal authorities to adjudicate marriage arrangements and local disputes in the vicinity of their hillside homes, although their areas of jurisdiction are only vaguely defined. These so-called customary or *adat* chiefs have never been formed into a central council that pontificates on the traditions and customary law of the Lauje people. Nor do they have much sense of Lauje adat or tradition as something distinctive, autochthonous, or essential to Lauje identity. Several adat chiefs I spoke to in various parts of the hills are of the opinion that, to the extent that they adhere to any fixed procedures and fines, these were established and given to them by the government, personified by the headman of the local administrative unit, the *desa*. They regard their authority to settle disputes as a power granted by the village administration, ultimately backed by the civil, police, and military authorities of the district.

For their part the desa headmen, all of whom belong to the coastal elite, routinely ignore the people in the interior. They encounter them in the coastal markets, and know a few by name, but are not much concerned about ordering their lives. They deal with them most directly during election campaigns, since they are responsible to the ruling party for delivering the vote. They find exercises such as census-taking extremely onerous, requiring effort disproportionate to the rewards received, and they generally invent the population, production, and other data that they are expected to file with their superiors. They have been under pressure to collect taxes on hillside land, but uncertainty about the legal status of the land (which is customary property within official state forest boundaries) and the concern that, even if owners are registered, they will not pay up, makes it more convenient to leave land and people alone. The hill people whose land is registered have come forward voluntarily, in the hope of increasing their tenure security vis-à-vis the state but also, and often more significantly, vis-à-vis their kin and neighbors.[9] What exists, then, is a situation in which the state institutions designed to monitor populations and order their relationship to natural resources are present, but not well developed. However, their underdevelopment is a result of limited state investment in territorialization, not opposition from a preformed community already in place.

SUBSISTENCE ISOLATION OR MARKET ENGAGEMENT?

The Lauje hills remain, by Indonesian standards, rather inaccessible. They are connected to the coast only by rough foot trails. On one of the rivers it is possible to float rafts downstream; going upstream it is necessary to ford the rivers multiple times, hazardous or impossible when they are high, and particularly dangerous when there are flash floods originating from the headwaters. This is perhaps the kind of place where one might expect to encounter so-called subsistence farmers, only weakly connected to coastal marketplaces and to regional and international trade systems. But this is not the case. The people living farthest inland in the most inaccessible places (about six to sixteen hours' hike) have long gathered forest products for sale to merchants on the coast, and purchased items they regard as essential (clothing, salt, knife and axe blades) as well as a growing list of luxuries (sugar, dried fish, coconut oil, kerosene, flashlights and batteries, pressure lamps, and cassette players). They grow their own staples (maize, tubers, rice) and sell these on the coast if they need cash urgently enough to make the effort of carrying these bulky products worthwhile. In the middle hills (two to six hours' hike) they have grown shallots, garlic, and groundnuts for at least fifty years, and frequently buy staples to supplement their own production. For at least two hundred years, farmers in the dry foothills have produced tobacco for regional trade on a scale significant enough to be noted in Dutch sources (Nourse 1999).

Besides cash crops, wage labor away from home is a very significant income source for Lauje men.[10] Between about 1920 and 1980, they were recruited in large numbers to extract ebony for city-based merchants. Mechanisms of labor recruitment included the need to pay head taxes, the use of cash advances, and the institutionalization of gambling. Since about 1980, ebony has been replaced by rattan as the premier export, making the headwaters of the Lauje river system and the neighboring, less populated areas very busy and crowded places. When returns to labor have been good, some men have not bothered to clear gardens at all, leaving their wives to farm in second- or third-year swiddens or to beg for cleared land from neighbors and kin.[11]

Since the early 1990s, cloves, cocoa, cashews, and kapok have been planted on hillside land by the residents and by coastal people who are beginning, for the first time, to take a direct interest in the resources of the interior. In order to accommodate these new crops, hillside residents have enclosed and effectively privatized the swidden land to which they formerly held undivided rights with the other descendants of the ancestor who first cleared it. In some cases, they have sold land and trees to outsiders (Li 1996a, 1997). But, in view of the history of market involvement I have described, as well as the active role of Lauje people in bringing about these changes, it makes little sense to regard the ensuing transformations as the result of capitalism or the penetration of market forces into communities from the outside. Now, as in the past, it makes more sense to acknowledge that people live in these places because of the productive possibilities they present, including those that involve markets.

SACRED TIES AND CONSERVATION?

As long as anyone can remember, the value of land and other natural resources has been assessed in relation to the goods they can produce, whether for immediate use or sale. Although individuals who sell land are regarded as feckless and foolish, or sometimes just unfortunate, I am not aware that they are seen to be transgressing some sacred tie between Lauje people, singly or collectively, and the land upon which they live and work. To make space for cocoa, some high-risk areas such as steep riverbanks have been cleared, but again, the critique of neighbors is that the effort will probably be wasted when the young trees together with the field slide down into the river. No sacred sanctions or environmental ethic are involved. There are taboos against cutting particular large trees, usually a small stand on the ridge of a hill, but the reasons for this are again pragmatic: The spirits living in those trees are capable of causing illness, death, and destruction. Even so, some of these trees have been cut, and if no disasters befall, the person who cut them is invited to clear other trees on the principle that his power must be greater than that of the relevant spirits, or his magic sufficient to placate them.

In terms of imagined futures, many Lauje living in the hills dream of a time when they can move down to the coast and have the pleasure of eating rice and fresh fish daily. Others say they prefer to live in the hills where the air is cool and they can farm, but they would like to have a house down below to use on market days, to show that they are the class equals of the coastal people who have long despised them. They are attached to the places where they were born and have grown up, to the trees and graves of ancestors, and to the pleasures of living close to kin and good neighbors. But, as far as I can tell, their attachments do not amount to boundaries, to a sense of a distinct community separate from, or opposed to, that which lies beyond.

FORMING COMMUNITIES FOR "DEVELOPMENT"

Contrary to the usual narrative that views communities as natural units subject to penetration by states, it is the increased interaction between state institutions and hillside residents in the context of recent "development" initiatives that has led the formation of more distinct, bounded units at the neighborhood level. In many parts of Indonesia, especially in upland areas where territorializing processes have been increasing in intensity, self-conscious, organized local communities have formed in order to contest state projects such as hydro dams, or state-sponsored settlement, logging, mining, or estate development (Li 1999, 2000). The Lauje area has not been burdened with such intrusive state schemes. Nevertheless, hill people have begun to form themselves into more orderly units in order to be more effective in making claims upon the state for access to "development": schools, health services, and agricultural programs. At the same time, state institutions charged with delivering "development" have been anxious to identify and pin down appropriate target groups for their activities and interventions. Community formation is therefore occurring due to a (partial, provisional, and contingent) conjuncture of state and local interests.

Under the aegis of the Directorate General for Regional Development, in collaboration with a Canadian aid program, the Lauje area was flagged for a development boost beginning in 1990. Attention was initially drawn to the area because of the perceived poverty and backwardness of the mountain farmers, the general development deficit of the region when compared with neighboring transmigration sites, and evidence of environmental degradation in the hills (Strachan et al. 1989). The program eventually designed for the area involved supporting farmers interested in planting estate crops by giving them training and free inputs. There was also a program to clarify traditional land rights by listing owners, mapping plots, and eventually issuing letters of acknowledgment that could translate into individual titles. The demand for clarification of tenure arose from the Estate Crops Department, unused to dealing with smallholders *in situ,* and aware that a program to assist mountain dwellers in planting trees would have the effect of consolidating their hold over the land (Babcock and Ruwiastuti 1993). Once the hill farmers were defined as the effective target group, there was a new interest from state agencies in regularizing their position and making them legitimate beneficiaries and recipients of state development assistance. To do this, the nature and location of target communities had to become better specified (Li 1996a). For the first time, officials began to hike into the hills and to acknowledge that there were thousands of people living and farming there, rather than the few wandering primitives they had been led to imagine. The sketch-mapping and list-making efforts of a team conducting a participatory rural appraisal helped officials to reconceptualize their target in terms of definite social groups occupying specific and named areas of the hills: real people in real places. The term "lingsos" (*lingkunan sosial*) was coined by program planners to refer to such social/ecological units.

The lingsos was, in a sense, a new form of community created at a conjuncture when official planners and mountain dwellers saw their respective
interests served by increased communication under the rubric of "development." It was a constructed term for a newly conceptualized entity, yet the
entity it attempted to capture promised to be more grounded in actual social
relationships than the normal official structure of subvillage units, represented
by improbable straight lines on the map on the wall of the village office. The
village leadership has long required its designated hamlet chiefs to keep lists of
mountain households, and be ready to mobilize "the community" to undertake labor duties or pay taxes. Yet the results (both the lists themselves, and
the readiness) were consistently disappointing. With the new program some
hill people, for the first time, anticipated that they would receive some benefits in return for state allegiance, and were therefore willing to be mapped and
listed, their households grouped as communities and pinned down on paper.
Still, there was considerable flux between one list-making exercise and the
next, indicating both the continued mobility of hillside farmers and their
reassessments of the costs and benefits of engagements with state authority
and "development." Besides the estate crop inputs, they have shown some
interest in the creation of small mountain schools, and can readily see that a
concentration of school-aged children (substantiated by the collection of
hundreds of names on a list) at or near enough to a particular named place is
essential to their claim upon the state for the necessary resources.

COMMUNITY-BASED NATURAL RESOURCE MANAGEMENT?

Now that communities have begun to form in the Lauje hills in the context,
and for the purpose, of engagement with the state bureaucratic apparatus, one
could imagine a discussion about resource management and conservation taking place. There are environmental problems that loom large for the hill farmers, not least of which are the diseases afflicting their cocoa groves and the
insecure yield from the new tree crops when compared with the swidden crops
(food and cash) that they have displaced. To resolve these problems, they
would be very interested in outside assistance. But hill farmers are uncon-
cerned about environmental "problems" that might loom large for outsiders:
deforestation, loss of biodiversity, erosion. Coercive conservation measures,
such as a ban on planting steeply sloping land, exclusion from the remaining
forests, or a requirement to move out of the hills to the coast would likely
provoke the formation of a more clearly bounded, oppositional community
capable of articulating both an identity and a set of interests in opposition to
the state. Such a community may even begin to present itself in a rhetoric of
"indigenous people" in touch with their environment in contrast to a distant,

unknowing, and uncaring state. Precisely this process has occurred in another area of Central Sulawesi, as I have documented elsewhere (Li 2000). Where "development" has, in the Lauje case, brought hill folk and state authorities together, conservation would likely drive them apart, forming definite but difficult communities in the process.

Conclusion

Even among the indigenous hill farmers of Sulawesi, and more so where populations are differentiated by class and ethnicity and have histories of hostile engagement with state authorities, conjunctures in which the conservation mandate or agenda of state-institutions and the interests of a specific group of resource users are (or could become) congruent or perhaps complementary are not easy to find. My earlier analysis, and the Lauje case presented, strongly suggest that conservation efforts that are consistent with the market-related economic strategies of resource users are more likely to be effective than those that overlook them, or bury them in a rhetoric of subsistence. The resulting initiatives may bear little resemblance to those imagined in the communities literature. Identifying them will not bring about radical change, although it could help in meeting the equity and efficiency goals toward which the proponents of community-based natural resource management strive. In many cases, they will increase rather than decrease the intensity of state involvement in local affairs. However carefully they are crafted, conservation initiatives and institutional arrangements that assume or impose a separation between "community" and "market" or "state" have no prospect. If they are designed on the assumption that all rural people are fully implicated in economic and political processes of a powerful and sometimes overwhelming nature, they could make a difference.

Notes

I would like to thank Arun Agrawal and Donald Moore for their detailed comments on earlier versions of this chapter, and for stimulating discussions on these topics. I have adopted the term "boundary work" from Moore (email, April 23, 1997).

1. I focus upon boundaries here, rather than the (equally important) "internal" inequities of communities, because boundaries have received relatively less attention. As Moore (email, April 23, 1997) points out, there is a parallel with the literature that critiqued "households as natural units," which explored the internal dynamics of households but paid less attention to their boundaries or the histories of their constitution as units, thereby (inadvertently) contributing to their further reification. I have attempted some boundary work on households in Li (1996b), and I discuss the internal dynamics of communities in Li (1996a, 1997).

2. Leach et al. (1997) succeed in avoiding some of the binaries set up by community and radically rethinking basic assumptions, including "the assumption that a distinct community exists" (1997, 3). To do this, they bring in a quite different set of terms—about endowments, entitlements, institutions, landscapes, and "people in places" as "part of history." They do not reject the term "community," although they "contextualize it by describing a more or less temporary unity of situation, interest or purpose among particular groups of social actors" (1997, 7), a unity that is apparent only from some perspectives and at particular scales of analysis.

3. See my discussion in Li (1996a).

4. Note that, as Massey goes on to reject the idea of boundaries that counterpose an inside and outside, scare quotes reappear, and the limits of language are again apparent: community is defined "through the particularity of linkage to that 'outside.' "

5. Pigg (1992) makes such observations in her insightful discussion of "villageness" in relation to development. She describes the ways in which lower-level functionaries, urban elites, and donors filter out the complexities (as well as the flows, travel, and relationships) that they know to exist in villages, and construct instead "the Nepali village," a typified, simplified, generic, and isolated other-world. The latter, she argues, is not the world in which villagers actually live, but a mythic place that exists only from the perspective of developed, nonvillage places, and can only be seen by people who see themselves as nonvillagers (see also Ferguson 1994; Gupta and Ferguson 1992).

6. Abrams (1988) makes a useful distinction between the idea of "the state" as a unified source of intention and power, which is an ideological construct or mask, and the state-system, which is composed of institutions of political and executive control and their key personnel. The state-system, through its everyday operations, produces (and disguises) the relations of power on which the reified idea of "the state" is based (see also Joseph and Nugent 1994; Mitchell 1991).

7. "When there are many 'external' agents and processes refracted through (no matter how much one wants to problematize its boundaries, constitution, etc.) a 'community', [it is] interesting to note how often [it is] the 'state' that represents the prototypical outsider" (Moore, email, April 23, 1997).

8. Sivaramakrishnan (1996) provides an analysis along these lines for the project of joint forest management in India.

9. For a detailed account of local struggles over land and shifting tenure see Li (1996a, 1997).

10. It took me some time to recognize the importance of this, since I took with me to the field the assumption that farming and the use of forest products would be central to livelihoods, especially in such an isolated, back-woodsy place.

11. The gender division of labor and conditions of household formation are described in Li (1996b, 1998).

Bibliography

Abrams, Philip. 1988. "Notes on the Difficulty of Studying the State." [1977] *Journal of Historical Sociology* 1(1):58–89.

Angelsen, Arild. 1995. "Shifting Cultivation and 'Deforestation': A Study from Indonesia." *World Development* 23(10):1713–1729.

Babcock, Tim, and Maria Ruwiastuti. 1993. "'Indigenous Peoples' dan Penguasaan atas Tanah." *Kompas* 29 April.

Bernstein, Henry. 1990. "Taking the Part of the Peasants?" In *The Food Question*, ed. Henry Bernstein et al., 69–79. New York: Monthly Review Press.

Breman, Jan. 1980. *The Village on Java and the Early-Colonial State*. Rotterdam: Comparative Asian Studies Programme.

————. 1988. *The Shattered Image: Construction and Deconstruction of the Village in Colonial Asia*. Dordrecht, The Netherlands: Foris Publications.

Brow, James. 1990. "Notes on Community, Hegemony, and the Uses of the Past." *Anthropological Quarterly* 63(1):1–6.

Brown, Elaine. 1994. "Grounds at Stake in Ancestral Domains." In *Patterns of Power and Politics in the Philippines*, ed. James Eder and Robert Youngblood, 43–76. Temple: Arizona State University.

Carrier, James. 1992. "Occidentalism: The World Turned Upside Down." *American Ethnologist* 19(2):195–212.

Comaroff, John, and Jean Comaroff. 1992. *Ethnography and the Historical Imagination*. Boulder, Colo.: Westview Press.

Corrigan, Philip. 1994. "State Formation." In *Everyday Forms of State Formation*, ed. Gilbert Joseph and Daniel Nugent, xvii–xix. Durham, N.C.: Duke University Press.

Davies, Susanna. 1994. "Information, Knowledge and Power." *IDS Bulletin* 25(2): 1–13.

Dove, Michael R. 1993a. "A Revisionist View of Tropical Deforestation and Development." *Environmental Conservation* 20(1):17–24, 56.

————. 1993b. "Smallholder Rubber and Swidden Agriculture in Borneo: A Sustainable Adaptation to the Ecology and Economy of the Tropical Forest." *Economic Botany* 47(2):136–147.

Enters, Thomas. 1994. "Now You See It, Now You Don't: The Effects of the Ecocrisis Theory on Research." Paper presented at the IUFRO, FORSPA, CIFOR, FAO/RAPA Workshop on The Barriers to the Application of Forestry Research Results, 24–28 October 1994, Bangkok.

————. 1995. "The Token Line: Adoption and Non-Adoption of Soil Conservation Practices in the Highlands of Northern Thailand." Paper presented at the International Workshop on Soil Conservation Extension: Concepts, Strategies, Implementation and Adoption, 4–11 June, Chiang Mai, Thailand.

Escobar, Arturo. 1984–85. "Discourse and Power in Development: Michel Foucault and the Relevance of His Work to the Third World." *Alternatives* 10:377–400.

————. 1992. "Planning." In *The Development Dictionary: A Guide to Knowledge as Power*, ed. Wolfgang Sachs, 131–145. London: Zed Books.

Ferguson, James. 1994. *The Anti-Politics Machine*. Minneapolis: University of Minnesota Press.

Fisher, William. 1996. "Native Amazonians and the Making of the Amazon Wilderness: From Discourse of Riches and Sloth to Undevelopment." In *Creating the Countryside*, ed. E. Melanie DuPuis and Peter Vandergeest. Philadelphia: Temple University Press.

Foucault, Michel. 1981. *Power/Knowledge*. New York: Pantheon Books.

Gordon, Robert. 1992. *The Bushman Myth*. Boulder, Colo.: Westview.

Gupta, Akhil, and James Ferguson. 1992. "Beyond 'Culture': Space, Identity, and the Politics of Difference." *Cultural Anthropology* 7(1):6–23.

Hart, Gillian. 1989. "Agrarian Change in the Context of State Patronage." In *Agrarian Transformations: Local Processes and the State in Southeast Asia*, ed. Gillian Hart et al., 31–52. Berkeley: University of California Press.

Healey, Christopher. 1985. "Tribes and States in Pre-Colonial Borneo: Structural Contradictions and the Generation of Piracy." *Social Analysis* 18:3–39.

Hefner, Robert. 1990. *The Political Economy of Mountain Java: An Interpretive History*. Berkeley and Los Angeles: University of California Press.

Hirsch, Philip. 1989. "The State and the Village: Interpreting Rural Development in Thailand." *Development and Change* 20:35–56.

Hitchcock, Robert, and John Holm. 1993. "Bureaucratic Domination of Hunter-Gatherer Societies: A Study of the San in Botswana." *Development and Change* 24:305–338.

Hoben, Allan. 1995. "Paradigms and Politics: The Cultural Construction of Environmental Policy in Ethiopia." *World Development* 23(6):1007–1021.

Joseph, Gilbert, and Daniel Nugent. 1994. *Everday Forms of State Formation.* Durham, N.C.: Duke University Press.

Kahn, Joel. 1993. *Constituting the Minangkabau: Peasants, Culture and Modernity in Colonial Indonesia.* Providence, R.I.: Berg.

Kemp, Jeremy. 1991. "The Dialectics of Village and State in Modern Thailand." *Journal of Southeast Asian Studies* 22(2):312–326.

Leach, Melissa, and James Fairhead. 1994. "Natural Resource Management: The Reproduction and Use of Environmental Misinformation in Guinea's Forest-Savanna Transition Zone." *IDS Bulletin* 25(2):81–87.

Leach, Melissa, Robin Mearns, and Ian Scoones. 1997. "Environmental Entitlements: A Framework for Understanding the Institutional Dynamics of Environmental Change." *IDS Discussion Paper* 359. Sussex, U.K.: Institute of Development Studies.

Lee, Richard, and Irven DeVore eds. 1976. *Kalahari Hunter-Gathering.* Cambridge, Mass.: Harvard University Press.

Li, Tania Murray. 1996a. "Images of Community: Discourse and Strategy in Property Relations." *Development and Change* 27(3):501–527.

———. 1996b. "Household Formation, Private Property and the State." *Sojourn* 11(2):259–87.

———. 1997. "Producing Agrarian Transformation at the Indonesian Periphery." In *Economic Analysis Beyond the Local System*, ed. Richard Blanton et al., 125–146. Lanham, Md.: University Press of America.

———. 1998. "Working Separately but Eating Together: Personhood, Property, and Power in Conjugal Relations." *American Ethnologist* 25(4):675–694.

———. 1999. "Marginality, Power and Production: Analyzing Upland Transformations." In *Transforming the Indonesian Uplands: Marginality, Power and Production*, ed. Tania Murray Li. Amsterdam: Harwood Academic Press.

———. 2000. "Articulating Indigenous Identity in Indonesia: Resource Politics and the Tribal Slot." *Comparative Studies in Society and History* 42(1):149–179.

Lynch, Owen J., and Kirk Talbott. 1995. *Balancing Acts: Community-Based Forest Management and National Law in Asia and the Pacific.* Washington, D.C.: World Resources Institute.

Massey, Doreen. 1993. "Power-Geometry and a Progressive Sense of Place." In *Mapping the Futures: Local Cultures, Global Change*, ed. Jon Bird et al., 59–69. London: Routledge.

Mitchell, Timothy. 1991. "The Limits of the State: Beyond Statist Approaches and Their Critics." *American Political Science Review* 85(1):77–96.

Moniaga, Sandra. 1993. "Toward Community-Based Forestry and Recognition of Adat Property Rights in the Outer Islands of Indonesia." In *Legal Frameworks for Forest Management in Asia: Case Studies of Community-State Relations*, ed. Jefferson Fox. Honolulu: Environment and Policy Institute, East-West Center.

Nourse, Jennifer. 1994. "Textbook Heroes and Local Memory: Writing the Right History in Central Sulawesi." *Social Analysis* 35:102–121.

———. 1999. *Conceiving Spirits: Birth Rituals and Contested Identities among Lauje of Indonesia.* Washington, D.C.: Smithsonian Institution.

Nugent, David. 1994. "Building the State, Making the Nation: The Bases and Limits of State Centralization in 'Modern' Peru." *American Anthropologist* 96(2):333–369.

Nugent, Daniel, and Ana Maria Alonso. 1994. "Multiple Selective Traditions in Agrarian Reform and Agrarian Struggle: Popular Culture and State Formation in the *Ejido* of Namiquipa, Chihuahua." In *Everday Forms of State Formation,* ed. Gilbert Joseph and Daniel Nugent, 209–246. Durham, N.C.: Duke University Press.

Pigg, Stacy Leigh. 1992. "Inventing Social Categories Through Place: Social Representations and Development in Nepal." *Comparative Studies in Society and History* 34(3):491–513.

Rahnema, Majid. 1992. "Participation." In *The Development Dictionary,* ed. Wolfgang Sachs, 116–131. London: Zed Books.

Rangan, Haripriya. 1993. "Romancing the Environment: Popular Environmental Action in the Garhwal Himalayas." In *Defense of Livelihood: Comparative Studies on Environmental Action,* ed. John Friedmann and Haripriya Rangan, 155–181. West Hartford, Conn.: Kumarian Press.

Roseberry, William. 1989. *Anthropologies and Histories.* New Brunswick, N.J.: Rutgers University Press.

Schuurman, Frans. 1993. "Introduction: Development Theory in the 1990s." In *Beyond the Impasse,* ed. Frans Schuurman, 1–48. London: Zed Press.

Sellato, Bernard. 1994. *Nomads of the Borneo Rainforest: The Economics, Politics and Ideology of Settling Down.* Honolulu: University of Hawaii Press.

Sivaramakrishnan, K. 1996. "Participatory Forestry in Bengal: Competing Narratives, Statemaking, and Development." *Cultural Survival Quarterly* 20(3):35–39.

Strachan, Lloyd, Jeremy Stickings, and Peiter Prins. 1989. *Provincial Development Status Review Sulawesi Tengah.* Jakarta: University of Guelph and the Directorate General of Regional Development, Department of Home Affairs, Government of Indonesia.

Tomich, Thomas, and Meine van Noordwijk. 1995. "What Drives Deforestation in Sumatra." Paper presented at Regional Symposium on Montane Mainland Southeast Asia in Transition, 13–16 November, Chiang Mai, Thailand.

Tsing, Anna Lowenhaupt. 1993. *In the Realm of the Diamond Queen.* Princeton, N.J.: Princeton University Press.

Vandergeest, Peter, and Nancy Peluso. 1995. "Territorialization and State Power in Thailand." *Theory and Society* 24:385–426.

Williams, Raymond. 1976. *Keywords.* London: Fontana/Croom Helm.

Wilmsen, Edwin. 1989. *Land Filled with Flies.* Chicago: University of Chicago Press.

Wolf, Eric. 1982. *Europe and the People Without History.* Berkeley: University of California Press.

Zerner, Charles. 1994. "Through a Green Lens: The Construction of Customary Environmental Law and Community in Indonesia's Maluku Islands." *Law and Society Review* 28(5):1079–1122.

Conclusion	Community and the Commons

BONNIE J. MCCAY

Romantic and Other Views

In September 1990 I had the privilege of being a discussant at the plenary session of the first Common Property Conference of a new organization, the International Association for the Study of Common Property, at Duke University, Durham, North Carolina (McCay 1990). A decade later I have the privilege of writing a concluding chapter to an important volume on community-based conservation.

This volume is an excellent if inadvertent response to the challenge I posed at the very first Common Property Conference in 1990. There I spoke at some length, in response to excellent papers by leaders in the new field of common property studies—Daniel Bromley, Elinor Ostrom, Ronald Oakerson, David Feeny—about "romancing the commons." I will address this before focusing on my main objective, which is to discuss varying perspectives on the place of "community" in resource management and conservation.

Romancing the Commons

My comments at Duke University in 1990 centered upon the idea that those of us gathered there were engaged in the enterprise of romanticizing "the commons." The idea of the "commons" harkens to a mythic time—before The Fall or before Capitalism or before The Gods Became Crazy—when people lived in harmony with each other and with nature and hence there was no need for the institutions of private property. Myths about the past can be charters for the future, but myths they are. The romantic appeal of "the commons" is doubtless part of the old Western suspicion that "individualism" is flawed (Bloch 1930), and that a better way of life could be found in small rural communities where people shared in common even the very land upon which they depended (Fernandez 1987).

The narrative developed at the conference and in subsequent work locates "indigenous resource management" in early human history and tribal, non-Western cultures, and autonomous, self-regulating village communities in more recent history. It goes on to show very convincingly how, in specific cases in Africa and India and other places, the "common property institutions" involved withered away or were stamped out, creating tragedies of the commons. At the end of this perverse and tragic process, the victims of it are blamed for trying to make a living from degraded and highly restricted communal resources and have few alternatives and hardly any way to regulate the commons left to them.

The message is powerful and important, but romanticization of prestate, preindustrial, pre-Columbian, pre-whatever human society is central to this narrative. It may also be found in some otherwise excellent and valuable attempts to revise our perceptions of the workings of the English village commons (Cox 1985; Hanna 1990). Romancing the commons is also evident in the tendency to treat "user communities" or "appropriators" as homogeneous, cooperative, and inclined to solidarity when needed. None of the speakers at the 1990 conference did this, and none would accept such a portrait, which must seem suspicious to any methodological individualist, but there is a tendency that is reinforced by the habit of referring to "community of users" without much further analysis. What about heterogeneity within the commons? Is it just the difference between free-riders and good citizens, between cooperators and defectors? Are there not other differences that affect potentials for collective action and its consequences? Differences of class, ethnicity, and gender; subcultural differences such as occupational identification; and critical social relationships that define situations of production, reproduction, and exchange? The answer provided by the authors of this book is a resounding yes.

No one, even the most neoclassical economist, would deny the importance of social and other differentiation. However, because these factors become absorbed and simplified into discussions of prisoners' dilemmas and free-riding and institutional arrangements, the unintended message may be that class, gender, and ethnicity have very little to do with resource conservation and management. This book shows otherwise.

The romantic alternative to the gloomier assessment of the commons is also found in claims about how premodern peoples live harmoniously with their environments, the tendency to find conservation value for all "traditional" resource use systems even when they are in fact organized for other purposes (Carrier 1987), as well as grand appeals to "the divine comedy of community" (Boulding 1977). The facts are otherwise. For instance, pre-[whatever] communities and agrarian villages varied greatly, and over time, and communal resources were sometimes used wastefully and abominably (it would seem from certain archaeological records) or in any case could not be prevented from decline and destruction by people and their institutions. And, as authors in this book show, community can be as much the site of everyday trials and triumphs and all too human tragedies as of divine or other comedies.

Another romanticizing act is to dichotomize the actors into the locals and the government. Guess who are the good guys and who the villains? Just because people live in a small, local community does not mean that they are particularly wise and adept in how they manage the resources on which they depend, and just because other people work for the government or a multinational corporation or the World Bank does not mean that they are particularly uncaring and inclined toward ineptitude or avarice. More important, they do not and cannot any longer live in isolation from one another, and our task requires appreciation of their necessary interactions and how those affect common resource use and conservation, as shown, for example, in Sara Singleton's chapter in this book.

Romancing the commons also occurs when we dichotomize "knowledge," as indigenous or traditional on the one hand, and technical or modern on the other. The point is to recognize the value of indigenous or traditional knowledge, but the danger is that when this seems to be absent or woefully wrong or underdeveloped, all attention is shifted to specialized expertise from the outside. What about the processes whereby new knowledge is created, fragments of old knowledge are constructed into new forms, new understandings of nature and human relationships to nature? And how can commons institutions not only build upon "traditional" knowledge but be designed to help people develop knowledge about their environments?

"People without history" (Wolf 1982), whose lives and institutions and landscapes have been so radically transformed by the European encounter and postcolonial globalizing forces, deserve greater respect. They deserve careful and accurate analysis of the conditions under which institutions arose and were sustained or lost and the conditions under which common pool resources were used, abused, managed and mismanaged, or simply ignored. The tendency to romanticize human communities and their resource management abilities can be corrected by bringing empirical, theoretically informed research to those questions (McCay and Acheson 1987b). Romanticism, like the skepticism of the tragedy of the commons model, should provoke concern and critical commentary, as in the chapters of this book, not wild claims and overreliance on a few good stories.

Romancing the commons is not all bad. The romantic perspective leads us to a more optimistic view of human nature and potentials. We are open to the possibility of "comedy" in an encyclopedia definition of comedy as "the drama of humans as social rather than private beings, a drama of social actions having a frankly corrective purpose" (cited in Smith 1984). The individual herdsman in the model popularized by Garrett Hardin (1968) becomes a person who is, among other things, a member of a community of herders with more or less shared interest in managing the common pasture. Or so it might be. We must find out.

THE PHRASE "COMMUNITY-BASED CONSERVATION" in the subtitle of the book deserves more reflection. In most policy circles the phrase is "community-based natural resource management" or "community-based coastal resource management." Evident in this lexical shift is a powerful, although subtle, transnational cultural movement away from the traditional enterprise of resource management (as in fisheries, forestry, water, and other ministries) to the newer enterprise of conserving valued species, habitats, biodiversity (with less clear status in national and provincial ministries and more force in international conventions and the actions of powerful nongovernmental organizations [NGOs]). Granted, the word "conservation" can stand for either notion, the utilitarian, commodity-oriented one or the more protectionist perspective. Its choice, at this time and in this geopolitical context, which is increasingly dominated by a few very powerful private foundations and their dependents, suggests the latter, however. That is interesting. One of the ways the focus on conservation rather than resource management ties in with the "community" theme of the book is that the best known representation of this new perspective, "ecosystem management," gives far greater space to local communities, as well as public participation, than does the more traditional notion of forestry, fisheries, and wildlife administration (McCay and Wilson 1997).

Community and the Commons

The special place of "community" in resource management and rural development is the outcome of a loosely woven transnational movement unified by goals such as social justice, environmental health, and sustainability. It has a

complex and multistranded history. Its sources include frustrations of conservationists forced to recognize the need to involve local people in order to protect biodiversity and valued habitats, attempts to empower local groups
against state and transnational forces, indigenous rights claims, and more
(Brosius et al. 1998). My premise is that "community-based natural resource
management" or "community-based conservation" is also an outgrowth of and
intersects with critical thinking about "the commons."

"Everyone's right, no one's responsibility" is a popular understanding of
the problem of the commons. What is meant is that when people share rights
to a resource and no one has a secure and exclusive claim to its future benefits,
no one has a reason to take care of it. Experiments in laboratories and games
such as the "prisoners' dilemma" have shown the structure of this situation
and supported older understandings of "the tragedy of the [unmanaged] commons" (Hardin 1968, 1994; Lloyd 1837).

Emphasis on communities comes in part from reactions to the paradigm
of neoclassical economics, which is dominant in environmental and resource
economics and plays a strong hand in national and transnational policy formation, including International Monetary Fund and World Bank requirements of structural adjustment and privatization. In that paradigm, problems
of resource overuse and environmental destruction are believed to come
about because of the lack of clearly defined and defended exclusive property
rights, which create perverse incentives for individual behavior (Bromley
1989; Demsetz 1967). Markets depend on such rights in order to function;
according to this line of thought the pricing that would occur through the
market exchanges made possible by property rights would lead to wiser and
more sustainable uses.

In this analysis, tragedies of the commons are instances of "market failure." The ideal solution is to privatize the commons. In its extreme, privatization is part of the libertarian program of "free market environmentalism"
(Anderson and Leal 1991), which advocates free markets and trade as solutions to rather than causes of environmental problems. Less extreme is the
argument for finding ways to "internalize externalities," or at least use some
semblance of the security and tradeability of private property to improve the
stewardship incentives of resource users (Young and McCay, 1995).

However, enclosure is not always politically feasible; it is easily seen as
causing "tragedies of the commoners" and thus may be protected against by
law and custom (McCay 1998). It also may not be economically feasible,
given the high transaction costs of imposing or changing property rights
(Anderson and Hill 1990; Libecap 1989). Second best, in the economics
model of the commons, is using the powers of government to manage the

commons. To the extent that resource users are thought of at all, it is assumed that resource users or their communities cannot manage the commons because of the "free-rider" effect and other perversities of public goods and common rights.

The economistic interpretation of natural resource and environmental problems has been challenged for many reasons. Laboratory experiments and game theory show dilemmas of the commons that lead to suboptimal decisions, but they can also show potentials for cooperation with regard to common resources (or threats, as in the prisoners' dilemma) (Axelrod and Dion 1988; Ostrom et al. 1994). Key to more cooperative solutions is the possibility of observing and communicating with each other, the fundamental underpinnings of community. In the "thought experiment" offered by Hardin (1968), communication is absent among the herders making decisions about how many animals to put on the communal pasture. Yet in the real world, knowledge, risk, and estimates about the behavior of others make a great difference to such decisions (Runge 1981). In my own classrooms at Rutgers University, prisoners' dilemma exercises show that several other components of community also make a difference, including whether those playing have known each other in the past, whether they expect to know each other in the future, and whether they share certain values. What better definition of community than shared past, present, and future?

People are assumed to be isolated, calculating individuals of the species *homo economicus* in the "tragedy of the commons" model, rather than social and cultural beings affiliated through kinship, ethnicity, neighborhoods, work, and other ties. In the economic model they are also presumed to have a specific preference-ordering, despite the existence of numerous other possibilities. If *homo economicus* with a strong preference for winning at least cost, rather than others with other preferences (including making sure that others are at least as well off as oneself) (Rose 1994), then no wonder community is absent from the model.

The neoclassical approach can be criticized at a deeper theoretical and philosophical level. It is neither new nor earthshaking to observe the absence of communication and community in prisoners' dilemma games and other social dilemmas with the features of the tragedy of the commons. Any modeling must simplify and abstract from reality. Moreover, as noted above, adding elements of community has the powerful effect of showing conditions for cooperation. However, the choice of modeling forms of explanation is often part of a broader intellectual program, one in which community is viewed as the aggregate outcome of the choices and behaviors of individuals.

This methodological and radical individualism contrasts markedly with critical and social theory emphasizing the irreducibility of social experience and its embeddedness in webs of meaning, not just calculations of costs and benefits. From that perspective, the social relationships, institutions, and culture that make up community have profound effects on individual choice and behavior (McCay and Jentoft 1998; Pálsson 1991). By simplifying out the multiple goals, roles, sources of identity and affiliation, and worldviews within which the so-called rational decision-making of economic actors is embedded, we lose all but peripheral vision of the roles of social factors and community in how people relate to and deal with their commons.

Moreover, the neoclassical interpretation dismisses the possibility of common property— that is, institutions which assign rights of use and possibly ownership to members of a group, and thus which can be engaged in protecting resources and wilderness (Berkes 1989; Ciriacy-Wantrup and Bishop 1975; McCay and Acheson 1987a; Ostrom 1990). "The commons" is not a situation defined by the lack of restriction or ownership claims; instead, a "commons" is a place or activity marked off and given meaning by institutions that establish rights of access and use (among which may be free and open access) and that may or may not provide some degree of cooperative or communal restraint on individual behavior. To the extent that the institutions identify boundaries, excluding some from the commons, one can argue that property has been created. If that is so, we can argue that there are many kinds of property besides private property, and they all have potentials to help or hurt resource management (Berkes et al. 1989).

Just as laboratory studies and simulations suggest potentials for cooperation, case studies support the idea that community in the abstract, and communities in the particular, can be sources and sites of common resource management (Berkes 1989; Bromley et al. 1992; McCay and Acheson 1987a). In addition, case studies provide material for analyses of conditions for the emergence and maintenance, as well as decline and failure, of institutions for managing common resources in local communities (McKean 1992; Ostrom 1990; Wade 1988;) as well as comanagement arrangements (Baland and Platteau, 1996; Pinkerton 1994). This line of argument dovetails with the rise of policy interest in community-based management in many parts of the developing world, as shown in this book.

Without dismissing the importance of property rights, I wish to make another point about the neoclassical way of interpreting commons problems, namely its overwhelming focus on property rights. Should we not ask whether there are other causes of resource decline and environmental damage, causes that replace or intersect with the property rights problem? The metaphor of "community failure," in contrast to "market failure," is appropriate (McCay and Jentoft 1998). If there is a resource or environmental problem, we should not stop at the property rights question, which can be a red herring (Emmerson 1980). Rather, we should assume some capacity of communities to manage the resources upon which they depend and the ecosystems they value, just as we make assumptions about the workings of markets. When and where there is an environmental problem, the question becomes why community failure rather than why market failure. We might ask why the communities involved have not acted to prevent or mitigate those problems, whether their actions were sufficient to the task, whether communities can be helped to strengthen their resource management capabilities, and other such questions. Property rights—private, common, state, or otherwise—may or may not play a major role in a particular instance of "community failure" (or, by implication, community success). However, so might the workings of markets, ironically, and configurations of power, wealth, and authority—not to mention the forces of nature. And these in turn can have great effect on property rights and other determinants of access to and the motivation and power to manage common resources.

Romancing Community?

That said, a focus on community, and community failure, can be as red a herring as the focus on property rights and market failure can be. This point can be made in two very different and opposing ways. One is political ecology; the other is "against political ecology." The political ecology perspective as represented by Michael Goldman (1998), who criticizes "human ecologists" or those who have contributed field-based case studies to discourse on the commons, for being too focused on social and ecological relations in local sites, and not enough on "the dialectic relations between local and nonlocal" (1998, 27). Like other political ecologists, he calls for greater attention to externally generated political influences on human/environment interactions as well as a more critical "analysis of modernity, development and its institutions" and the roles of commons experts—of whatever school—within them (41). The very ideas of "market failure" and "community failure" would be construed as expressions of a dangerous "resource managerialism" that is part of hegemonic processes that themselves have major roles in destroying common lands and resources. Either community is beside the point, or we need to look at a wider set of communities, including those of power brokers, researchers, nongovernmental organization actors, entrepreneurs, and others, in order to be able to understand what is happening and why.

Similarly raising questions about a focus on community while armed to the teeth against political ecology is the work of Andrew P. Vayda and his associates. Their general concern is overreliance on *a priori* judgments, theories, and biases about what is important in understanding environmental changes. Among those biases is that of political ecologists, who claim that external political-economic forces are always important and should be given priority in research. Vayda and Walters (1999) argue that this is an instance of "question-begging research (i.e., for concentrating on factors assumed in advance to be important and for thus missing both other factors and the complex and contingent interactions of factors whereby environmental changes often are produced)" (1999, 168). Anyone focusing on either market failure or community failure could be accused of the same untoward bias (McCay and Vayda 1992).

To understand this critique fully, one must recognize and accept that the object of explanation is environmental change. Environmental change, not institutional change. Environmental change, not the effects of the penetration of capital. Environmental change, not capacities for or failures of collective action. The program for research is to identify particular environmental events (i.e., a decrease or increase in the abundance or diversity of forest life, or fisheries, in an area) and then try to construct chains of causes and effects, which may or may not include distant political forces and the hegemony of communities of experts, funders, and practitioners, or coalitions of the agents of multinational businesses with local elites, or whatever.

The point is the "whatever." The research task is to discover not to prescribe. From this perspective, much of the "community-based natural resource management" work may be important, insofar as it influences the rate and nature of environmental changes in particular areas. Whether this is so is an empirical question. It is possible that environmental changes are occurring for other reasons (as Walters found in his study of mangroves in the Philippines) (Vayda and Walters 1999). Moreover, it might be beside the point, if deforestation is occurring because people other than community members are working the forests for charcoal and the local community does not have the power to detect or stop these actions. Political ecologists, "communitarians," and "neoclassical economists" can all be suspected of wearing convenient, attractive, and possibly very misleading blinders. We should do whatever we can to respect the realities of peoples' lives and actions and how they affect and are shaped by their natural and political environments.

Respect, Clarity, and Criticism

My closing message is about empathy, respect, and humility: empathy and respect for the realities of the lives of people other than ourselves and humility about what we as researchers and practitioners can do. The theories, models, methods, and biases we bring to our work as researchers and writers may or may not help the people with whom we work, and they may or may not serve us as we try to express what we experienced, heard, and recorded during our research. A second point is the need to be very clear about what it is we are trying to explain, and why. Do we agree that environmental change should be the explanandum, or would some of us insist that variation in the workings of local-level community-based management systems—or degrees of interference from outside sources of political power or capitalism—should be the explanandum? What about the incomes and health status of people in communities as the explanandum? These questions are assumed or backgrounded in obeisance to the notion of "sustainable development."

A third closing point is the need, as analysts, to be critical and open about the very idea of community. There are communities of place and of interest; there are communities of people who share experiences focused on a particular issue, and some of these are "virtual" in the sense of relying on Internet and telecommunications technology for most interactions. Some of these are deserving of being "romanced." Much more work needs to be done to enable and encourage more widespread information!

Bibliography

Anderson, Terry L., and Peter J. Hill. 1990. "The Race for Property Rights." *Journal of Law and Economics* 33(April): 177–197.

Anderson, Terry L., and Donald R. Leal. 1991. *Free-Market Environmentalism*. Boulder, Colo.: Pacific Research Institute for Public Policy and Westview Press.

Axelrod, Robert, and Douglas Dion. 1988. "The Further Evolution of Cooperation." *Science* 242:1385–1390.

Baland, Jean-Marie, and Jean-Philippe Platteau. 1996. *Halting Degradation of Natural Resources: Is There a Role for Rural Communities?* Oxford, U.K.: Clarendon Press, and FAO, UN.

Berkes, Fikret, ed. 1989. *Common Property Resources: Ecology and Community-Based Sustainable Development*. London: Belhaven Press.

Berkes, Fikret, David Feeny, Bonnie J. McCay, and James M. Acheson. 1989. "The Benefit of the Commons." *Nature* 340(July 13): 91–93.

Bloch, Maurice. 1930. "La lutte pour l'individualisme agraire dans la France de XVIIIe siècle." *Annales d'histoire économique et sociale* 11:329–383, 511–556.

Boulding, Kenneth E. 1977. "Commons and Community: The Idea of a Public." In *Managing the Commons*, ed. G. Hardin and J. Baden, 280–294. San Francisco: W. H. Freeman.

Bromley, Daniel W. 1989. *Economic Interests and Institutions: The Conceptual Foundations of Public Policy*. New York: Basil Blackwell.

Bromley, Daniel W., et al., eds. 1992. *Making the Commons Work: Theory, Practice, and Policy*. San Francisco: Institute for Contemporary Studies Press.

Brosius, J. Peter, Anna Lowenhaupt Tsing, and Charles Zerner. 1998. "Representing Communities: Histories and Politics of Community-Based Natural Resource Management." *Society and Natural Resources* 11:157–168.

Carrier, James G. 1987. "Marine Tenure and Conservation in Papua New Guinea: Problems in Interpretation." In *The Question of the Commons*, ed. B. McCay and J. Acheson, 142–167. Tucson: University of Arizona Press.

Ciriacy-Wantrup, S., and R. Bishop. 1975. "'Common Property' as a Concept in Natural Resources Policy." *Natural Resources Journal* 15:713–727.

Cox, Susan J. Buck. 1985. "No Tragedy on the Commons." *Environmental Ethics* 7:49–61.

Demsetz, Harold. 1967. "Toward a Theory of Property Rights." *American Economic Review* 62(2):347–359.

Emmerson, Donald K. 1980. "Rethinking Artisanal Fisheries Development: Western Concepts, Asian Experiences." World Bank Staff Working Paper no. 423. Washington, D.C.: World Bank.

Fernandez, James W. 1987. "The Call to the Commons: Decline and Recommitment in Asturias, Spain." In *The Question of the Commons*, ed. B. McCay and J. Acheson, 266–289. Tucson: University of Arizona Press.

Goldman, Michael. 1998. "Inventing the Commons." In *Privatizing Nature: Political Struggles for the Global Commons*, ed. Michael Goldman, 20–53. New Brunswick, N.J.: Rutgers University Press.

Hanna, Susan. 1990. "The Eighteenth Century English Commons: A Model for Ocean Management." *Ocean and Shoreline Management* 14:155–172.

Hardin, Garrett. 1968. "The Tragedy of the Commons." *Science* 162:1243–1248.

———. 1994. "The Tragedy of the Unmanaged Commons." *Trends in Ecology and Evolution* 9:199.

Libecap, Gary. 1989. *Contracting for Property Rights*. New York: Cambridge University Press.

Lloyd, William Forster. 1837 [1968]. Lectures on Population, Value, Poor-Laws, and Rent, Delivered in the University of Oxford during the Years 1832, 1834, 1835, & 1836. Reprint. New York: Augustus M. Kelley.

McCay, Bonnie J. 1990. "Romancing the Commons: Discussant's Remarks." First International Conference on Common Property Resources, 28–30 September, Duke University, Durham, North Carolina.

———. 1998. *Oyster Wars and the Public Trust: Property, Law, and Ecology in New Jersey History*. Tucson: University of Arizona Press.

McCay, Bonnie J., and James M. Acheson. 1987a. *The Question of the Commons: The Culture and Ecology of Communal Resources*. Tucson: University of Arizona Press.

———. 1987b. "Human Ecology of the Commons." In *The Question of the Commons*, ed. B. McCay and J. Acheson, 1–34. Tucson: University of Arizona Press.

McCay, Bonnie J., and Svein Jentoft. 1998. "Market or Community Failure? Critical Perspectives on Common Property Research." *Human Organization* 57(1):21–29.

McCay, Bonnie J., and Andrew P. Vayda. 1992. "The Ecology of Natural Resource Management." Paper presented at the annual meetings of the American Anthropological Association, 3 December 1992, San Francisco.

McCay, Bonnie J., and Douglas Wilson. 1997. "'Ecosystem Management' for US Fisheries." Paper presented to the Annual Meeting of the Society for Applied Anthropology, 4–9 March 1997, Seattle, Washington.

McKean, Margaret A. 1992. "Success on the Commons: A Comparative Examination of Institutions for Common Property Resource Management." *Journal of Theoretical Politics* 4(3):247–281.

Ostrom, Elinor. 1990. *Governing the Commons: The Evolution of Institutions for Collective Action*. New York: Cambridge University Press.

Ostrom, Elinor, Roy Gardner, and James Walker. 1994. *Rules, Games, and Common-Pool Resources*. Ann Arbor: University of Michigan Press.

Pálsson, Gisli. 1991. *Coastal Economies, Cultural Accounts: Human Ecology and Icelandic Discourse*. Manchester, U.K.: Manchester University Press.

Pinkerton, Evelyn. 1994. "Local Fisheries Co-Management: A Review of International Experiences and Their Implications for Salmon Management in British Columbia." *Canadian Journal of Fisheries and Aquatic Sciences* 51:1–17.

Rose, Carol M. 1994. *Property and Persuasion: Essays on the History, Theory, and Rhetoric of Ownership*. Boulder, Colo.: Westview Press.

Runge, C. F. 1981. "Common Property Externalities: Isolation, Assurance, and Resource Depletion in a Traditional Grazing Context." *American Journal of Agricultural Economics* 63:595–606.

Smith, M. Estellie. 1984. "The Triage of the Commons." Paper presented at the Annual Meeting of the Society for Applied Anthropology, 14–18 March 1984, Toronto.

Vayda, Andrew P., and Bradley B. Walters. 1999. "Against Political Ecology." *Human Ecology* 27(1):167–179.

Wade, Robert. 1988. *Village Republics: Economic Conditions for Collective Action in South India*. New York: Cambridge University Press.

Wolf, Eric R. 1982. *Europe and the People Without History*. Berkeley: University of California Press.

Young, Michael D., and Bonnie J. McCay. 1995. "Building Equity, Stewardship, and Resilience into Market-Based Property Rights Systems." In *Property Rights and the Environment: Social and Ecological Issues,* ed. Susan Hanna and Mohan Munasinghe, 87–102. Washington, D.C.: World Bank.

About the Contributors

Arun Agrawal is an associate professor of political science at Yale University. He has written about the politics of development, conservation, indigenous knowledge, and common property. His recent book, *Greener Pastures: Politics, Markets, and Community among a Migrant Pastoral People* (Duke University Press, 1999) focuses on raika pastoralists in India, and examines their lives in the related institutional contexts of markets, states, and community. His recently coedited *Agrarian Environments* (with K. Sivaramakrishnan) explores how the separation of agrarian and environmental studies has been instrumental in creating obfuscating dichotomies between community and state, local and global, and indigenous and scientific.

Clark C. Gibson is an assistant professor of political science at Indiana University. Much of his research explores the institutions and politics of natural resources, especially forests and wildlife in Africa and Latin America. His recent book, *Politicians and Poachers: The Political Economy of Wildlife Policy in Africa* (Cambridge University Press, 1999), examines the politics of wildlife management at multiple levels in Zambia, Kenya, and Zimbabwe. A recent coedited volume, *People and Forests: Communities, Institutions, and Governance* (MIT Press, 2000) (coeditors Elinor Ostrom and Margaret A. McKean), explores the governance of forests at the local level.

Hsain Ilahiane is an assistant professor of anthropology at Iowa State University. His research focuses on ethnicity and natural resource management in southern Morocco, Native American natural resource management in the southwestern United States, and the historiography of New Spain. This work has appeared in *The Journal of Political Ecology, Ethnology, The International Journal of Middle Eastern Studies*, and the *Journal of North African Studies*. He has also authored and coauthored chapters on urbanism in *Charting Memory:*

Recalling Medieval Spain and "Rapid Rural Appraisal Methods of Arid Land Irrigation" in *Canals and Communities*.

Tania Murray Li is an associate professor in the Department of Sociology and Social Anthropology, Dalhousie University, Halifax, Canada. Her research concerns questions of cultural and economy in rural Southeast Asia and in urban settings (*Malays in Singapore*, Oxford University Press, 1989). She has been adviser to various rural development programs in Indonesia.

Bonnie J. McCay is Board of Governors Distinguished Service Professor at Rutgers, the State University of New Jersey, in the Department of Human Ecology. She was trained as an ecological anthropologist and has worked mainly in fisheries. She has published numerous articles on common resource management and fisheries. Her books on the topic are *The Question of the Commons* (coedited with J. Acheson, University of Arizona Press, 1987), *Community, State, and Market in the North Atlantic Fisheries* (coauthored with R. Apostle et al., University of Toronto Press, 1998), and *Oyster Wars and the Public Trust* (University of Arizona Press, 1998).

Melanie Hughes McDermott is a postdoctoral fellow at the Center for Environmental Communication of Rutgers, the State University of New Jersey. She holds a M.Sc. degree in forestry from the University of Oxford and a Ph.D. from the Department of Environmental Science, Policy and Management at the University of California at Berkeley. She has conducted field research and worked in community development in the Philippines, Mozambique, Zimbabwe, California, and New Jersey. Her publications concern nontimber forest products in Southeast Asia and indigenous peoples' land rights and forest management in the Philippines.

Ruth Meinzen-Dick is a senior research fellow at the International Food Policy Research Institute, where she conducts research on collective action, property rights, water resource management, and gender issues. She holds a Ph.D. in development sociology from Cornell University, and has worked extensively in South Asia and Southern Africa. Her publications include numerous articles and books, especially on water management in India, Pakistan, and Zimbabwe, and a recent coedited volume on *Negotiating Water Rights* (IT Press and Vistaar, 2000).

Bettina Ng'weno is completing graduate work in the department of anthropology at Johns Hopkins University. Her intellectual interests lie in the study of various forms of property and governance. She has worked with the National Museums of Kenya and the African Center for Technology Studies (ACTS) on issues of culture and intellectual property rights and is presently working on ethnicity based territorial claims by Afro-Colombians in the southwestern Colombian Andes. Some of her research appears in *African Economic History*.

Elinor Ostrom is Arthur F. Bentley Professor of Political Science at Indiana University, where she codirects both the Workshop in Political Theory and Policy Analysis, and the Center for the Study of Institutions, Population, and Environmental Change. She is the author of *Governing the Commons* (Cambridge University Press, 1990) and *Crafting Institutions for Self-Governing Irrigation Systems* (Institute for Contemporary Studies Press, 1992), and has published numerous articles and chapters on issues of collective action and resource management.

Sara Singleton is an assistant professor of political science at Tulane University. Her research explores the links between institutions and outcomes in natural resource management, particularly fisheries, and the effects of inequality on institutional design and implementation. Her recent book, *Constructing Cooperation: The Evolution of Institutions of Comanagement* (University of Michigan Press, 1998), is a study of the development of a regulatory regime in which twenty Pacific Northwest Indian tribes comanage a large, biologically complex and highly valuable transboundary salmon fishery together with state, federal, and international regulatory agencies.

Margreet Zwarteveen is a lecturer and researcher at the Irrigation and Water Engineering Group at the Department of Environmental Sciences at the Wageningen Agricultural University and Research Centre, the Netherlands. She holds an M.Sc. in irrigation and development studies, and is working toward a Ph.D. in irrigation and gender studies at the same university, based on field research in South Asia and West Africa. She has published a number of articles and reports on gender and irrigation management.

Index

Abrams, Philip, 176n. 6
actors: concept of, 12–13; institutional role of, 14–15; multiplicity of, 13, 20, 23–24n. 42. *See also* community; indigenous peoples; tribes; *specific groups*
agriculture: domain of interaction and, 78; female-headed farms and, 71, 80–81; in Philippines, 6, 53, 162; subsistence-and-conservation agendas in, 161–162, 172. *See also* boundaries and boundary work; irrigation management; market interactions
agroforestry programs, 162
almaciga resin trade (Philippines), 53–54, 56, 60n. 23
Amazonia, "subsistence" in, 160
Amung-me people (Irian Jaya), 11
Ancestral Domain Management Plan (ADMP, Philippines), 40, 54, 59–60n. 9
ancestral domains: context of policy on, 32–33, 58; definitions of, 38, 56; lack of boundedness and homogeneity in, 48–49; state control of, 41–42. *See also* Certificate of Ancestral Domain Claim (CADC, Philippines)
Antiquities and Monuments Act (Kenya), 111–112, 132
Arab people (Morocco): agriculture of, 89–90; customary law of, 98–105; status of, 95–98, 105–108
Ascher, William, 10–11
Atran, Scott, 129
authority, group membership and, 125–127, 133–134

Baland, Jean-Marie, 71, 78, 142
Batak people (Philippines), 46–52
Beidelman, T. O., 133
Berber people (Morocco): agriculture of, 89–90; customary law of, 98–105; status of, 95–98, 105–108
Berry, Sara, 113
biodiversity: human manipulation of, 6; limits on maintaining, 21n. 17; local priorities and, 163; as rationale for protection, 112
Borneo Dayak people, 160
boundaries and boundary work: ancestral domains and, 48–49; approach to, 157–158, 175n. 1; example of particular place of, 167–175; kin ties across, 52; locating historic, 47, 60n. 19; of state and community, 38, 163–167, 172; subsistence and, 159–163; terminology in, 158–159
Bowen, John R., 113, 117
Brandon, Katrina, 5
Brantley, Cynthia, 134n. 2
Breman, Jan, 165
Brown, Elaine, 162

CAMPFIRE wildlife program (Zimbabwe), 22n. 30
categorical identity, definition of, 112, 113
Central Bank of Kenya, 122
Certificate of Ancestral Domain Claim (CADC, Philippines): conceptions of community in, 37–39; description of, 32; evaluation of, 43, 51–52; evolution of, 33–37; misrepresentation of

Certificate of Ancestral Domain Claim (CADC, Philippines) (*continued*) community in, 43–44, 46–51; obstacles in, 60n. 12; resource control and, 52–58; rights granted in, 39–40

Chanock, Martin, 123

choice-theoretic foundation, concept of, 6–7

citizenship, 124, 167. *See also* community membership

Coastal Forest Conservation Unit (CFCU, Kenya): challenges for, 116; forest protection under, 111–112, 132; significance of, 126, 131, 134n. 11

collective action: capacity for, 33, 139, 140–142; effects of, 154n. 1

Collier, J., 120

colonialism: ethnic and spatial divisions under, 36; forest policy as legacy of, 34–35; indirect rule under, 169–170; land policies under, 120–121; "subsistence" and, 159–160; villages created under, 165

comedy, definition of, 183

common property: community and, 183–187; devolution programs and, 85n. 2; forms of, 112–114, 127–129; kinship's role in, 116–118; legal system and, 118, 131–134; romanticization of, 180–183; stealing of, 106–107, 123, 128, 130. *See also* boundaries and boundary work; inheritance disputes (Kenya); Kayasan (Palawan, Philippines); salmon fisheries (Pacific Northwest); water users' organizations (South Asia); Zaouit Amelkis Village (Morocco)

Common Property Conference, 85n. 5, 180

commons: enclosure of, 184–185; use of term, 180–181, 186. *See also* common property

community: approach to, 15–20, 189; authority linked to membership in, 125–127, 133–134; choice-theoretic foundation for, 6–7; common property and, 183–187; components of, 1–2,

7–15, 22n. 28, 185; definitions of, 8–12, 22nn. 29–30, 112–114, 139–142; formation of, 168–170, 172–174; gender's link to, 66, 69–71, 81–84; historic role in conservation, 3–7, 23n. 37; history of concept, 2–3; indigenous cultural, defined, 37, 41–43, 58; outside threats to, 45–46, 60n. 14; patriarchal control and, 66–69; as problematic concept, 43–44, 57–58; romanticization of, 187–188; state's construction of, 32–43, 46–52, 57–58; state's link to, 158–159, 182; terminology for, 158–159, 176n. 2; unitary model of, 65–66. *See also* boundaries and boundary work; indigenous peoples; institutions

community-based natural resource management, use of term, 183, 184. *See also* common property; community; resource conservation and management

community capacity, concept of, 33. *See also* collective action

community-environment relationship: dynamism of, 43, 48–49; misconceptions of, 33, 39, 41, 44, 50

community membership: authority and, 125–127, 133–134; dynamism of, 47; indigenous vs. migrant in, 48, 49, 53, 56

conservation, use of term, 183. *See also* resource conservation and management

Constitution (Lgara), 105, 106

Constitution (Philippines), 34–35, 36, 41

Cook, Carolyn, 11

cooperatives, women's participation in, 72

Cultural Survival Quarterly, 21–22n. 18

culture, men linked to, 66–67, 69

dams, repair of, 105–106

Death Donation Societies, 77, 85n. 11

decentralization. *See* devolution programs

decision-making: in fisheries industry, 155n. 7; shared norms and, 11; state's assignment of, 38–39, 42–43; theories on, 185–186

deforestation, 23n. 37, 34, 35

democratization, 5, 21–22n. 18

De Monts de Savasse, R., 101–102

Denevan, William M., 6

DENR. *See* Philippines Department of Environment and Natural Resources (DENR)

density, as issue, 9

development policy: community formation and, 172–174; ethnopolitics of, 89–90; failure of, 1; subsistence and, 159–163; terminology of, 176n. 5; women's oppression and, 67–68

devolution programs: decentralization in, 166–167; description of, 63–65; gender relations in, 69–71, 81–82; local-level involvement in, 153–154; recommendations for, 82–84

Dewey, John, 3

Digo people (Kenya): "common title" and, 129–130; context of, 111–114; description of, 114–116; gender relations among, 130–131; identity of, 125–127; Islamic vs. customary law for, 118–120; kinship among, 116–118, 127–129; land registration/adjudication and, 120–122, 124–125, 128–129; meaning/authority and, 125–127, 133–134; population of, 134n. 8; present claims of, 122–125

Directorate General for Regional Development (Indonesia), 173

Dolgin, Janet, 125

domain of interaction, concept of, 77–79

Dominguez, Virginia, 127

Dove, Michael, 23n. 36, 161

Dublin Statement on Water and the Environment, 72

Durkheim, Émile, 3

Duruma people, 128, 134n. 2, 134n. 8

Eagleton, Terry, 23–24n. 42

ecofeminism, 68–69

economics, neoclassical, as model, 184–187. *See also* market interactions

Eder, James, 46

efficiency-enhancing principles, 147–148

Elizalde, Manuel, 60n. 17

environments: changes in, 188; population growth's impact on, 4; pristine type of, 5–6. *See also* biodiversity

ethnic identity: access to land/resources based on, 47–48; lack of articulation of, 168–169; significance of, 15; social stratification and, 95–98

family, definitions of, 125–127, 130–131. *See also* kinship

Farm Bill (U.S., 1985), 21n. 15

feminism, 67–68

fisheries industry: conflicts in, 143–144, 145; hatcheries and, 155n. 8; individual transferable quotas in, 147; largest catches in, 155n. 6; open access rule in, 147; property rights in, 139, 148–149; river-by-river-based decisions in, 155n. 7. *See also* salmon fisheries (Pacific Northwest)

Fishery Conservation and Management Act (U.S., 1976), 145

folk model, of irrigation management, 100, 104

Food and Agriculture Organization (FAO), 1

forest ecosystems and management: agroforestry programs for, 162; colonialism's legacy for, 34–35; indigenous knowledge and control of, 50–51; protection of, 111–112, 116, 132; as sacred, 11, 118; sustainability of, 44, 81; as virgin vs. human-influenced, 6. *See also* palm grove (Morocco); Philippine land and forest policy

forest products: access, management, and environmental status, 53–55, 56; land/water rights system and, 103; norms for/against cutting trees as, 11–12; "subsistence orientation" and, 161

Fox, Robert, 46, 49

Ganyuma vs. Mohamed (Eastern Africa), 118–120, 126
Gellner, E., 96
Gemeinschaft, 8, 20–21n. 6. *See also* social structure
gender relations: community's link to, 66, 69–71, 81–84; in determining power, 78; inheritance disputes and, 116–118, 130–131; marginalization and, 64–65; significance of, 15; spending habits and, 65. *See also* patriarchy; water users' organizations (South Asia)
Gesellschaft, 20–21n. 6. *See also* community
Gluckman, Max, 118
Goldman, Michael, 187
Grossi, Paolo, 120

Hammoudi, A., 99–100
Haratine people (Morocco): agriculture of, 89–90; exclusion of, 104–107; land acquired by, 107–108; status of, 97–98, 102–103; water rights and, 99–100
Hardin, Garrett, 4, 183, 185
Hassan Addakhil dam, 93–94
Hassan al-Dakhali dam, 103
Haugerud, Angelique, 128
Hefner, Robert, 161–162
heterogeneity: economic inequality and, 141–142; evidence of, 181; in resource use, 71, 78. *See also* community; indigenous peoples; tribes
homogeneity: absence of, 48–49, 57, 165; assumptions of, 64, 65–66, 181; collective capacity and, 141–142; in community definitions, 9–10, 37–38
households: in Berber social organization, 96; definition of, 60n. 16, 175n. 1; as domain of interaction, 77–78; unitary model of, 65–66; women's role in, 70–71
Huk rebellion, 35

identity: categorical type of, 112, 113; defined by religion, 124–127, 169. *See also* ethnic identity

illiteracy, 76
India, water users' organizations in, 73t, 74, 77
indigenous, use of term, 59n. 2
indigenous peoples: approach to, 189; community formation of, 168–169; conservation ethic and, 23n. 37; international support for, 41; knowledge of, 22n. 19, 182; marginalization of, 159–160; native reserves for, 121; romanticization of, 180–183; stewardship role of, 5; strategies of, 36–37, 43. *See also* ancestral domains; tribes
Indigenous People's Rights Act (1997, Philippines), 59n. 7
Indonesia: agroforestry programs in, 162; beliefs in, 22n. 27; development program in, 173; Dutch rule in, 169–170; "subsistence" in, 160. *See also* Sulawesi hill farmers (Indonesia)
Industrial Forest Management Agreement (Philippines), 60n. 11
inequality, economic, 141–142
inheritance: equal distribution of, 127–128, 131; importance of land, 117–118; *inter vivos* distribution of, 126–127
inheritance disputes (Kenya): common property's role in, 113–114; "common title" and, 129–130; context of, 111–113; customary vs. Islamic law in, 118–120; evaluation of, 131–134; gender relations and, 116–118, 130–131; kinship's role in, 116–118, 127–129; land registration/adjudication issues in, 120–122, 124–125, 128–129; meaning/authority and, 125–127; present claims in, 122–125; settlement of, 123
institutions: actors' role in, 14–15; definition of, 14, 24n. 46; design issues and, 166; international, 4–5; local-level processes and, 13–14; significance of, 20. *See also* nongovernmental organizations (NGOs); state
Integrated Social Forestry Program (Philippines), 35

international agencies, 4–5. *See also* non-governmental organizations (NGOs)

International Association for the Study of Common Property, 85n. 5, 180

irrigation management: description of, 98–103; men's and women's roles in, 70–71; overview of, 89–90; social organization of, 104–108; women's participation in, 71–80. *See also* water users' organizations (South Asia); Zaouit Amelkis Village (Morocco)

Islam: customary law vs., 114, 118–120, 123–127, 135n. 19, 135n. 22; family defined by, 130–131; forest's meaning and, 116; identity defined by, 124–127, 169

isolation, assumptions of, 5–6

Israel, land registration in, 129

Jarmonia dam (Morocco), 100–101

Java, village creation in, 165

Juang people (Orissa), 11

Kalahari San people, 159–160

Kantu people (Kalimantan), 23n. 36

katutubo, definition of, 60n. 20

Kayasan (Palawan, Philippines): approach to, 33; CADC's impact on, 51–52; definitional issues and, 43–44; description of, 44–46; fieldwork in, 59n. 3, 60n. 16; funds for, 56–57, 61n. 26; implications of case, 57–58; resource control and, 52–57; state's "community" compared to, 46–51

Kaya Tiwi, 115, 118

Keisi, Mzee, 119–120

Kenya: colonialism in, 120–121; description of, 115; forest protection in, 111–112; land policies in, 121–122; laws in, 114, 118–120, 123–127, 135n. 19, 135n. 22. *See also* Digo people (Kenya)

kinship: gender relations in, 130–131; inheritance disputes and, 116–118, 127–129; intertribal, in Pacific Northwest, 146–147; for Lauje people, 168–169

knowledge, dichotomy of, 22n. 19, 182

Kome, A., 78

land resources: access to, 53, 126–127; "common title" for, 129–130; customary law on, 99, 101–105; importance of, 117–118; insecurity about, 114, 128–129, 131, 132–133; migration's impact on, 107–108; Native American use of, 23n. 39; registration/adjudication of, 120–122, 124–125, 128–129. *See also* agriculture

Lauje people (Indonesia): concept of community for, 168–169; development schemes and, 172–174; income sources of, 171–172; resource management and, 174–175; state interactions with, 169–170

law: claims vs. rights in, 124; customary, 169–170; customary vs. Islamic, 114, 118–120, 123–127, 135n. 19, 135n. 22

lbayoud disease (date palm fungus), 94–95

Leach, Melissa, 176n. 2

leadership: as political institution, 49–50; state's definition of indigenous, 38–39, 42–43; value of, 77

Lerner, Daniel, 21n. 7

local organizations: for death benefits, 77, 85n. 11; devolution programs and, 153–154; effectiveness of, 80–81; irrigation management by, 105; women's participation in, 71–72. *See also* tribes; water users' organizations (South Asia)

Long, N., 74–75

Louisiana, inheritance in, 127

MacKenzie, Fiona, 128, 132

Maine, Henry, 2, 20n. 3

Maluku Islands (Indonesia), beliefs in, 22n. 27

Marcos, Ferdinand, 36

market interactions: community's link to, 158–159; resource management and, 174–175, 184–185; significance of, 15; state and community separated

market interactions (*continued*)
from, 22–23n. 31; state's role in, 164;
"subsistence" and, 160–162, 171–172.
See also forest products
Marx, Karl, 3
Massey, Doreen, 158
matrilinealism: challenge to, 118–120,
123; description of, 116–118; female
landholders and, 129–131
Maurer, B., 120
men, culture linked to, 66–67, 69
Mezzine, L., 104–105
microcredit programs, 72
migration, land use impacted by,
107–108
Mijikenda peoples (Kenya), 111–112,
134n. 2. *See also* Digo people (Kenya)
Mijikenda Union, 115
Mining Act (1995, Philippines), 42,
60n. 11
Mishra, Smita, 11
Moore, Donald, 175n. 1
Moore, Sally Falk, 117
Morocco. *See* Zaouit Amelkis Village
(Morocco)
Moser, C.O.N., 71–72
Murphree, Marshall, 22n. 30
mythic community, vision of, 19–20. *See
also* commons: use of term

Narayan, D., 85n. 6
Native Lands Registration Ordinance
(1959, Kenya), 121
Native Land Tenure Rules (1956,
Kenya), 121
NATRIPAL (United Tribes of Palawan),
50, 52, 54–57
Natural Resources Management Program
(NRMP, USAID), 37, 59n. 8
nature, women linked to, 66–69
Navaz, L. S., 120
Nepal: forest management in, 81; water
users' organizations in, 73t, 74–75,
76–77, 78
Neupane, N., 80
New People's Army (Philippines), 35
nongovernmental organizations

(NGOs): indigenous peoples supported by, 5; intervention of, 83; in
post-Marcos Philippines, 36–37,
54–57
norms, community, 10–12
Northwest Indian Fisheries Commission
(NWIFC), 149–150
Nourse, Jennifer, 168

Oendo, Ayuko, 116, 128, 131
Okoth-Ogendo, H.W.O., 121–122
Olson, Mancur, 142
Orissa, tribal norms in, 11
Ostrom, Elinor, 141
ownership, concept of, 118. *See also*
property rights

Pacific Fisheries Management Counsel
(PFMC), 144–145, 155n. 7
Pacific Salmon Treaty, 144
Pakistan, water users' organizations in,
73t, 74
Palawan, 45f. *See also* Kayasan (Palawan,
Philippines)
Palawan Council for Sustainable Devel-
opment, 60–61n. 24
palm grove (Morocco): customary law
on, 98–99; irrigation of, 99–103; steal-
ing from, 106–107
Parsons, Talcott, 3, 20–21n. 6
patriarchy, 66–69, 80
Peluso, Nancy, 164, 165
People Power revolution (Philippines),
36
Peters, Pauline, 21–22n. 18
Philippine Development Forum, 59n. 8
Philippine land and forest policy, com-
munity constructed in, 32–43. *See also*
Kayasan (Palawan, Philippines)
Philippines: agriculture in, 6, 53, 162;
forest products of, 53–55, 56; population of, 59n. 2; resettlement schemes
in, 47
Philippines Department of Environment
and Natural Resources (DENR):
Department Administrative Order
No. 2 (DAO 2) of, 37–44, 46, 52,

54–56; licensing by, 54, 60–61n. 24; objectives of, 41–43, 52–53; programs of, 34, 35, 59n. 6. *See also* Certificate of Ancestral Domain Claim (CADC, Philippines)

Pigg, Stacy Leigh, 176n. 5

place, definitions of, 51–52

Platteau, Jean-Philippe, 71, 78, 142

political ecology perspective, 187–188

politics: of access to forest products, 54–55; as context for local-level processes, 14; definitions of, 113; of development policy, 89–90; terminology in, 158–159

Posey, Darrell, 6

power: distribution and context of, 112–113; gender as determinant of, 78; of state, 4–6; symbolic type of, 104–105; variability of, 13; visibility of, 24n. 44, 64. *See also* state

Pradhan, N. C., 75, 78

principle of subsidiarity, 85n. 1. *See also* devolution programs

private property: preference for, 131–134; resistance to, 128–129, 131

privatization: in Kenya, 121–122; rationale for, 184–185; in Sulawesi hills, 171–172. *See also* devolution programs

processes, local-level, 13–14, 20

property, types of, 120–122, 186. *See also* common property; private property

property rights: control of, 104–105; defense of, 154–155n. 2; as disincentives, 4; in fisheries, 148–149; gender and, 70–71, 129–131; theories of, 23n. 39, 186–187. *See also* inheritance disputes (Kenya); irrigation management

Rajasthan, norms in, 11

Ranger, Terence, 123

rattan trade (Philippines), 53–55

Regalian Doctrine (Spanish), 34–35

Registered Land Act (1963, Kenya), 122

resettlement schemes, 47

resource conservation and management: as alienating influence, 174–175;

approach to, 19–20, 63–65; definition of, 20n. 1; economic paradigm for, 184–187; failure of, 1, 5; history of community in, 3–7, 23n. 7; shared norms and, 10–12; state objectives in, 41–43, 52–53; subsistence and, 161–162, 172. *See also* common property; community

resource management organizations: evaluation of, 69, 80–82; recommendations for, 82–84; women's participation in, 69, 71–80. *See also specific groups*

resources: access to, 47–48, 53–55, 69, 71, 79–80, 126–127; community size and, 8–9; heterogeneous use of, 71, 78; symbolic, 55–57. *See also* common property; fisheries industry; forest ecosystems and management; land resources; water resources

revenue-sharing schemes, 22n. 30

Revised Forestry Code (Philippines), 34, 35

rights: claims vs., 124; in fisheries industry, 139, 143–144; water, 99–103. *See also* Certificate of Ancestral Domain Claim (CADC, Philippines); property rights

Romania, land registration in, 129

Sahara Desert, French control of, 95, 97, 98. *See also* Zaouit Amelkis Village (Morocco)

Salhiya dam (Morocco), 100

Salish people (Pacific Northwest), 142–143, 155n. 5

salmon fisheries (Pacific Northwest): approach to, 138–139; comanagement issues for, 142–152; concept of community and, 139–142; evaluation of, 152–154

Saora people (Orissa), 11

Sarin, M., 81

sasi, images of, 22n. 27

SATRIKA (Tribal Association of Kayasan), 50, 52, 54–56

segmentary lineage model, 96

Shipton, Parker, 130
Singleton, Sara, 22n. 28
social structure: changes in, 2–3, 14;
    continuity in, 112, 113, 116, 117–118;
    as domain of interaction, 78–79;
    homogeneity in, 9–10, 37–38; legit-
    imization of, 126; local-level processes
    and, 13–14, 20; market, state, and
    community separated in, 22–23n. 31;
    order in, 41; stratification in, 66,
    95–98; water rights linked to, 99–103.
    See also ethnic identity; inheritance;
    kinship
soils, in Ziz Valley, 92–93
South Asia. See water users' organiza-
    tions (South Asia); specific countries
Spencer, Herbert, 3
Sri Lanka, water users' organizations in,
    73t, 74–75, 76, 77, 78
stakeholder participation, 64
state: community as constructed by,
    32–43, 57–58; community boundary
    with, 22–23n. 31, 163–167; commu-
    nity formation and, 169–170; commu-
    nity's link to, 158–159, 182; fisheries
    comanagement issues for, 144–146,
    152–154; objectives of, 41–43, 52–53;
    power of, 4–6; state-system vs. idea of,
    176n. 6
subsistence: market interactions vs.,
    171–172; use of term, 159–163
Succession Act (1981, Kenya), 122, 124,
    125, 129, 135n. 22
Sulawesi hill farmers (Indonesia): com-
    munity formation and, 169–170; con-
    cept of community and, 168–169;
    description of, 157; development
    schemes and, 172–174; fieldwork
    among, 167; resource management
    and, 174–175; subsistence vs. market
    interactions for, 171–172
Sumatra, social continuity in, 117
Swynnerton Plan (Kenya), 121

Tagbanua people (Philippines): descrip-
    tion of, 46–48; as migrants, 53; net-
    works of, 56–57; political institutions

of, 49; as social unit, 51–52; sustain-
    ability issues and, 50–51
Taylor, Michael, 22n. 28
Tengger highlanders (Indonesia), 161–162
territorialization, concept of, 164–167
Thailand, conservation farming in, 162
Tönnies, Ferdinand Julius, 2, 3, 8
transboundary resources. See boundaries
    and boundary work; salmon fisheries
    (Pacific Northwest)
tribes: collective capacities of, 139,
    140–141; comanagement issues for,
    142–144, 152–154; concept of com-
    munity and, 139–140; internal fish-
    eries management of, 150–152; norms
    of, 11; relations among, 146–150;
    social homogeneity and, 141–142;
    state institutions and, 144–146
Tsing, Anna Lowenhaupt, 170
Tully, James, 23n. 39

USAID, 61n. 26. See also Natural
    Resources Management Program
    (NRMP, USAID)

Vandergeest, Peter, 164, 165
Vayda, Andrew P., 188
Verdery, Katherine, 129
villageness, concept of, 176n. 5

Wade, R., 85n. 7
Walters, Bradley B., 188
Washington (state). See salmon fisheries
    (Pacific Northwest)
water resources: access to/control of, 71,
    79–80; centrality of, 64; rights to,
    99–103; stealing of, 80–81, 106–107.
    See also water users' organizations
    (South Asia); Zaouit Amelkis Village
    (Morocco)
water users' organizations (South Asia):
    disputes in, 75; evaluation of, 80–84;
    membership of, 73–75; overview of,
    71–73; participation in, 75–80
Watts, Michael, 23–24n. 42
Wells, Michael, 5
wildlife: hunting/fishing's impact on,

155n. 3; norms for/against killing, 11–12. *See also* fisheries industry

Williams, Brackette F., 112–113

Williams, Raymond, 157

Willis, Justin, 126

women: land titles of, 129–131; nature linked to, 66–69; as resource users and managers, 70–71. *See also* water users' organizations (South Asia)

Zaouit Amelkis Village (Morocco): description of, 89–95; irrigation system of, 98–103; social organizations and, 104–108; social stratification in, 95–98

Zerner, Charles, 22n. 27

Ziz Valley (Morocco), 91f. *See also* Zaouit Amelkis Village (Morocco)

Zwarteveen, M., 80